The divergent trajectories of the EU and Russia in the early 2000s set the two entities on the path of confrontation. In this detailed empirical study, Anna-Sophie Maass convincingly demonstrates that a series of external shocks helped reshape their relationship at the same time as the internal evolution of the two brought about a new understanding of their respective actorness in a system in which no fundamental mode of reconciliation had been devised. This important work represents essential reading for anyone seeking to understand the dynamics of the relationship between the EU and Russia.

Richard Sakwa, *University of Kent, UK*

The question of why the EU's and Russia's relations ended up on a conflictual path is one of the most pressing ones for our generation. This book provides a multi-layered analysis of the road from initial promise to the current bitter mutual disappointment and recrimination. It is a sobering account that should be required reading for everyone interested in the future of EU–Russia relations.

Hiski Haukkala, *University of Tampere, Finland*

This is an important book that speaks to a wide audience across disciplinary boundaries. Expertly following the contours of the EU's troubled relationship with Russia over the past two decades, Maass' analysis is rigorous and based on a wealth of primary material. Its value goes well beyond a simple retrospective of recent conflicts and diplomatic impasses; this is a study that contextualizes the current 'ice age' in the EU's relations with Russia and offers significant insights into the dynamics that have contributed to its emergence.

Dimitris Papadimitriou, *University of Manchester, UK*

EU–Russia Relations, 1999–2015

This book traces the development of EU–Russia relations in recent years. It argues that a major factor influencing the relationship is the changing internal dynamics of both parties: in Russia's case an increasingly authoritarian state, in the case of the EU an increasing coherence in its foreign policy as applied to former Soviet countries which Russia regarded as interference in its own sphere. The book considers the impact of conflicts in Kosovo, Chechnya, Georgia and Ukraine, discusses the changing internal situation in both Russia and the EU, including the difficulties in overcoming fragmentation in EU policy making, and concludes by assessing how the situation is likely to develop.

Anna-Sophie Maass is a Post-Doctoral Research Fellow in the European Neighbourhood Policy Chair at the College of Europe, Warsaw, Poland.

Routledge Contemporary Russia and Eastern Europe Series

58 **Fashion and the Consumer Revolution in Contemporary Russia**
Olga Gurova

59 **Religion, Nation and Democracy in the South Caucasus**
Edited by Alexander Agadjanian, Ansgar Jödicke and Evert van der Zweerde

60 **Eurasian Integration – The View from Within**
Edited by Piotr Dutkiewicz and Richard Sakwa

61 **Art and Protest in Putin's Russia**
Lena Jonson

62 **The Challenges for Russia's Politicized Economic System**
Edited by Susanne Oxenstierna

63 **Boundaries of Utopia – Imagining Communism from Plato to Stalin**
Erik van Ree

64 **Democracy in Poland**
Representation, participation, competition and accountability since 1989
Anna Gwiazda

65 **Democracy, Civil Culture and Small Business in Russia's Regions**
Social processes in comparative historical perspective
Molly O'Neal

66 **National Minorities in Putin's Russia**
Federica Prina

67 **The Social History of Post-Communist Russia**
Edited by Piotr Dutkiewicz, Richard Sakwa and Vladimir Kulikov

68 **The Return of the Cold War**
Ukraine, the West and Russia
Edited by J. L. Black and Michael Johns

69 **Corporate Strategy in Post-Communist Russia**
Mikhail Glazunov

70 **Russian Aviation, Space Flight and Visual Culture**
Vlad Strukov and Helena Goscilo

71 **EU–Russia Relations, 1999–2015**
From courtship to confrontation
Anna-Sophie Maass

EU–Russia Relations, 1999–2015

From courtship to confrontation

Anna-Sophie Maass

LONDON AND NEW YORK

First published 2017
by Routledge
2 Park Square, Milton Park, Abingdon, Oxon OX14 4RN

and by Routledge
711 Third Avenue, New York, NY 10017

Routledge is an imprint of the Taylor & Francis Group, an informa business

© 2017 Anna-Sophie Maass

The right of Anna-Sophie Maass to be identified as author of this work has
been asserted by her in accordance with sections 77 and 78 of the
Copyright, Designs and Patents Act 1988.

All rights reserved. No part of this book may be reprinted or reproduced or
utilised in any form or by any electronic, mechanical, or other means, now
known or hereafter invented, including photocopying and recording, or in
any information storage or retrieval system, without permission in writing
from the publishers.

Trademark notice: Product or corporate names may be trademarks or
registered trademarks, and are used only for identification and explanation
without intent to infringe.

British Library Cataloguing-in-Publication Data
A catalogue record for this book is available from the British Library

Library of Congress Cataloging-in-Publication Data
Names: Maass, Anna-Sophie, author.
Title: EU-Russia relations, 1999–2015 : from courtship to confrontation /
Anna-Sophie Maass.
Other titles: European Union-Russia relations, 1999–2015
Description: Abingdon, Oxon ; New York, NY : Routledge, 2016. | Series:
Routledge contemporary Russia and Eastern Europe series ; 71 | Includes
bibliographical references and index.
Identifiers: LCCN 2016005448| ISBN 9781138943698 (hardback) |
ISBN 9781315672274 (ebook)
Subjects: LCSH: European Union countries–Foreign relations–Russia
(Federation) | Russia (Federation)–Foreign relations–European Union
countries.
Classification: LCC D1065.R9 M33 2016 | DDC 341.242/20947–dc23
LC record available at http://lccn.loc.gov/2016005448

ISBN: 978-1-138-94369-8 (hbk)
ISBN: 978-1-315-67227-4 (ebk)

Typeset in Times New Roman
by Wearset Ltd, Boldon, Tyne and Wear

To my parents
With my deepest gratitude and love.

Contents

	Acknowledgements	x
	List of abbreviations	xii
	Introduction	1
1	EU–Russian diplomacy during the Kosovo War	8
2	Overcoming the 'Chechnya Irritant' in EU–Russia relations	28
3	Russia and the politics of EU eastern enlargement	57
4	The threat to EU–Russia relations of EU enlargement in the Orange Revolution	84
5	Towards confrontation: 2006–2008	113
6	The repercussions of EU diplomacy in Georgia	137
7	The point of no return? EU–Russia relations after the Euro-Maidan	164
	Conclusions	191
	Appendix: list of interviews	199
	Index	200

Acknowledgements

This monograph has travelled a long way. The spark to embark on this journey was lit by Professor Elizabeth de Zutter and Dr Tom Casier at the University of Maastricht. At La Trobe University in Melbourne, the foundations for this book were laid by my PhD research. Throughout its candidature I have incurred many debts. I owe so much to my supervisor Dr Robert Horvath. The shaping of my argument greatly benefited from his constructive scepticism. I am equally grateful for the support of my co-supervisor Professor Nick Bisley. Dr Philipp Bull's and Dr Stefan Auer's efforts and enthusiasm for enhancing European Studies at La Trobe laid the foundations for my development. I am also very thankful to Dr Adrian Jones and his family.

A close circle of wonderful friends made my time in Australia the most cherished period of my life. Especially Shihan George Ciechanowicz and Dr Grainne Oates are a source of immense support, wisdom and kindness. Sempai George Dixon, Dr Kyra Giorgi, Elizabeth Hill, Kylie Mason, Dr Russel Marks and Danielle Vida enrich my life.

This monograph reached its final destination at the College of Europe's Natolin campus in Warsaw. I am very grateful to Mrs Vice Rector Ewa Ośniecka-Tamecka and Professor Dr Tobias Schumacher for granting me a Post-Doctoral Fellowship in the European Neighbourhood Policy Chair which provided the academic liberty to work on this monograph. In Natolin I was very fortunate to work with Professor Hiski Haukkala. Our discussions on EU–Russia relations, teaching tutorials and the guidance of students in their MA theses research were enriching. I am very thankful to Professor Dimitris Papadimitriou from the University of Manchester. His initiation of my appointment as an Honorary Research Fellow at his Jean Monnet Centre of Excellence broadened my horizon. I am grateful to my interviewees, several officials in the EU institutions, who deepened the shaping of my argument. I appreciate all efforts of Lucy McClune and Peter Sowden from Routledge.

Dr Dimitris Bouris, Dr Irene Fernandez-Molina, Dr Michal Natorski and Max Wright have become close friends with whom I spent great moments in Warsaw. I am very grateful to have met you.

Without the support of my parents I would not have been able to reach any of the above mentioned destinations. I am deeply indebted to you. Your constant support, encouragement, advice, kindness and patience helped me overcome obstacles I encountered on parts of my academic journey. The least I can do in a humble attempt to express my gratitude is to dedicate this book to you.

I am also very grateful to my brother, whose professional endeavours were a source of inspiration in my pursuits. I am grateful to Yves Brand, my aunt Monika as well as my friends in Melbourne, Warsaw, Exeter and Maastricht for enriching my life.

Abbreviations

AA	Association Agreement
CEC	Central Election Commission
CFSP	Common Foreign and Security Policy
CIS	Commonwealth of Independent States
DCFTA	Deep and Comprehensive Free Trade Area
EaP	Eastern Partnership
ECT	European Energy Charter Treaty
ENP	European Neighbourhood Policy
EU	European Union
EUMM	European Union Monitoring Mission
FSB	Federalnaya Sluzba Bezopasnosti
FTD	Facilitated Transit Document
KFOR	NATO's Kosovo Force
MAP	Membership Action Plan
NATO	North Atlantic Treaty Organisation
NGO	non-governmental organisation
OSCE	Organisation for Security and Cooperation in Europe
PACE	Parliamentary Assembly of the Council of Europe
PCA	Partnership and Cooperation Agreement
PfM	Partnership for Modernisation
RMTS	Russian Medium Term Strategy
SES	Single Economic Space
TACIS	Technical Assistance to the Commonwealth of Independent States

Introduction

In 1999 EU–Russia relations were marked by great expectations. At the end of the Yeltsin era, Russian leaders aspired to join the EU and courted it as a negotiating partner during the Kosovo crisis. During the early years of Putin's presidency, this rapport developed into a 'strategic partnership' that was founded upon gas deals, cooperation in the 'war on terror' and silence about human rights abuses in Chechnya. But by the end of Putin's second term as president, this relationship was in trouble. The EU–Russia summits were dominated by acrimonious clashes over Russia's use of energy as a geopolitical weapon and the withering of Russian democracy. In Russian policy-making circles, the EU was increasingly regarded as a hostile power. During Medvedev's presidency, this perception intensified when the EU's development of political and economic integration projects with countries in the former Soviet space became a major source of confrontation in EU–Russia relations. The emergence of the Ukraine crisis in November 2013 has distorted Javier Solana's 1999 vision of an EU–Russian 'strategic partnership' as 'the greatest opportunity to affect the cause of world affairs for the better'.[1] By 2015, this 'strategic partnership' seems to have reached the point of no return.

The purpose of this monograph is to explain the reasons for this spectacular reversal in EU–Russia relations from courtship in 1999 to confrontation in 2015. The book's central contention is that the deterioration of the relationship was shaped by the divergent internal transformations of both the EU and Russia. The nature of the EU's change was both territorial and institutional. As a territorial entity, the EU expanded to Russia's borders, absorbing members of the Warsaw Pact and former republics of the Soviet Union. This enlargement had three major repercussions for EU–Russia relations. First, it paved the way for the EU's increasing influence in Russia's 'near abroad'. Second, the proximity of the EU created a mass of new possibilities for friction, for instance, free transit for Russian citizens to neighbouring states, including the Russian exclave of Kaliningrad. Third, the EU exerted influence in the former Soviet successor states by establishing the European Neighbourhood Policy (ENP) and the Eastern Partnership (EaP), the latter aimed primarily at enhancing political and economic cooperation with Armenia, Azerbaijan, Belarus, Georgia, Ukraine and Moldova.[2]

Another component of the EU's internal transformation was changes in its institutional structure. In 1999 the establishment of the office of the High

2 Introduction

Representative for the Common Foreign and Security Policy (CFSP) was a significant step towards both rendering EU foreign policy more coherent and enhancing the EU's visibility in its external relations. Javier Solana's appointment as High Representative of the CFSP and Secretary-General of the European Council in October 1999 had a crucial role in shaping EU foreign policy.[3] Solana demonstrated his capacities by playing a critical role in the negotiations that sealed Putin's geopolitical defeat in the Orange Revolution in Ukraine. When Solana also mediated in the resolution of a revolution in Kyrgyzstan in 2005, the Kremlin's hostility towards EU interference in the post-Soviet space increased significantly.

No less important for the breakdown of the EU–Russia 'partnership' was the transformation of Russia into an increasingly authoritarian state. A widening gap emerged between the values the EU sought to promote in its relations with Moscow and political reality in Russia. While the EU attempted to promote economic and political reforms in Russia as a price for a future in an integrated Europe, the Kremlin was not receptive to this lure. It sought to maintain autonomy in domestic and foreign policy as reflected in the Russian Medium Term Strategy for its relations with the EU. Increased state control over its energy market and the pursuance of an aggressive foreign policy in the post-Soviet space became hallmarks of Russian foreign policy between 2000 and 2015.

During this period, the Putin regime was increasingly hostile towards liberal democracy and the West. Unlike the Yeltsin regime, it did not regard the EU as a collaborator in the construction of Russia's sovereign democracy. With this concept – sovereign democracy, which reflected Russia's hostility towards the West's interference in Russian domestic affairs – the Kremlin justified its increasing authoritarianism.[4] Human rights abuses by Russia, which also manifested themselves in violent dispersals of peaceful demonstrations against the opposition to the Putin regime, provoked growing conflict between Russia and the EU. Simultaneously Russia attempted to reconstitute itself as a great power on the international arena. Its blatant interference in election campaigns in Georgia and Ukraine, its use of energy policy as a means to enforce its hegemony in the region, and the pressure it exerted on heads of government in former Soviet satellite states who aimed to align themselves with the EU within the EaP framework, were all attempts to keep these countries within the Kremlin's orbit.

This book illuminates the repercussions of the divergence of the EU and Russia as political entities by examining the evolution of their diplomatic relations between 1999 and 2015. In 1999, for Russian policy makers, the military might of the USA and NATO constituted the principal threat to their national interests. In contrast, they treated the EU as a benign, amorphous entity: a diplomatic channel to maintain relations with the West. By 2005, the Kremlin perceived the EU as a harmful actor whose increasing influence in the former Soviet space impinged upon the Putin regime's objectives in this region. The EU's tangible interference in the resolution of the political crisis in Ukraine in 2004 was the most evident demonstration of its influence over the post-Soviet space. It resulted in open confrontation with the Kremlin.

Introduction 3

In addition to the EU's increasing influence in the post-Soviet space, its normative appeal to some former Soviet successor states was another factor which contributed to the deterioration of EU–Russia relations. During Putin's presidency, the EU's gravitational pull – its allure to countries in the post-Soviet space – was perceived as a threat by the Kremlin. The Orange Revolution was perceived as confirmation of the ideational impact of the EU, with EU flags symbolising the aspirations of a proportion of the Ukrainian population and the political elite for integration of the Ukraine into the EU. At the same time, the increasing gap between the EU's limited attempt to promote its values in relations with Moscow on the one hand, and Russia's political reality on the other, contributed to the worsening of EU–Russia relations.[5]

By examining various facets of the transformation of EU–Russia relations, this monograph attempts to deepen and widen scholarship on this topic. Two major books are at the core of this academic literature. On one hand, Hiski Haukkala assesses how differences in world view and power between the EU and Russia underpin their failure to institutionalise their relations.[6] In order to approach this research issue, Haukkala analyses the relationship through case studies including the Chechen War in 1999 and the Northern Dimension Policy, for instance.[7] On the other hand, in his monograph on conflicts in EU–Russia relations, the Russian scholar Sergei Prozorov has chosen to examine, among other examples, enlargement of the EU, tensions between sovereignty and integration, as well as asymmetries in EU–Russia relations to illuminate inherent conflicts in the relationship.[8]

There is a limited range of scholarly articles which explore the factors influencing the reversal of EU–Russia relations from courtship to confrontation, and they tend to focus on either limited time periods or narrow issues. Several studies, for instance, focus on EU–Russian diplomacy during the Chechen War.[9] Another group of scholars concentrate on EU–Russia energy relations. Among this group, Faber van der Meulen assesses the EU and Russia's trade in gas.[10] In a different vein, Andrew Monaghan, Roland Goetz, Andrei Belyi and Steve Wood examine energy security.[11] Other studies assess the EU's and Russia's approaches to their shared neighbourhood, as well as the political and economic repercussions of the EU's eastern enlargement for EU–Russia relations.[12]

Similarly, literature on Russian foreign policy also examines the transformation of EU–Russia relations within a narrow time frame.[13] A prominent example is Janusz Bugajski, who claims that during Putin's presidency, Russia has been threatening the West through diplomacy intended to fracture the EU and NATO by using energy policy as a geostrategic weapon.[14] As in this book, Bugajski claims that in the mid to late 1990s the Kremlin regarded the EU as a useful counterpart to the US and NATO's influence due to its soft security policies. However, by the late 1990s, the EU was perceived by the Kremlin as impinging upon Russia's policy interests by becoming a magnet attracting the former Soviet space.[15] In this way, Bugajski acknowledges the transformation of EU–Russia relations but without assessing the reasons for this development, which this monograph endeavours to elucidate.

4   *Introduction*

Taking a different approach to Bugajski, Andrei Tsygankov treats EU–Russia relations as a subset of Russia's relations with the West.[16] According to Tsygankov, who assesses Russian foreign policy during the Yeltsin and Putin eras, the Kremlin prefers to keep the EU at arm's length when it considers that the EU is infringing upon Russian interests.[17] Tsygankov analyses Russia's integration with the West and its 'great power balancing' during Yeltsin's presidency and the 'great power pragmatism' that marked the Putin era.[18] One of Tsygankov's conclusions is that Moscow's political and diplomatic weight, its possession of natural resources and its military power have undermined the capacity of the West to impact upon developments in Russia.[19] Contrary to Tsygankov, this book aims to illuminate the evolution of EU–Russian diplomatic relations.

In an assessment of the reasons for the transformation of this relationship, this book takes domestic factors and the role of civil society into account. Civil society in the West exerted pressure on the EU's political elite to take a tougher stance on Russia during the second Chechen War. This book takes into consideration the influence of prominent European political leaders, who played a significant role in maintaining cordial relations with Putin at a time of severe clashes in EU–Russia relations. Domestic factors in Russia that influenced the development of EU–Russia relations included the significant role played by political technologists in the Kremlin such as President Putin's close adviser Gleb Pavlovsky. In 2004, he strongly supported the presidential election campaign of the pro-Russian candidate in Kiev. The Kremlin's heavy investment in this election was made redundant by the EU's interference in the political crisis in Kiev which resulted in the victory of the pro-Western presidential candidate and obstructed Russia's geopolitical interests in Ukraine. As a consequence, the first major political crisis between the EU and Russia since 1999 emerged.

There were two main factors which triggered the worsening of this relationship. On the one hand, the EU's absorption of states from Central and Eastern Europe, three of them belonging to the post-Soviet space, exemplified its enhanced influence in the region. Due to their Soviet past, several of the 'new' member states took a more confrontational stance towards Russia than the 'old' EU member states. As a consequence, they jeopardised the Kremlin's foreign policy objective to impose its hegemony over the former Soviet space. The most significant confirmation of the influence of 'new' member states on the EU's foreign policy towards Russia was the central role played by Poland and Lithuania in the EU's diplomatic mission to Kiev during the Orange Revolution in November 2004. At the same time, the establishment of both the ENP and the EaP enabled the EU to exert influence in the region, either through direct political and economic integration initiatives, or through the implicit export of the EU's values in the framework of these regional policy frameworks. The Kremlin perceived the ENP as an imposition of the EU's will in some countries of the former Soviet space. When the EaP promised to result in concrete integration plans between the EU and some post-Soviet states, it marked a new era of confrontation in EU–Russia relations.

Introduction 5

On the other hand, the EU's ideational component – its intention to seek to harmonise certain political, economic, judicial standards in the countries belonging to the EaP and its ability to act as a role model for some former Soviet satellite states – together with the EU's ability to increase influence in the post-Soviet space, contributed to the deterioration of EU–Russia relations. The Putin regime perceived the attractiveness of the EU's values to countries in the post-Soviet space as a threat. It regarded the EU as a rival actor intending to shape values in Russia's near abroad, and hence potentially jeopardising the Kremlin's dominance over the region. The EU used the opportunity created by its ideational appeal to countries in the former Soviet space such as Ukraine, both during and after the Orange Revolution, to enhance its relations with these states, despite the vociferous objections of the Kremlin. The Kremlin reacted by unleashing a propaganda campaign against the EU, a development which would have been unthinkable at the end of the Yeltsin era in 1999.

Notes

1 Solana (1999).
2 Other members of the ENP are Algeria, Egypt, Israel, Jordan, Lebanon, Libya, Morocco, Tunisia, the Occupied Palestinian Territory, Syria and Tunisia (European Commission (2004)). For a scholarly account of the ENP and its challenges for the EU, see Dannreuther (2006).
3 Smith (2008), p. 42. Solana coordinated EU foreign policy in cooperation with the current, past and future rotating European Council Presidency as well as the European Commission.
4 Surkov (2008).
5 Tom Casier has argued that in 2008 'normative objectives ... even if not always backed up by real pressure or strict conditionality ... have now moved to the periphery of the agenda'. He exemplifies his argument by referring to both the EU–Russia Joint Statement of the summit in June 2008 and the European Commission's review of Russia's policy of the same year. See Casier (2013).
6 Haukkala (2010), p. 1.
7 The Northern Dimension Policy is a political and economic programme between Russia, the Baltic States and Scandinavia established by the EU in 1999.
8 Prozorov (2006), p. 6.
9 Forsberg and Herd (2005), p. 455; Francis (2008); Haukkala (2009); Smith (2005).
10 Van der Meulen (2009), p. 833.
11 Belyi (2003); Goetz (2009); Johnson (2005); Monaghan (2006).
12 Averre (2005a); Averre (2009), p. 1692; Flenley (2008). Averre has also examined EU–Russia relations by focusing on security (see Averre (2005b), pp. 73–92; Casier (2007), p. 73). For economic repercussions of the EU's eastern enlargement, see Breuss (2002); Sulamaa and Widgren (2004).
13 Bugajski (2008), p. 6.
14 Bugajski (2008), p. 18.
15 Ibid.
16 Tsygankov (2006), p. XXIV.
17 Tsygankov (2006), pp. 140, 141.
18 Ibid.
19 Tsygankov (2006), p. 182.

6 *Introduction*

Bibliography

Averre, D. (2005a). Russia and the European Union: Convergence or divergence? *European Security* 14(2): 175–202.

Averre, D. (2005b). The EU–Russian relationship in the context of European security. In Johnson, D. and Robinson, P. (2005). *Perspectives on EU–Russia Relations. Europe and the Nation State*. London and New York: Routledge.

Averre, D. (2009). Competing Rationalities: Russia, the EU and the 'shared neighbourhood'. *Europe–Asia Studies* 61(10): 1689–1713.

Belyi, A. (2003). New Dimensions of Energy Security of the Enlarging EU and their Impact on Relations with Russia. *Journal of European Integration* 25(4): 351–369.

Breuss, F. (2002). Benefits and Dangers of EU Enlargement. *Empirica* 29(3): 245–274.

Bugajski, J. (2008). Introduction. Russia resurgent. In *Expanding Eurasia. Russia's European ambitions*. Washington DC: Centre for Strategic Studies.

Casier, T. (2007). The clash of integration processes? The shadow effect of the enlarged EU on its eastern neighbours. In Malfielt, K., Verpoest, L. and Vinokurov, E. (eds). *The CIS, the EU and Russia. The challenges of integration.* Studies in Central and Eastern Europe. New York: Palgrave Macmillan. pp. 73–94.

Casier, T. (2013). The EU–Russia Strategic Partnership: Challenging the normative argument. *Europe–Asia Studies* 65(7): 1377–1395.

Dannreuther, R. (2006). Developing the alternative to enlargement: The European Neighbourhood Policy. *European Foreign Affairs Review* 11(2): 183–201.

European Commission. (2004). The European Neighbourhood Policy. http://ec.europa.eu/world/enp/policy_en.htm

Flenley, P. (2008). Russia and the EU: The clash of new neighbourhoods? *Journal of Contemporary European Studies* 16(2): 198–202.

Forsberg, T. and Herd, G.P. (2005). The EU, Human Rights and the Russo-Chechen conflict. *Political Science Quarterly* 120(3): 455–478.

Francis, C. (2008). 'Selective Affinities': The reactions of the Council of Europe and the European Union to the Second Armed Conflict in Chechnya (1999–2006). *Europe–Asia Studies* 60(2): 317–338.

Goetz, R. (2009). Pipeline-Popanz. Irrtümer der europaeischen Energiedebatte. *Osteuropa.* Special Issue: Am Rad drehen. *Energie, Geschichte, Ideologie* 9(1): 3–18.

Haukkala, H. (2009). Lost in Translation? Why the EU has failed to influence Russia's development. *Europe–Asia Studies* 61(10): 1757–1775.

Haukkala, H. (2010). *The EU–Russia Strategic Partnership. The limits of post-sovereignty in international relations.* London and New York: Routledge.

Johnson, D. (2005). EU–Russia energy links. In Johnson, D. and Robinson, P. (eds) *Perspectives on EU–Russia Relations. Europe and the nation state*. London and New York: Routledge. pp. 175–194.

Monaghan, A. (2006). Russia–EU Relations: An emerging energy security dilemma. Carnegie Endowment Centre for International Peace. http://carnegieendowment.org/files/EmergingDilemma1.pdf

Prozorov, S. (2006). Approaching EU–Russian conflicts. In *Understanding Conflicts between Russia and the EU. The limits to integration.* London and New York: Routledge.

Smith, H. (2005). The Russian Federation and the European Union: the shadow of Chechnya. In Johnson, D. and Robinson, P. (eds). *Perspectives on EU–Russia Relations. Europe and the nation state.* London and New York: Routledge.

Smith, K.E. (2008). *European Union Foreign Policy in a Changing World.* Cambridge: Polity.

Solana, J. (1999). The EU–Russia Strategic Partnership. Speech by High Representative designate of the European Union for Common Foreign and Security Policy. Council of the European Union. Stockholm, Wednesday 13 October 1999. Retrieved 25 April 2015 from: www.consilium.europa.eu/uedocs/cms_data/docs/pressdata/EN/discours/59417.pdf

Sulamaa, P. and Widgren, M. (2004). EU-enlargement and Beyond: A simulation study on EU and Russia integration. *Empirica* 31(4): 307–323.

Surkov, V. (2008). Russian Political Culture. The view from Utopia. *Russian Politics and Law* 46(5): 10–26.

Tsygankov, S. (2006). *Russia's Foreign Policy. Change and continuity in national identity.* Lanham, MD: Rowman and Littlefield.

Van der Meulen, E.F. (2009). Gas supply and EU–Russia relations. *Europe–Asia Studies* 61(5): 833–856.

1 EU–Russian diplomacy during the Kosovo War

NATO's intervention in Kosovo precipitated the most serious crisis in Russia's relations with the West since the end of the Cold War. The rupture began with a symbolic gesture. No sooner had the first cruise missiles struck targets in Serbia on 24 March 1999 than the Russian Prime Minister, Yevgeny Primakov, aborted a visit to the United States. He ordered his plane to be turned around over the mid-Atlantic. By April, President Yeltsin was warning of the possibility of Russian military intervention and 'a European war or even a world war'.[1] The seriousness of this threat became clear on 12 June, when a contingent of 200 Russian paratroopers seized Pristina's airport before the arrival of NATO forces. The result was a protracted military stand-off between Russia and NATO.

This chapter seeks to explain why the breakdown of Russia's relations with NATO and the US coincided with a remarkable development in cooperative EU–Russian diplomacy. At a time when both the EU and Russia were facing internal political and economic challenges, they realised their potential for cooperation when faced with the breakout of the Kosovo War. It was settled because of the establishment of a peace plan by Russia's envoy for Kosovo, Viktor Chernomyrdin, and the Finnish president, Martti Ahtisaari, who negotiated on behalf of the EU.

The chapter argues that despite being the most severe crisis in Russia's relations with the US and NATO since the end of the Cold War, the Kosovo conflict became a catalyst for significant EU–Russian cooperation due to three factors. First, in Russian policy-making circles the EU was perceived as a passive actor that was neither a belligerent power nor a focused diplomatic presence. In early March, this impression was reinforced by the lack of leadership in the EU following the sacking of the European Commission over a corruption scandal. While Russian policy-making circles were vociferous in their denunciation of an 'aggressive' NATO, the EU remained the acceptable face of the West at the height of the Kosovo crisis.

The second contributing factor was Germany's Presidency of the European Council. Like Russia, Germany was opposed to a ground war. Hence, during Germany's chairmanship of the European Council, Russian policymakers regarded the EU as the acceptable partner in the West before and during the Kosovo War, which facilitated EU–Russian diplomacy. At the same time,

Germany had close ties with Russia. Since the severe economic crisis in Russia in 1998, Germany had been Russia's largest foreign creditor. The close personal relationship between the German chancellor and chairman of the European Council Presidency, Gerhard Schroeder, and Yeltsin fostered EU–Russian cooperation.

Third, the Yeltsin administration was preoccupied with resolving domestic problems and thus faced two major difficulties in dealing with the Kosovo crisis on its own. Yeltsin was under threat from a nationalist-inclined State Duma which used the Kosovo War to whip up national condemnation of his administration. The State Duma instigated an impeachment process against Yeltsin in March. At the same time, Russia was facing the repercussions of its 1998 economic crisis. On both levels cooperation with the EU offered a way of defusing a war.

Laying the groundwork for EU–Russian collaboration

Being faced with the emerging international crisis in Kosovo, domestic political turmoil paired with economic problems in Russia and Yeltsin's cordial relations with Schroeder enhanced the EU and Russia's determination to develop a partnership. The EU–Russia summit in Moscow on 18 February 1999, the third to take place since the Partnership and Cooperation Agreement (PCA) – the legal basis for EU–Russia relations – entered into force in 1997, laid the groundwork for the partners' diplomacy before the Kosovo War. The summit's joint statement proclaimed that an EU–Russian 'partnership', which initiated 'common approaches to tackle the 21st century's challenges, [was a] fundamental factor of peace and stability on the European continent'.[2] In the press conference, Schroeder characterised the summit as a 'political sign' of the willingness to engage in enhanced cooperation.[3] As a way of contrasting Russia's relations with the US with those with the EU, Yeltsin expressed his strong opposition to NATO's intervention in Kosovo in front of Schroeder. He declared that in giving US President Clinton his opinion on the possibility of the US launching airstrikes against Serbia, he had warned that 'we [would not] stand for this.... We [would not] let them touch Kosovo'.[4]

Yeltsin's outspoken warning to NATO not to interfere in Kosovo stood in contrast to his political self-identification with the EU. He lamented that 'regrettably the Russian Federation [was] not a member of the European Union'.[5] Yeltsin's friendly sentiments were reciprocated by Schroeder. He announced that Germany would be 'Russia's advocate' [Anwalt] in the West during negotiations to reschedule Russia's debt repayments.[6] Russia's economy at the beginning of the Kosovo War was characterised by trade deficits, the flight of capital in response to shrinking reserves in Russia's central bank, as well as price increases, simultaneous decreases in salaries, the devaluation of the rouble, massive foreign debts and inflation.[7] According to Boris Fyodorov, Russia's former Finance Minister, 'the government [was] basically bankrupt'.[8]

This auspicious dialogue between Schroeder and Yeltsin coincided with the first attempt by the Kosovo Contact Group to develop an 'Interim Agreement for Peace

10 *EU–Russian diplomacy in Kosovo War*

and Self-Governance' in Rambouillet on 6 February. These talks, led by Contact Group members Germany, Italy, France, the US and the UK, aimed to negotiate by 19 February a three-year peace agreement that would guarantee autonomy to Kosovo.[9] The negotiations, mediated by Boris Mayorski from Russia, Chris Hill representing the US, and the EU Special Representative on Kosovo, Dr Wolfgang Petritsch, broke down.[10] According to Mayorski, the possibility of adopting an agreement was unlikely because the negotiators were 'working under conditions [with] quite a high level of mistrust'.[11] Petritsch explained that the reason the negotiations broke down was that politicians in the former Yugoslavia would 'rather be defeated than compromise'.[12] The continuation of talks in a further round of negotiations in Paris brought Kosovo to the brink of war due to the stalemate among the negotiators.[13] On the last day of the negotiations, on 23 March, the US envoy Richard Holbrooke declared that an agreement between the Organisation for Security and Cooperation in Europe (OSCE) and the Yugoslav government regarding the deployment of a mission in Kosovo in compliance with UN security resolutions had been violated by Serb and Albanian military groups. As a result, Holbrooke stated that the interim peace agreement could not be implemented without the 'presence of foreign military forces'.[14]

Meanwhile, the EU's diplomatic role, which had been limited at the negotiations in Rambouillet and Paris, was further undermined by the resignation of the European Commission in March. A report from the European Court of Auditors provided evidence of missing EU funds, disloyalty, corruption and a lack of transparency.[15] The European Commission resigned collectively on 15 March.[16] The fact that the Commission stepped down at a time when the CFSP had not yet been developed undermined the EU's capabilities in external relations. The post of EU High Representative of the CFSP, responsible for the coordination of EU foreign policy in cooperation with the current, past and future rotating European Council Presidencies and the European Commission, was not established until October 1999.[17] Before this, European Commissioners responsible for this policy domain played a significant role in shaping EU foreign policy. Among those Commissioners was Hans van den Broek, who was responsible for coordination of the EU's foreign affairs in Central and Eastern Europe and the former Soviet Union, foreign and security policy, and human rights.[18] Van den Broek played an important role in managing EU external relations, especially with Russia. He represented the EU at some of the EU–Russia summits including that of February 1999.[19] He also witnessed the entry into force of the EU–Russian PCA at the summit on 1 December 1997.[20]

Although the EU reacted quickly to appoint an interim Commission the day after their resignation, its ability to act was limited. Under European Commission Vice President Michel Marin's leadership, the interim Commission was merely in caretaker mode.[21] It served until 13 September 1999, when new members were appointed. Nine days after the Commission's resignation, the former Italian Prime Minister Romano Prodi was appointed by European governments as the European Commission's new president. His election was only endorsed by the European Parliament on 6 May.[22]

The EU – the acceptable face of the West

Russia's suspicions about NATO were heightened by the accession of Poland, Hungary and the Czech Republic to the alliance on 12 March, about two weeks before the launch of air strikes against Serbia. To many Russian observers, NATO's enlargement represented a flagrant violation of the accords reached between Mikhael Gorbachev and Western leaders during the dismantling of the Warsaw Pact and the Soviet withdrawal from Eastern Europe.

This simmering resentment exploded into public outrage when NATO launched air strikes on Serbian targets on 24 March. The Russian Prime Minister Yevgeny Primakov, who was on a flight to New York, ordered his plane to return immediately to Moscow when he received news of the bombing.[23] The implication of Primakov's gesture was made explicit in a speech given by the Russian Foreign Minister Igor Ivanov to the Duma on 27 March in which he condemned NATO for 'the act of aggression [which] ha[d] created a real threat to world peace'.[24] Ten days later he accused NATO's leadership of seeking 'with maniacal stubbornness to erase Yugoslavia and its peoples off the face of the earth'.[25] Shortly after NATO's intervention, Russians protested in front of the US embassy in Moscow and there were grenade attacks on the building.[26]

The seriousness of the crisis in relations between Russia and NATO culminated in a formal institutional break. On 24 March Yeltsin withdrew Russian representatives from the NATO–Russia Permanent Joint Council, a forum for regular consultation on security issues of common concern.[27] In addition, Sergey Kislyak, Russia's permanent representative to NATO, was called back from his military responsibilities, but maintained his duties regarding political representation.[28]

At the height of this explosion of anti-NATO sentiment, the EU became the acceptable face of the West for Prime Minister Primakov. Within days of his mid-Atlantic gesture, Primakov expressed his determination to develop an EU–Russian partnership, stating: 'I confirmed my opinion – to develop relations with the European Union'.[29] On 30 March, Primakov flew to Belgrade acting 'on the president's instructions ... to find a political settlement, so that this barbaric bombing can be stopped'.[30] After six hours of talks with President Milosevic, he flew to Bonn for discussions with Chancellor Schroeder.[31] According to the newspaper *Kommersant*:

> the German chancellor had not been chosen by accident as the main partner. He was the chairman of the European Union. For Primakov, it was important to negotiate on the playing field of the Organisation for Security and Cooperation in Europe. And to show at the same time, that he was not negotiating with the 'aggressor', NATO, but with the European Union.[32]

The need for EU–Russian cooperation was emphasised by the Russian Deputy Prime Minister Vladimir Bulgak. He declared that only EU–Russian 'joint efforts ... give us the possibility of resolving the [Kosovo] conflict by political means'.[33]

12 *EU–Russian diplomacy in Kosovo War*

Meanwhile, proposals brought forward by the Duma put Yeltsin under pressure to react to the war. The Duma issued a resolution on 7 April outlining its intention to provide Yugoslavia with armaments, although it did not move to implement its resolution until 15 April.[34] Yeltsin denounced these proposals as 'politicised, aggressive and unrealistic', and a 'slow drawing of Russia into the war'.[35] In contrast, the chairman of the Duma, Gennady Seleznyov, declared that the supply of arms was aimed at stopping NATO aggression.[36]

The EU and Russia: emerging diplomatic partners

While Russian policymakers continued to denounce NATO as an aggressor responsible for killing Russia's Slavic brothers, they perceived the EU as its very antithesis. This clear distinction between Russia's relations with the US and NATO on one hand and with the EU on the other was emphasised by the Russian Foreign Minister Igor Ivanov. He contrasted the breakdown of the Russian government's relations with NATO to its cordial relations with the EU in a press conference with German foreign minister Fischer, who was representing the European Council Presidency. Ivanov stated that 'at present Russia's relations with NATO are suspended, [whereas] those with the EU continue with an intensive dialogue'.[37] He warned that the atmosphere of Russian–US relations would 'undoubtedly be damaged' as a consequence of NATO's bombing. He stressed that this severe deterioration in relations would not be Russia's fault because it had not been '[its] choice'.[38]

With the Yeltsin administration coming under increasing pressure, it was vital for Russian policymakers to engage with the EU in order to deal with the Kosovo crisis. Tensions between Yeltsin and the Duma culminated in his impeachment. The charges Yeltsin faced concerned misconduct in the undeclared war on Chechnya from 1994 until 1996, and the use of force against hardline lawmakers.[39] Yeltsin sought to dismiss these accusations by declaring that, having lost the first and second presidential elections,

> the Communists began to look for any means to destroy the president, any way to remove him from his post. They exploited everything – the fall of the USSR was declared a 'conspiracy', the mistakes of the first Chechen campaign were called a 'crime'; economic difficulties were called 'the genocide of the Russian people'.[40]

On 15 May, the Duma deputies failed to impeach Yeltsin on any of the charges against him because they were unable to achieve the necessary two-thirds majority in favour of impeachment.[41]

The Duma's demands for a stronger stance on the Kosovo conflict made the Yeltsin administration vulnerable. According to Yeltsin's Press Secretary Dimitri Yakushkin, Kosovo was the 'most difficult crisis because … it [was] inflaming our internal politics – you can hear the speeches [given] in the State Duma'.[42] He declared that there '[was] a whole range of measures in reserve.…

EU–Russian diplomacy in Kosovo War   13

Nothing is ruled out. Of course, Yeltsin [would] not allow Russia to be dragged into a war'.[43]

In fact, pressure from the Duma had the opposite result and instead inspired peace-making efforts as demonstrated by Yeltsin's appointment of Viktor Chernomyrdin as his representative in Yugoslavia on 14 April.[44] The pressure Yeltsin was facing became evident when he declared that the Russian envoy should 'just end [the war because] it [was] ruining everything'.[45] According to Yeltsin, 'Russian people were alarmed and tense [because they] took the Yugoslav tragedy to heart'.[46] He recalled that , as a consequence, he 'was operating in two directions, putting pressure on NATO and on Milosevic. We had to stop this war no matter what'.[47]

According to Dr Wolfgang Petritsch, the EU's Special Representative for Kosovo, Chernomyrdin's appointment helped the peace negotiations gain momentum. Petritsch declared that Chernomyrdin's role was significant because he was 'transmitting Yeltsin's frank messages to Milosevic, whereas during the negotiations in Rambouillet in February 1999, Yeltsin had not been willing to disengage from Milosevic'.[48]

Chernomyrdin's authority as Yeltsin's representative was enhanced by the dismissal of Prime Minister Yevgeny Primakov on 12 May. Addressing Primakov, Yeltsin stated that he had 'fulfilled [his] mission' and that it now seemed he had to resign.[49] Having been advised to write a 'request to resign, stating any reason', Primakov was succeeded by the former Interior Minister Sergei Stepashin from mid-May until the beginning of August 1999, when Vladimir Putin assumed his post as Prime Minister.[50]

Chernomyrdin was an ideal appointment for the development of Kosovo peace negotiations with the EU. As Russia's former premier from 1992 until 1998, he was a major figure with political clout within the Russian elite and on the international stage.[51] As premier Chernomyrdin had been an ardent advocate of Russia's membership of the EU. At a news conference on 18 July 1997 he announced that 'Russia should be in the EU with all the implications and consequences', even though the complete fulfilment of membership obligations might be difficult.[52]

Obviously feeling the impact of the Duma's pressure on the Yeltsin administration, Chernomyrdin requested a negotiation partner in the peace-making efforts. He advised the G7 states that he wanted to include a 'neutral international figure', who would accompany him in diplomatic mediations with Milosevic.[53] According to Chernomyrdin, the inclusion of a third party in the negotiations would provide President Yeltsin with much needed political cover in the face of intense domestic outrage over NATO's offensive.[54]

Chernomyrdin's 'neutral international' negotiating partner

Chancellor Gerhard Schroeder played a crucial role in securing the appointment of a negotiating partner for Chernomyrdin. In a meeting with Finnish President Martti Ahtisaari in Helsinki in May, he declared that

14 *EU–Russian diplomacy in Kosovo War*

we give our support to the Finnish President, and I give this support in my capacity as ... the country which chairs the European Union.... This means that he has the full support of the European Union in the peace negotiations which he is carrying out together with Chernomyrdin.[55]

In his memoirs, he recalled that he was convinced that Ahtisaari, the 'diplomat who had gained experience in international diplomacy, would be the right man for mediating on behalf of the EU'.[56] Schroeder stated that Ahtisaari had the 'appropriate negotiating power when talking to the Yugoslav government. His aura of neutrality, [due to the fact that he represented a non-NATO state] guaranteed Ahtisaari's [impartiality] in the negotiations'.[57]

Ahtisaari's role as mediator was decisive for several reasons. First, the German government had sensed that the resolution of the Kosovo War required the involvement of Russia. Michael Steiner, foreign policy adviser to the German chancellor, backed up Schroeder's assumption that a resolution could only be found if it was possible to 'get Russia on board'.[58] Second, Ahtisaari was a skilful diplomat. He had made a career out of conflict resolution in Bosnia and in the crisis between Namibia and South Africa in the late 1980s. From 1992 until 1993, he gained additional experience chairing the Bosnia working group at the International Conference on the former Yugoslavia.[59] Third, Ahtisaari had made himself known as a friend of Russia even before he was suggested as Chernomyrdin's potential negotiating partner. At the opening session of the Finnish Parliament in February 1999, Ahtisaari stressed that Finland had been trying to 'strengthen cooperation between the [EU] and Russia'.[60] Chernomyrdin expressed his appreciation for Ahtisaari's appointment as mediator. He stated that he was 'a good politician, and it was a pleasure to work with him'.[61] He added that Finland had 'always conducted itself respectfully toward Russia ... and Ahtisaari had excellent relations with Yeltsin'.[62]

Although the EU instigated Ahtisaari's assumption of the role of envoy, his actual status remained unclear. This was partly due to the fact that Chancellor Schroeder appointed him without an official mandate as mediator on behalf of the EU in Kosovo. Unlike Dr Wolfgang Petritsch, who had been officially appointed as the EU's High Representative for Kosovo on March 30 after having been the European mediator of the Contact Group at Rambouillet, Ahtisaari was never formally chosen to act as EU Special Representative in the peace negotiations.[63] Another reason for the ambiguity of Ahtisaari's role was the fact that his appointment as negotiator had also been supported by the US government.[64] When US Deputy Secretary of State Strobe Talbott proposed Ahtisarri to act as envoy in the mediations, Ahtisaari stated that he was prepared to assume this post as long as he had the backing of the EU.[65] He acknowledged the EU's role in his appointment by saying that 'the EU countries and the European Council confirmed the German EU Presidency's decision to appoint me. It was the first time when in a trilateral form we were trying to solve the problems'.[66] The Slovenian foreign minister, Eduard Kukan, who was one of the two UN special envoys to Kosovo, acknowledged that Ahtisaari had 'received the European Union's blessings ... to become its Kosovo envoy', but simultaneously asserted that '[his] mandate was not very clear'.[67] In international media coverage of the peace negotiations in Kosovo, Ahtisaari was invariably referred to as the 'EU's envoy'.[68]

His role provoked confusion in Russia. In an article titled 'Who are you, President Ahtisaari?' the newspaper *Sankt-Peterburgie Vedomosti* expressed uncertainty about whether he represented the EU, the UN, the OSCE or the G8.[69] This article reflects the EU's lack of visibility in its foreign policy in Kosovo. About three years after this war, in the preparation phase for eastern enlargement of the EU, often considered by analysts as the EU's most crucial foreign policy tool, the EU gained both more visibility and capacity in its external relations. A major source of confrontation in EU–Russia relations emerged once Russian policymakers became aware of the repercussions of the EU's increasing influence in Russia's 'near abroad' as a consequence of its eastward expansion. This book demonstrates how the EU's eastern expansion and other sources of confrontation resulted in increasing strain following the initially cordial relationship that characterised Ahtisaari and Chernomyrdin's diplomacy.

Several obstacles marked Ahtisaari's and Chernomyrdin's negotiations. The first was NATO's accidental bombing of the Chinese embassy in Belgrade on 7 May. Wesley Clark, NATO's Supreme Allied Commander for Europe, had authorised the attack, but the embassy was bombed instead of the Federal Directorate of Supply and Procurement, responsible for the management of arms trafficking, because CIA maps had not been updated.[70]

Another impediment to the mediation efforts was Yeltsin's threat to boycott the peace negotiations. Yeltsin had the impression that Russia's concerns regarding Kosovo had been disregarded. He stated that '[i]t must be clear that if Russia's efforts continue to be ignored, we will leave the reconciliation process with all of its consequences'.[71] A Kremlin spokesman quoted Yeltsin's reasons for his intended withdrawal from the negotiations. He declared that 'our calls and repeated suggestions [were] clearly not reaching somebody'.[72] The reason for Yeltsin's stance was an EU–Russian disagreement concerning the constitution of Kosovo's peacekeeping mission. The Yeltsin administration was opposed to a NATO-led peacekeeping mission, and preferred one under the auspices of the UN. Russia's foreign minister Igor Ivanov explained to Chernomyrdin that the UN 'must be the leading' institution in this operation.[73] Chernomyrdin was concerned that 'if Yeltsin agree[d] to subordinate Russian troops to the alliance, which ha[d] been waging this war, the impeachment process against him [would] start all over again'.[74]

A further obstacle for Ahtisaari and Chernomyrdin in their attempt to find a political solution to the Kosovo War was the indictment of Milosevic by the International Criminal Tribunal. He was accused of the expulsion of 740,000 refugees from Kosovo since the beginning of 1999 and the murder of 340 Kosovar Albanians. According to Yeltsin's spokesman Yakushkin, 'all attempts to solve the crisis in the Balkans without Milosevic's participation were bound to fail'.[75] The Russian Foreign Ministry declared in a statement that Milosevic's indictment would 'create additional obstacles on the path to the resolution of the Yugoslav situation'.[76]

16   *EU–Russian diplomacy in Kosovo War*

The peace plan

Despite these obstacles, the fourth round of tripartite talks between Ahtisaari, Talbott and Chernomyrdin in Bonn on 1 June resulted in the formulation of a list of non-negotiable objectives. The goal of Ahtisaari and Chernomyrdin's mission was to put the following three-point plan into practice: first, the Serbian government should withdraw paramilitary as well as Serbian troops from Kosovo; second, the Yugoslavian government should agree to allow Kosovo to be administered under a UN mandate; third, Belgrade should accept an international military presence under NATO's command.[77]

The EU and Russia had played a crucial role in the development of the peace plan. Schroeder, as chairman of the European Council Presidency, praised Russia's contribution to the development of the plan. He declared that 'from the very outset Germany and the European Union [counted on] using our traditionally good relations with Russia in the interest of achieving a solution to the Kosovo conflict'.[78] He stressed that the German government was 'sure that peace and peaceful development in the Balkans cannot be ensured without Russia's participation'.[79] He was appreciative of Chernomyrdin's diplomacy, saying that 'we were glad that a politician appeared in the person of Viktor Chernomyrdin, enjoying the confidence of the Russian president, who [shares our] perspective of Southeast Europe as we see it'.[80]

On the same day, Ahtisaari and Chernomyrdin's successful diplomacy resulted in Milosevic's capitulation. Despite his intention to amend the plan, Ahtisaari and Chernomyrdin managed to convince Milosevic to accept their peace plan, which the G8 states had already agreed.[81] This plan called for ceasing NATO bombing, an end to violence and repression, the withdrawal of troops, the deployment of international civilian and security presences under the UN's auspices, an international security presence with the essential contribution of NATO aimed at the safe return of refugees and displaced persons to their homes under the supervision of the UN High Commissioner for Refugees, the establishment of an interim administration for Kosovo decided by the UN Security Council as well as unfettered access for humanitarian organisations to Kosovo.[82] After having submitted the peace plan to the Serbian Parliament for approval, it was accepted on 2 June.[83]

The success of EU–Russian diplomacy was reflected in the Serbian government's announcement of the acceptance of the peace plan. No sooner had Milosevic capitulated than Schroeder rang Yeltsin to express his gratitude for the Russian government's successful diplomatic efforts. He thanked Yeltsin for Russia's 'constructive and peace-making role'.[84] At a news conference with Ahtisaari, he emphasised that this 'was a political breakthrough'.[85]

A day after the acceptance of the peace plan, Russia and the West managed to overcome the stalemate on the constitution of Kosovo's peacekeeping mission. The text on the deployment of NATO's Kosovo Force (KFOR), the retreat of Serbian forces and the establishment of a civil administration was adopted. Kosovo was divided into five zones, one for each member of the Contact Group.

Chernomyrdin had agreed that the international security presence in Kosovo should be provided by NATO within the framework of UN Security Council Resolution 1244. Under this resolution, roles were assigned to different international organisations for the provision of a civil and military presence in post-war Kosovo.[86] However, details of Russia's participation in the security presence had yet to be determined 'in order to prevent this issue from holding up the overall settlement'.[87]

Despite having overcome the deadlock over the formation of a peacekeeping mission, the EU and Russia clashed over Kosovo's post-war reconstruction. The EU became a primary financial contributor to Kosovo's reconstruction, providing the UN Interim Administration Mission in Kosovo with €243.7 million in 1999 for humanitarian aid, reconstruction and special financial assistance.[88] The European Commission also developed a reconstruction and development strategy for 1999 worth €5 million.[89] While the EU took responsibility for Kosovo's economic reconstruction, KFOR,[90] under the command of the UN, took responsibility for maintaining security.[91]

At the same time, the EU was developing plans for closer integration with the Balkan states. On 10 June 1999, about a week after the Kosovo War had been resolved, the European Council signed the Sarajevo Summit Declaration approving the purposes and principles of the Stability Pact for South Eastern Europe, which focused on the stabilisation of Albania, Bosnia and Herzegovina, Croatia, the Federal Republic of Yugoslavia and the Former Yugoslav Republic of Macedonia.[92] The Stability Pact was led by EU member states, the US, Russia and eight south-eastern European nations in cooperation with the World Bank and the International Monetary Fund (IMF).[93] It offered those countries the opportunity of signing Stabilisation and Association Agreements with the EU, which opened up the possibility of their accession to the EU.[94] These agreements aimed to foster peace, democracy, respect for human rights and economic prosperity in order to achieve stability through political and economic reforms, as well as the promotion of development and security in the Balkans.[95]

Despite the EU's efforts in restoring security in the Balkans, a further clash between NATO and Russia reflected continuing struggles over Kosovo's post-war reconstruction. The Russian government's request to participate in the NATO-led peacekeeping mission had been accepted by NATO member states, but the scope of its participation had not been clarified.[96] The severity of the clash over Russia's involvement in post-war reconstruction was made clear when on 12 June, 200 Russian paratroopers, who were engaged in peacekeeping for NATO's Stabilisation Force of Bosnia and Herzegovina, detached themselves from the Russian military and seized Pristina airport before the arrival of KFOR. As a result, they became the first foreign troops to march into Kosovo, and Serbs based at the airport in Pristina hailed the Russian paratroopers as liberators.[97] According to Marc Webber, the so-called 'dash to Pristina' was 'seemingly ... designed as a unilateral attempt to set up a Russian sector'.[98] The Yeltsin administration insisted that Russian troops should maintain a part of Kosovo under their command.[99]

18 *EU–Russian diplomacy in Kosovo War*

For Yeltsin, the 'dash to Pristina' had more symbolic than practical significance. He declared that Russia

> must make a crowning gesture, even if it had no military significance. It was not a question of specific diplomatic victories or defeats; it was a question of whether we had won the main point. Russia had not permitted itself to be defeated in the moral sense. It had not let itself be split. It had not been dragged into the war. This last gesture was a sign of moral victory in the face of the enormous NATO military, all of Europe, and the whole world.[100]

The next day, representatives of the Clinton administration confirmed the widely held view that the dash reflected US–Russian tensions over Russia's involvement in the peacekeeping mission in Kosovo. US Secretary of State Madeleine Albright stated that Russia and the US had gone from 'celebrating victory to a farcical Cold War encore'.[101] At a meeting between the US Defence Secretary William Cohen and his Russian counterpart Igor Sergeyev six days after the dash to Pristina, the US and Russia agreed on the deployment of Russian troops to Kosovo under the leadership of the national commanders of other members of the Kosovo Contact Group. [102]

While Russia, the US and NATO were competing over their involvement in post-war Kosovo, EU–Russia relations consolidated. The launch of the 'EU's Common Strategy on Russia' on 4 June had sent out a clear message of commitment to enhancing relations with Russia. According to NATO Secretary-General Javier Solana, the Common Strategy sought to 'cement the partnership between the EU and Russia'.[103] The fact that this strategy was the first document of its kind adopted by the EU highlighted the significance of Russia as a partner.[104] It had been prepared by the European Council in late 1998 as a response to the economic collapse of Russia that year.[105] Hence, it was not an EU response setting out further objectives for enhancing its relations with Russia immediately following the success of EU–Russian diplomacy in terminating the Kosovo War. The EU Common Strategy on Russia, launched during the Austrian European Council Presidency, stressed the

> Union's solidarity with Russia and its people during the present economic crisis.... The European Council underline[d] the EU's readiness to help Russia in overcoming the crisis through credible and sustained market-based reforms, while respecting urgent social need, and a continued commitment to democracy including freedom of the media, the rule of law and respect for human rights.[106]

This quote reflects two aspects of the EU's political approach towards Russia. On the one hand, the EU expressed its support in light of the repercussions of the Russian economic crisis. On the other hand, this expression of solidarity was accompanied by a request to Russia to further pursue efforts to promote democracy. Both the rule of law and respect for human rights were a source of confrontation in the evolution of EU–Russia relations several months after the partners' successful diplomacy during the Kosovo War.

In addition to the divergence between the EU and Russia over human rights and the rule of law, the increasing prominence of the EU in external relations became a source for friction in EU–Russia relations about three years after the Kosovo War in the context of preparations for the eastward enlargement of the EU. The EU's foreign policy gained in prominence in two ways: First, the implementation of the Treaty of Amsterdam in May 1999 introduced EU Common Strategies, which intended to give a 'clearer focus to European foreign policy and to combine all the external policies of the EU into a single framework'.[107] According to a former official from the Directorate General for External Relations at the European Commission, Common Strategies sought to enhance the EU's leverage in external policy.[108] Second, another means to enhance EU foreign policy was the Amsterdam Treaty's introduction of the post of a High Representative, who was responsible for assisting the European Council in the formulation, preparation and implementation of decisions in foreign policy.[109] On June 4, Chancellor Schroeder announced that Javier Solana would become the High Representative for the CFSP in December 1999.[110] These two changes laid the institutional foundation for the EU's increasing ability to develop its external relations, as compared to its passivity prior to its involvement in the Kosovo peace mediations. As a consequence of the institutional underpinnings, the EU's foreign policy evolved to the extent that it had a direct impact on Russian citizens and policy makers. The latter perceived the EU's eventual increasing ability over the former Soviet space as an impingement of the Kremlin's interests. Hence, Russian policy makers' and diplomat's perceptions of the EU changed. This was one the main indicators of the gradual transformation of EU–Russia relations from courtship to confrontation, which the following chapters endeavour to trace.

Conclusion

This chapter has explained why the breakdown in Russia's relations with the US and NATO coincided with the emergence of cooperative diplomacy in EU–Russia relations. The partner's diplomacy was shaped by three factors: First, what had made the EU attractive for Russia during the Kosovo War was its initial role as a bystander at the beginning of the Kosovo crisis. While a dominant and 'aggressive' NATO was killing Russia's Slavic brothers in Serbia, the Russian political elite perceived the EU as a passive and benign actor. Russian policymakers declared that its relations with NATO were suspended but relations between Russia and the EU should be enhanced. As a consequence, these policymakers began to regard the EU as the 'acceptable face of the West'.

The second and third factors which fostered EU–Russian diplomacy, namely Russia's domestic political problems and the German European Council Presidency, were intertwined. While Yeltsin was under pressure from the Duma, which urged him to take a tougher stance on the Kosovo War and instigated an

20   *EU–Russian diplomacy in Kosovo War*

impeachment process against him, he realised that Russia could not deal with the Kosovo crisis on its own. He turned to the EU as a negotiating partner. Chancellor Schroeder's cordiality in his role as chairman of the German European Council Presidency was the third factor which laid the groundwork for EU–Russian diplomacy during the Kosovo War. In announcing that Germany would be Russia's 'advocate' in its negotiations with international financial institutions concerning the repayment of Russia's debts, Schroeder made himself known as a friend of Russia. Schroeder's appointment of Ahtisaari as the EU's special envoy for Kosovo, gave Chernomyrdin, Russia's mediator in Kosovo, a competent partner in the peace negotiations. Chernomyrdin and Ahtisaari developed a peace plan which resolved the Kosovo War and exemplifies success in EU–Russian diplomatic cooperation.

The Kosovo War was the embodiment of EU–Russian cooperation before the relationship became increasingly strained and ultimately confrontational in the years following the international crisis in Serbia. The second Chechen War, which erupted just a few months after the resolution of the Kosovo War, resulted in moments of severe tension followed by constructive engagement in the EU–Russia 'strategic partnership'.[111] This seeming paradox, which reveals several facets of the internal dynamics of EU–Russian diplomacy, is at the core of the next chapter.

Notes

1 BBC Summary of World Broadcasts. Source: Russian Public TV. Yeltsin warns NATO against unleashing world war. 12 April 1999.
2 European Council (1999). Joint statement by President of the Russian Federation, B.N. Yeltsin, President of the European Council, G. Schroeder and President of the European Commission, J. Santer. EU–Russia Summit, Moscow, February 1999. Emphasis added.
3 BBC Summary of World Broadcasts. Russia, EU leaders stress partnership as summit gets under way. 19 February 1999.
4 Akin (1999).
5 Isachenkov (1999a).
6 *Sueddeutsche Zeitung* (1999); Deutsche Presse Agentur (1999a).
7 Illarionov (1999), pp. 29–59.
8 Averre (2009), p. 577.
9 Weller (1999), p. 211; Truehart (1999).
10 Ginsberg (2001), p. 246.
11 BBC Monitoring Former Soviet Union – Political. Supplied by BBC Worldwide Monitoring. Source: NTV. Russian mediator says universal agreement 'unlikely' at Rambouillet talks. 10 February 1999.
12 Solioz and Petritsch (2003), p. 357.
13 BBC Monitoring Former Soviet Union. Supplied by BBC Worldwide Monitoring. Source: Radio Russia. Russian envoy denies backing Belgrade to accept international force in Kosovo. 15 March 1999.
14 BBC Monitoring Europe – Political. Supplied by BBC Worldwide Monitoring. Source: Radio B92 Belgrade. Holbrooke urges Serbs to accept foreign troops in Kosovo. 23 March 1999.
15 Nugent, Paterson and Wright (eds) (2003), p. 208.

EU–Russian diplomacy in Kosovo War   21

16 European Commission (1999).
17 Smith, K.E. (2008), p. 42.
18 *Daily Mail* (1999).
19 Akin (1999).
20 European Commission (1997).
21 BBC Monitoring Europe – Political. Supplied by BBC Worldwide Monitoring. Source: RNE Radio 1, Spain. Spanish European Commissioner to take over European Commission as caretaker. 7 May 1999
22 James and Schmid (1999); *Wall Street Journal* (1999). For Schroeder's explanation of the significance of Prodi's nomination, see: Deutsche Presse Agentur (1999b).
23 Surovell (2000), p. 244.
24 BBC Monitoring Former Soviet Union – Political. Source: Russia TV. Russian Foreign Minister Ivanov Kosovo crisis speech at Duma session. 29 March 1999.
25 Averre (2009), p. 578.
26 Reeves (1999).
27 NATO (2002). The justification for this withdrawal was that the Kremlin equated the lack of authorisation from the UN Security Council for NATO's bombing in Yugoslavia with a breach of the Permanent Joint Council's Founding Act, which stated that NATO and Russia would need to respect the UN's primary responsibility for the maintenance of international peace and security. See: Smith (2006), p. 75.
28 Leeurdijk and Zandee (2001), p. 190.
29 Ulyanova (1999).
30 Ibid.
31 BBC Monitoring Former Soviet Union – Political. Supplied by BBC Worldwide Monitoring. Source: ITAR-TASS news agency. Russian–Yugoslav talks over, Russian premier off to Bonn. 30 March 1999.
32 *Kommersant* (1999).
33 Interfax (1999).
34 BBC Monitoring Former Soviet Union. Source: ITAR-TASS news agency. Russian Parliament votes for military aid to Yugoslavia. 7 April 1999.
35 BBC Summary of World Broadcasts. Source: Interfax news agency. Yeltsin says Russia preparing new Yugoslav initiative, rules out arms supplies. 9 April 1999.
36 BBC Summary of World Broadcasts. Source: ITAR-TASS news agency Russia to vote military aid to Serbia if NATO troops go in. Seleznev. 27 April 1999.
37 Shevtsov (1999).
38 Ibid.
39 Associated Press (1999); Reuters (1999).
40 Yeltsin (2000), p. 133, 134.
41 *The Guardian.* (1999); Norris (2005), p. 107.
42 BBC Summary of World Broadcasts. Source: Ekho Moskvy. Yeltsin supports tough stand on Yugoslavia-spokesman. 27 March 1999.
43 Ibid.
44 Ibid.
45 Stigler (2002–2003), p. 141.
46 Yeltsin (2000), p. 260.
47 Ibid.
48 Email interview with Dr Wolfgang Petritsch, former European chief negotiator of the Balkan Contact Group and EU envoy for Kosovo from October 1998 until July 1999. Interview conducted on 20 August 2011.
49 Primakov (2004), p. 283, 309.
50 Ibid.
51 Yeltsin (2000), p. 261.
52 McEvoy (1997).
53 Norris (2005), p. 85; Talbott (2002), pp. 313, 314.

22 *EU–Russian diplomacy in Kosovo War*

54 Norris (2005), p. 85.
55 Ulbrich (1999).
56 Schroeder (2006), p. 139.
57 Ibid.
58 Ibid. p. 137.
59 Leopold (1999).
60 *Moscow Times* (1999).
61 Norris (2005), p. 87.
62 Talbott (2002), p. 314.
63 Council of the European Union (1999).
64 For details on the US government's approval for Ahtisaari's role as a mediator see: Albright (2003), p. 417.
65 Talbott (2002), p. 314.
66 Ibid.
67 CTK National Newswires (1999).
68 See for example. Lloyd (1999); Walker (1999a).
69 *SPB Vedomosti* (1999).
70 NATO (2000); Castle, Marshall, Reeves and Sylvester (1999).
71 Norris (2005), p. 121.
72 Perlez (1999).
73 Talbott (2002), p. 319; Isachenkov (1999b).
74 Talbott (2002), p. 320.
75 *Die Welt*. (1999).
76 Walker (1999b).
77 Schroeder (2006), p. 138.
78 BBC Monitoring Former Soviet Union – Political. Supplied by BBC Worldwide Monitoring. Source: ITAR-TASS. Russia, Finland, USA heading for solution on Kosovo-German chancellor. 2 June 1999.
79 Ibid.
80 Ibid.
81 European Commission (1999).
82 Sand (1999).
83 BBC Summary of World Broadcasts. Source: Tanjug news agency. Belgrade. Serbian assembly approves Kosovo plan. 5 June 1999; BBC Summary of World Broadcasts. Source: Tanjug news agency. Belgrade. Yugoslav government endorses Kosovo peace plan. 3 June 1999.
84 BBC Monitoring Europe – Political. Supplied by BBC Worldwide Monitoring. German leader thanks Russian president for Kosovo role. 4 June 1999.
85 Swardson (1999).
86 Wouters and Naert (2001), p. 561.
87 Smith (2006), p. 87.
88 Kramer (2000), p. 6 .
89 European Commission/World Bank (1999).
90 Tolksdorf (2007).
91 Wouters and Naert (2001), p. 561.
92 Auswaertiges Amt Deutschland (1999).
93 Schmid (1999).
94 European Commission (2009). EU in Southeast Europe. The Stabilisation and Association Process. Retrieved 31 March 2009 from: www.delalb.ec.europa.eu/al/eu_in_see/stabilisation.htm
95 Stability Pact for South Eastern Europe (2009).
96 Schmid (1999).
97 Bohlen (1999).
98 Webber (2000), p. 203.

EU–Russian diplomacy in Kosovo War 23

99 Deutsche Presse Agentur (1999c).
100 Yeltsin (2000), p. 266.
101 Albright (2003), p. 423.
102 Drozdiak (1999).
103 Solana (1999).
104 Email interview with Lars Grønbjerg. Former seconded national expert working at the Unit for Relations with Russia and the Northern Dimension Policy at the European Commission Directorate General for External Relations. Conducted on 4 January 2012.
105 Ibid.
106 European Council (1998).
107 Hix (2005), p. 390.
108 Email interview with Lars Grønbjerg. Conducted on 4 January 2012.
109 Ibid.
110 Deutsche Presse Agentur (1999d).
111 'The EU–Russia Strategic Partnership' was the title of a speech given by Javier Solana in October 1999. The fact that Solana – who had not yet assumed the post of EU High Representative for the CFSP – uses his speech to explain the significance of EU–Russia relations, and the mutual responsibility of the EU and Russia to use the opportunity to develop their partnership, demonstrates the importance of relations with Moscow on the EU agenda.

Bibliography

Akin, M. (1999). Yeltsin goes after NATO on Kosovo. *Moscow Times*. 19 February 1999.

Albright, M. (2003). *Madame Secretary. A Memoir*. London: Pan Macmillan.

Associated Press. (1999). Ilyukhin. Parliament may vote on impeachment in mid-March. 18 February 1999.

Auswaertiges Amt Deutschland. Sarajevo Summit Declaration. 30 July 1999. Retrieved 31 March 2009 from: www.auswaertigesamt.de/diplo/en/Aussenpolitik/Regionale Schwerpunkte/Suedosteuropa/ErklaerungSarajevo.pdf

BBC Monitoring Europe – Political. Supplied by BBC Worldwide Monitoring. Source: Radio B92 Belgrade. Holbrooke urges Serbs to accept foreign troops in Kosovo. 23 March 1999.

BBC Monitoring Europe – Political. Supplied by BBC Worldwide Monitoring. Source: RNE Radio 1, Spain. Spanish European Commissioner to take over European Commission as caretaker. 7 May 1999.

BBC Monitoring Europe – Political. Supplied by BBC Worldwide Monitoring. German leader thanks Russian president for Kosovo role. 4 June 1999.

BBC Monitoring Former Soviet Union. Supplied by BBC Worldwide Monitoring. Source: Radio Russia. Russian envoy denies backing Belgrade to accept international force in Kosovo. 15 March 1999.

BBC Monitoring Former Soviet Union. Source: ITAR-TASS news agency. Russian Parliament votes for military aid to Yugoslavia. 7 April 1999.

BBC Monitoring Former Soviet Union – Political. Supplied by BBC Worldwide Monitoring. Source: NTV. Russian mediator says universal agreement 'unlikely' at Rambouillet talks. 10 February 1999.

BBC Monitoring Former Soviet Union – Political. Source: Russia TV. Russian Foreign Minister Ivanov Kosovo crisis speech at Duma session. 29 March 1999.

BBC Monitoring Former Soviet Union – Political. Supplied by BBC Worldwide Monitoring. Source: ITAR-TASS news agency. Russian–Yugoslav talks over, Russian premier off to Bonn. 30 March 1999.

24 *EU–Russian diplomacy in Kosovo War*

BBC Monitoring Former Soviet Union – Political. Supplied by BBC Worldwide Monitoring. Source: ITAR-TASS. Russia, Finland, USA heading for solution on Kosovo-German chancellor. 2 June 1999.

BBC Summary of World Broadcasts. Russia, EU leaders stress partnership as summit gets under way. 19 February 1999.

BBC Summary of World Broadcasts. Source: Ekho Moskvy. Yeltsin supports tough stand on Yugoslavia-spokesman. 27 March 1999.

BBC Summary of World Broadcasts. Source: Interfax news agency. Yeltsin says Russia preparing new Yugoslav initiative, rules out arms supplies. 9 April 1999.

BBC Summary of World Broadcasts. Source: Russian Public TV. Yeltsin warns NATO against unleashing world war. 12 April 1999.

BBC Summary of World Broadcasts. Source: ITAR-TASS news agency. Russia to vote military aid to Serbia if NATO troops go in. Seleznev. 27 April 1999.

BBC Summary of World Broadcasts. Source: Tanjug news agency. Belgrade. Yugoslav government endorses Kosovo peace plan. 3 June 1999.

BBC Summary of World Broadcasts. Source: Tanjug news agency. Belgrade. Serbian assembly approves Kosovo plan. 5 June 1999.

Bohlen, C. (1999). Crisis in the Balkans; Russia: new distrust clouds between talks between the US and Moscow. *New York Times*. 13 June 1999.

Castle, S., Marshall, A., Reeves, P. and Sylvester, R. (1999). War in Europe: Diplomatic shuttle end triumphant; gradually, relentlessly – and then suddenly: after the week of talking comes; the peace negotiations. *Independent*. 6 June 1999.

Council of the European Union. (1999). Former Special Representatives. Joint Action. 1999/239. CFSP. OJ. L89. Retrieved 29 May 2011 from: www.consilium.europa.eu/showpage.aspx?id=442&lang=en

CTK National Newswires. (1999). Kukan starts his mission of UN envoy for Kosovo today. 18 May 1999.

Daily Mail. (1999). Downfall of the Brussels 20; Commissioners tainted Europe in crisis by fraud and cronyism scandal resign en masse. Europe in crisis. 16 March 1999.

Deutsche Presse Agentur. (1999a). Roundup: Germany promises to back Russia. 19 February 1999.

Deutsche Presse Agentur. (1999b). Prodi chosen for top EU job. 27 March 1999.

Deutsche Presse Agentur. (1999c). First roundup: Yeltsin, Schroeder say strike must end, Helsinki meeting postponed. 4 June 1999.

Deutsche Presse Agentur. (1999d). Solana M. 'Europe' Kosovo expected to remain on EU summit agenda. 4 June 1999.

Die Welt. (1999). Haager Tribunal klagt Milosevic des Mordes an; Kreml will Gespraeche abbrechen – Clinton plant 'Bodenkrieg'. 28 May 1999.

Drozdiak, W. (1999). US, Russia reach military agreement; Russian to patrol NATO sectors. *Washington Post*. 19 June 1999.

European Commission. (1997). Entry into force of Partnership and Cooperation Agreement with Russia. European Commission Press Release Database. ip/97/1052/REV. Brussels 28 November 1997. Retrieved 11 November 2008 from: http://europa.eu/rapid/pressReleasesAction.do?reference=IP/97/1052&format=HTML&aged=1&language=EN&guiLanguage=en

European Commission. (1999). General Affairs Council. Declaration on the resignation of the European Commission. March 1999. 2168th Council meeting. Brussels, 21/22 March 1999. European Council Press Release Database. C/99/76. 6776/99 (Presse 76).

European Commission. (1999). Declaration of the European Union on Kosovo. Section: Foreign Politics and Common Security. PESC: 99/53. Press release. 2 June 1999.

EU–Russian diplomacy in Kosovo War 25

European Commission. (2009). EU in Southeast Europe. The Stabilisation and Association Process. Retrieved 31 March 2009 from: www.delalb.ec.europa.eu/al/eu_in_see/stabilisation.htm

European Commission/World Bank. (1999). European Commission decision establishing a programme for exceptional targeted support for public services under the 1999 Kosovo budget. Economic Reconstruction and Development in South East Europe. Retrieved 4 February 2009 from: www.seerecon.org/kosovo/ec/ec_dec_pubserv.htm

European Council. (1998). Presidency Conclusions. XIII. External issues. Russia. Vienna European Council. 11 and 12 December 1998. Retrieved 30 March 2009 from: www.consilium.europa.eu/uedocs/cms_data/docs/pressdata/en/ec/00300-R1.EN8.htm

European Council. (1999). EU–Russia Summit (Moscow, February 1999). Joint statement by President of the Russian Federation, B.N. Yeltsin, President of the European Council, G. Schroeder and President of the European Commission, J. Santer. Retrieved 11 November 2008 from: www.consilium.europa.eu/uedocs/cms_data/docs/pressdata/en/er/99-02-18.sta.htm

Ginsberg, R.H. (2001). *The European Union in International Politics. Baptism by fire.* Lanham, MD: Rowman and Littlefield.

Guardian. (1999). Yeltsin impeachment hearings begin. Vote to remove the president could take place tomorrow. 13 May 1999.

Hix, S. (2005). *The Political System of the European Union.* New York: Palgrave Macmillan.

Illarionov, A. (1999). How the Russian Financial Crisis was Organized. *Problems of Economic Transition.* 41(11): 29–59.

Interfax. (1999). My kliuchevye partnery. 16 April 1999.

Isachenkov, V. (1999a). Yeltsin meets with German, EU leaders. Associated Press. 18 February 1999.

Isachenkov, V. (1999b). Three envoys on Kosovo confer in Moscow. Associated Press. 21 May 1999.

James, B. and Schmid, J. (1999). EU leaders unanimous: Prodi to run Commission; 'A great challenge', Ex-Italy Prime Minister says. *International Herald Tribune.* 25 March 1999.

Kommersant. (1999). Natovskie samolety sledili za nami v vozdukhe. 31 March 1999.

Kramer, H. (2000). The European Union in the Balkans: Another step towards European integration. *Perception: Journal of International Affairs.* 5(3). Retrieved 4 February 2009 from: www.sam.gov.tr/perceptions/Volume5/SeptemberNovember2000/VolumeVN3HEINZKRAMER.pdf

Leeurdijk, D. and Zandee, D. (2001). *Kosovo: From crisis to crisis.* Aldershot: Ashgate Publishing.

Leopold, E. (1999). Finnish president may be Kosovo point men for West. Reuters. 13 May 1999.

Lloyd, J. (1999). In Moscow. Moscow rivalry hampers envoy's effectiveness. *Financial Times.* 24 May 1999.

McEvoy, J. (1997). Russia restates EU membership ambitions. Reuters. 18 July 1997.

Moscow Times. (1999). Finland-led EU will seek closer links with Russia. 1 April 1999.

NATO (2000). Who is who at NATO? Supreme Allied Commander Wesley J. Clark., US Army. Retrieved 2 March 2009 from: www.nato.int/cv/saceur/clark.htm

NATO (2002). *NATO Handbook. Cooperation between NATO and Russia.* Chapter 3. The Opening up of the Alliance. The NATO–Russia Permanent Joint Council. NATO Publications. Retrieved 2 March 2009 from: www.nato.int/docu/handbook/2001/hb030304.htm

26 EU–Russian diplomacy in Kosovo War

Norris, J. (2005). *Collision Course. NATO, Russia and Kosovo*. Westport, CT: Praeger.

Nugent, N., Paterson, W.E. and Wright, V. (eds) (2003). *The Government and Politics of the European Union*. Fifth Edition. Basingstoke, UK and New York: Palgrave Macmillan.

Perlez, J. (1999). Upheaval in the Kremlin may add another obstacle to finding peace through negotiation. *New York Times*. 13 May 1999.

Primakov, Y. (2004). *Russian Crossroads. Toward the new millennium*. Trans. Felix Rosenthal. New Haven, CT and London: Yale University Press.

Reeves, P. (1999). Assault on the Serbs. Mortar attack bid on US embassy rocks Moscow. Anti-American protests. *Independent*. 29 March 1999.

Reuters. (1999). Yeltsin likely to face mid-March impeachment vote. 18 February 1999.

Sand, D.R. (1999). Yugoslavia bows to NATO's demands. White House 'hopeful', air strikes still continue. *Washington Times*. 4 June 1999.

Schmid, J. (1999). EU picks contentious aide to Schroeder to lead Balkan reconstruction. *International Herald Tribune*. 30 June 1999.

Schroeder, G. (2006). *Entscheidungen. Mein Leben in der Politik*. Hamburg: Hofmann und Campe.

Shevtsov, N. (1999). Vokrug konflikta. Evrosoyiuz – Eto ne NATO. Pul's planety. *Trud*. 9 May 1999.

Smith, K.E. (2008). *European Union Foreign Policy in a Changing World*. Cambridge: Polity.

Smith, M.A. (2006). *Russia and NATO since 1991: From Cold War through cold peace to partnership?* Abingdon, UK: Routledge.

Solana, J. (1999). The EU–Russia Strategic Partnership. Speech by the High Representative designate of the European Union for Common Foreign and Security Policy. Stockholm, Wednesday, 13 October 1999. Retrieved 25 April 2015 from: www.consilium.europa.eu/uedocs/cms_data/docs/pressdata/EN/discours/59417.pdf

Solioz, C. and Petritsch, W. (2003). The Interview. The fate of Bosnia and Herzegovina: An exclusive interview of Christophe Solioz with Wolfgang Petritsch. *Journal of Balkan and Near Eastern Studies*. 5(3): 355–373.

SPB Vedomosti. (1999). Kto vy president Akhtisaari? 26 May 1999.

Stability Pact for South Eastern Europe (2009). About the Stability Pact. Retrieved 31 March 2009 from: www.stabilitypact.org/about/default.asp

Stigler, A.L. (2002–2003). A Clear Victory for Air Power: NATO's empty threat to invade Kosovo. *International Security*. 27(3): 124–157.

Sueddeutsche Zeitung. (1999). Deutschland will der Anwalt Russlands sein. 20 February 1999.

Surovell, J. (2000). *Capitalist Russia and the West*. Aldershot, UK: Ashgate.

Swardson, A. (1999). EU applauds the unity its members showed; group's role in Kosovo pact brings 'good day for Europe' says Germany's Schroeder. *Washington Post*. 4 June 1999.

Talbott, S. (2002). *The Russia Hand. A memoir of presidential diplomacy*. New York: Random House.

Tolksdorf, D. (2007). Implementing the Ahtisaari proposal: the European Union's future role in Kosovo. Centrum für Angewandte Politikforschung (CAP) Policy Analysis. Munich: Centrum für Angewandte Politikforschung. Ludwigs-Maximilian Universitaet. Retrieved 4 February 2009 from: www.cap-lmu.de/publikationen/2007/cap-policy-analysis-2007-01.php

Truehart, C. (1999). Moving beyond history's shadows; Kosovo talks present new European focus. *Washington Post*. 10 February 1999.

Ulbrich, J. (1999). EU regrets Milosevic continues to fight, backs diplomatic efforts. AAP Newsfeed. 18 May 1999.

Ulyanova, Iu. (1999). ...to k Primakovu idet Kamdessiu. *Segodnya.* 26 March 1999.

Walker, M. (1999a). Russian deal takes shape; Diplomacy Moscow brings key concessions on both sides. *Guardian.* 27 May 1999.

Walker, M. (1999b). Moscow threatens to abandon talks. Diplomacy: As air raids reach new pitch, indictments could stall peace negotiations. *Guardian.* 28 May 1999.

Wall Street Journal. (1999). Italy's Prodi wins backing to head European Commission. 6 May 1999.

Webber, M. (2000). *Russia and Europe. Conflict or Cooperation?* Basingstoke, UK: Palgrave Macmillan.

Weller, M. (1999). The Rambouillet Conference on Kosovo. *International Affairs.* 75(2): 211–251.

Wouters, J. and Naert, F. (2001). How Effective is the European Security Architecture? Lessons from Bosnia and Kosovo. *The International and Comparative Law Quarterly.* 50(3): 540–576.

Yeltsin, B. (2000). *Midnight Diaries.* New York: PublicAffairs.

2 Overcoming the 'Chechnya Irritant' in EU–Russia relations[1]

Between the autumns of 1999 and 2001 EU–Russia relations developed from a spectacular clash over the second Chechen War to a strange courtship. During the early months of the war, the EU unleashed a barrage of criticism concerning Russian human rights violations in Chechnya which culminated in the imposition of sanctions against Moscow. Acrimonious exchanges between European and Russian diplomats reached their climax in the suspension of Russia's voting rights in the Parliamentary Assembly of the Council of Europe. By October 2000, the situation had radically changed. The focus had shifted from confrontation over Chechnya to the development of cordial relations between Russia's newly elected President Putin and the EU's powerbrokers.

This chapter examines the shift from confrontation over the Chechen War to a breakthrough in EU–Russian diplomatic relations. It argues that this alteration was shaped by three factors. First, the EU's ability to urge Russia to end the war was weakened by its internal divisions. While some EU institutions articulated clear condemnation of Russia's conduct in Chechnya and imposed sanctions, some leading EU functionaries and heads of state took a much more accommodating line. This incoherence both weakened the EU's stance and facilitated rapprochement between the EU and Russia.

Second, the EU began to prioritise economic and political benefits over humanitarian concerns. This prioritisation was acknowledged by Tuomas Forsberg and Graeme P. Herd who argued that during both Chechen Wars the EU 'sacrificed a coherent and systematic advancement of its normative agenda, [namely the protection of human rights], in favour of strengthening its relations with [Russia]'.[2] During the second Chechen War, economic factors contributed to a shifting balance of power between the EU and Russia. On the one hand, Russia's economic recovery made it less vulnerable to international pressure than it had been in the immediate aftermath of its default in 1998. This recovery put pressure on European businesses to exploit the opportunities offered by the modernisation of Russia's hydrocarbon sector. On the other hand, the impending enlargement of the EU increased concerns about energy security. This preoccupation encouraged a shift of emphasis from confrontation over Chechnya to the launch of the EU–Russian Energy Dialogue in October 2000.

Third, the terrorist attacks on and following 11 September 2001 lent plausibility to Russian policymakers' efforts to portray the subjugation of Chechnya as an anti-terrorist operation. EU leaders were receptive to this interpretation and increased their cooperation with Russia on international terrorism.

Before Putin's election (October–December 1999)

The EU's response to the Chechen War

The outbreak of war between Russia and the breakaway region of Chechnya confronted the EU with a dilemma. On the one hand, the brutality of Russia's military onslaught and the ensuing pacification campaign was an affront to the values that the EU aspired to uphold. On the other hand, Russia was a victim of aggression. The invasion of Chechnya had been triggered by the incursion of Chechen Islamist militants into Russian territory in Dagestan. Meanwhile, over 300 civilians died as a result of terrorist attacks on apartment buildings in Russian cities, which were widely blamed on the Chechen insurgents. The challenges posed by the war were compounded by the EU's internal division. The early phase of the war took place under the Finnish chairmanship of the European Council Presidency (June–December 1999), which was sympathetic towards Russia and unwilling to provoke confrontation. At the same time, the EU Commissioner for External Relations Chris Patten was well known for his principled position on human rights.

On 7 October, six days after Russia's invasion of Chechnya, the European Parliament responded cautiously to this incursion. In a resolution condemning the escalation of the conflict, it expressed its deep concern over both the war and Putin's refusal to negotiate a political solution with the Chechen president, Aslan Mashkadov.[3] The resolution announced the EU's readiness to provide humanitarian assistance to Chechnya.[4] In a nod to Russian sensitivities, the resolution affirmed that the EU was 'committed to strengthening the strategic partnership with Russia in terms of economic integration and cooperation while maintaining stability and security in Europe and beyond'.[5] This view was reiterated by the Finnish foreign minister, Tarja Halonen, speaking on behalf of the Finnish European Council Presidency. She explained the EU's cautious reaction to Russia's invasion of Chechnya by declaring that the 'West may have been slow to speak up [on Chechnya] out of sympathy for Russia in the wake of the terrorist campaigns'.[6] No less cautious than Halonen was the German foreign minister Joschka Fischer. He declared that the German government was interested in the respect of human rights and Russia's stability, but stated that 'our capabilities of acting from outside were limited because the Chechen conflict took place in Russian territory within established frontiers'.[7]

The first opportunity for high-level discussions about the crisis was provided at the EU–Russian summit in Helsinki on 22 October. Attention was focused on the carnage in Chechnya caused by a missile strike that killed hundreds of civilians in Grozny's market square.[8] Even before the summit had begun, an EU spokesman

30   Overcoming the 'Chechnya Irritant'

warned bluntly that 'we cannot do business as usual even though the deepening of EU–Russia relations [was] the basis of our ambitions for the summit'.[9]

The market place massacre provoked tense discussions between the EU troika (the chairmen of the previous, current and subsequent European Council Presidencies) and Vladimir Putin, who was representing President Yeltsin at the summit. The Finnish Prime Minister Paavo Lipponen, speaking on behalf of the European Council Presidency, urged Putin to hold 'immediate negotiations' with the Chechen authorities and emphasised that the EU '[did] not accept a military solution'.[10] In his memoirs Chris Patten, the Commissioner for EU External Relations, recalled the High Representative of the CFSP Javier Solana's queries to Putin regarding the Russian government's reports on the bombing of the market square in Grozny. Putin denied possessing information on this attack; instead he reiterated the Russian military official's declaration that Chechen rebels had been responsible.[11] Patten reflected that he had 'never been so blatantly lied to at a meeting like this before'.[12] In an obvious criticism of the cordial relations of EU heads of state with Putin, Patten stated that '[the European politicians] let [Putin] get away with it – on that occasion, and again and again'.[13] Certainly, the joint statement of the summit offered no breakthrough. Its signatories – EU President Romano Prodi, Lipponen, Solana and Putin – merely stated that EU and Russian representatives had 'exchanged views' concerning the 'situation' in Chechnya.[14]

Putin's stance at the summit was intransigent. At the press conference Putin rejected EU requests to negotiate a political solution. He stressed that the ultimate goal of the Russian operation in Chechnya was 'to destroy the bases of the gunmen that pose a threat both to Russia and the whole of Europe'.[15] Putin stated the Kremlin's position that the EU should refrain from interfering in Russian domestic politics, as outlined later in the 'Russian Medium Term Strategy for Developments of Relations between the Russian Federation and the EU (2000–2010)' issued in 2000 in response to the EU's Common Strategy on Russia published in June 1999. According to the Russian Medium Term Strategy (RMTS), EU–Russia relations

> would be based on treaty relations without mentioning the objective of Russia's accession to or 'association' with the EU. As a world power situated on two continents, Russia should retain its freedom to determine and implement its domestic and foreign policies, its status and advantages of an Euro-Asian state and the largest country of the Commonwealth of Independent States [CIS], independence of its position and activities at international organizations.[16]

Only eight months earlier, Yeltsin had lamented that Russia was not an EU member state.[17] Now Putin was publicly renouncing the goal of Russia's integration into the EU. By emphasising Russia's status as a 'Euro-Asian' state, the strategy reoriented Russian policy towards the former Soviet space and asserted Russia's prerogative as an autonomous actor on the world stage.

Overcoming the 'Chechnya Irritant' 31

The RMTS exemplified the vast gulf between Russian and EU aspirations for their relationship. It contradicted the principles laid out in the EU's Common Strategy on relations with Russia in two fundamental ways. First, unlike the Common Strategy, the RMTS did not mention closer integration with Europe as a priority but stressed that Russian foreign policy was focused on the former Soviet space. The RMTS stated that 'the development of a partnership with the EU should contribute to consolidating Russia's role as a leading power in shaping up a new system of interstate political and economic relations in the [CIS]'.[18] According to the RMTS, Russia's interests should be safeguarded in light of the 'ambivalent impact' of the EU's expansion on its cooperation with Russia, with Russia seeking to achieve the 'best advantages of such [enlargement] … while preventing, eliminating or setting off possible negative consequences'.[19] In contrast, the Common Strategy stated that a

> stable, democratic and prosperous Russia, firmly anchored in a united Europe free of new dividing lines, [was] essential to lasting peace on the continent. The issues which the whole continent [was facing could] be resolved only through ever closer cooperation between Russia and the [EU].[20]

The reference to 'ever closer cooperation' implied the progressive evolution of the relationship and affirmed the Common Strategy's main objective: Russia's integration into a ' "common economic and social area in Europe" through the achievement of a free trade area and the accommodation of Russian legislation to EU norms'.[21]

Second, a comparison of both strategies demonstrates the EU and Russia's diverging views on the importance of norms in their 'strategic partnership.' The Common Strategy stated that Russia had a European identity and shared values with the EU: 'The [EU] welcomes Russia's return to its rightful place in the European family in a spirit of friendship, cooperation, fair accommodation of interests and on the foundations of shared values enshrined in the common heritage of European civilisation'.[22] In contrast, the RMTS did not address this notion of 'shared values'.[23] Instead, it stressed the Kremlin's immunity to normative approximation with the EU. This was reflected in the RMTS statement that 'while preserving the independence of the Russian legal system … a line to its approximation and harmonization with the EU legislation in the areas of the most active EU–Russia cooperation should be pursued'.[24] The reference to both independence of Russian legislation and simultaneous legal approximation with the EU is contradictory. It lies beyond the scope of this chapter to research the areas in which Russia preferred to remain independent and those in which it favoured approximation. However, the reference to approximation with EU legislation is vague and raises doubts about the sincerity of intentions to pursue this approach. These doubts were confirmed when the following year, the Russian Federation's Foreign Policy Concept emphasised strengthening Russian sovereignty.[25] Divergence between the EU and Russia over Russia's approximation to EU norms contributed to increasing conflict over the following years.

32 Overcoming the 'Chechnya Irritant'

The shift in Russia's foreign policy from Yeltsin's regret that Russia was not an EU member to the Kremlin's rejection of further integration with the EU was reflected in the Foreign Policy Concept published a year after the EU Common Strategy on Russia. On one hand, it criticised the exclusionary nature of EU expansion: 'integration processes, in particular, in the Euro-Atlantic region often assume a selective and restrictive character'.[26] On the other, it denounced enlargement for 'belittling the role of the sovereign state' and thus 'creat[ing] the threat of arbitrary interference in internal affairs'.[27] According to the Kremlin, Russian foreign policy should emphasise the 'preserving and strengthening [of Russia's] sovereignty'.[28] This statement clearly demonstrated the Kremlin's opposition to sacrificing state sovereignty as the price for enhanced political and economic integration. Instead, the Kremlin emphasised the 'inviolability of Russia's sovereignty'.[29]

The concept of 'sovereign democracy' articulated by Vladislav Surkov, deputy head of the Putin administration, expressed the Kremlin's political ideology during Putin's presidency.[30] According to Surkov, sovereign democracy 'most closely corresponds to the foundations of Russian political culture' because it 'justifies centralization, concentration of the nation's material, intellectual, and power resources for the purposes of self-preservation and successful development of each citizen in Russia and of Russia in the world'.[31]

The Kremlin's push to 'preserve the sovereign' and the lack of a unified EU stance on Russia undermined the EU's ability to coerce Russia to end the Chechen War. The limited coercive power of the EU was exemplified when Russian foreign ministry spokesman Vladimir Rakhmanin dismissed an additional resolution from the European Parliament calling for an immediate ceasefire. The resolution, which alluded to the 'launching of a constructive dialogue with legitimate Chechen representatives without any unrealistic preconditions', provoked a furious reaction from Rakhmanin.[32] He declared that the Russian Foreign Ministry could not agree with the Parliament's 'accusations against Russia', which referred to the 'staging of combat operations against civilian[s] [and] distort[ed] the very meaning of what [was] going on in Chechnya. It [was] hardly probable that unbiased conclusions [could] be drawn on the basis of one-sided interpretations of those issues'.[33] Rakhmanin issued a warning about the future of EU–Russia relations by declaring that 'damage inflicted by such actions, usually affects both parties'.[34]

Confrontation at the OSCE summit

The OSCE summit in Istanbul on 18 to 19 November was the occasion for a major showdown between the West and Russia over Chechnya. In contrast to the confrontation at the EU–Russia summit, the discussion descended into acrimonious exchanges and public confrontation. Three days before the summit, Patten acknowledged that the unfolding situation in Chechnya put EU relations with Russia under considerable strain. 'The Russian authorities', he warned, 'must understand that their present action has an impact on their acceptance by the international community and Russia's credibility as a political and economic partner'.[35] Noting that the Chechen crisis would dominate the summit, in his speech to the same session, Javier Solana vowed 'to continue to put pressure on the Russians to reduce the intensity of the conflict and attempt to achieve a peaceful solution'.[36]

EU leaders used the OSCE summit to subject Yeltsin to a barrage of criticism. At the opening of proceedings, Romano Prodi, president of the European Commission, asserted the EU's normative authority as an organisation that 'embodies the hopes and aspirations of millions'.[37] He then addressed the Russian delegation:

> We have made our position crystal clear. We have condemned the indiscriminate use of force. We have asked Russia to ... [h]alt the military campaign. Begin immediate political dialogue, which is the only way to lasting peace. The EU has suggested a useful role for the OSCE, ... in contributing to a political solution of the crisis.[38]

The most strident European critic of Russia was French President Jacques Chirac, who declared that the Kremlin had to be 'forced in a friendly manner' to end the war.[39] In a less than friendly manner, he took an even harder line than other Western democracies, announcing that France would refuse to sign the Charter for European Security unless the Russian government agreed to include a passage in the summit's communiqué that obliged the Kremlin to start peace negotiations with the Chechen authorities.[40]

Solana communicated a more moderate message to Russia. He declared that the EU wanted to 'continue to talk to our Russian friends and put pressure on them'.[41] In a clear attempt to dispel any doubts regarding the EU's capacity to exert pressure on Russia, Solana noted that the EU had the 'appropriate opportunities and structures' to do so. He emphasised the EU view that

> this war is not the solution to their problem, a real problem that is connected to terrorism.... We have to continue to make the Russian authorities feel that the direction they are taking is not a great one and that there was no military solution to the conflict.[42]

But in private, Solana was more cautious. He requested an informal meeting with Vladimir Lukin, the liberal chairman of the Duma's International Affairs Committee, and told him that 'the European Union is moving full steam towards its own foreign policy and would very much like to cooperate with Russia on that'.[43] According to Lukin, Solana emphasised that 'he is a friend of our country'.[44] Lukin sought to read between the lines of his conversation with Solana to predict the EU's response to the Chechen War. 'I gathered from this that there is an intention to chide us, but not to go too far'.[45] Several weeks later, Lukin's assumption about the EU's shift to a moderate stance regarding Chechnya proved to be correct.

34 *Overcoming the 'Chechnya Irritant'*

The results of the OSCE summit were mixed. It was neither a victory for Russia nor for the West. The Russian government gave in to the West's repeated requests to allow human rights monitors from the OSCE to visit Chechnya. At the same time, the foreign ministers of Russia, France, the UK, Germany and Italy signed the Charter for European Security.[46] In what might be regarded as a justification for signing the document, the Russian foreign minister, Ivanov, declared that the OSCE could contribute to the provision of humanitarian aid and the support of refugees who had fled Chechnya.[47] However, the lack of detail in the Charter about the OSCE's contribution to a political solution to the Chechen War meant that the Russian government felt under no obligation to resolve the conflict. Russia maintained its refusal to negotiate a political solution. Ivanov stressed that the Russian government was opposed to the OSCE's political mediation in the Chechnya conflict as well as to any interference in Russian Federation affairs.[48] The Russian government's intransigence was exemplified two days after Ivanov signed the Charter, when Putin declared that the 'anti-terrorist operation' in Chechnya would continue at the same pace as before until all 'terrorist bases ... [were] wiped out for good'.[49]

The Grozny ultimatum

The EU–Russian confrontation over Chechnya reached its climax when the Kremlin issued an ultimatum on 6 December warning the inhabitants of Grozny that they would be treated as terrorists if they did not leave the city within five days.[50] The ultimatum provoked a brief moment of consensus on the EU's stance towards Russia, which resulted in discussions on the imposition of sanctions.

Some heads of government of EU member states sought to persuade the Kremlin to revoke the ultimatum. In a letter to Yeltsin and Putin, the German chancellor, Schroeder, and foreign minister, Fischer, called for the ultimatum to be rescinded.[51] In a letter to his counterpart Ivanov, Fischer denounced the ultimatum as an 'act of barbarism' which was 'out of proportion [because it could not] be equated with crushing terrorism'.[52]

No less critical was the response of the French government. In an address to the French Senate, Foreign Minister Hubert Védrine criticised the ultimatum as a 'brutal military action which hit the population in a very severe manner and was totally indiscriminate'.[53] He demanded the withdrawal of the ultimatum. Védrine called upon the EU to confront Russia in a 'more blunt and stronger' way.[54] The EU would have to 'methodologically examine the relations we have with Russia' because it could not 'cooperate as usual with Russia under these conditions as if nothing had happened when they refused to listen to the pressure from the international community'.[55]

There were two major divisions in the EU regarding its stance towards Russia during the Chechen War. On the one hand, contrary to Védrine, European Commission President Prodi sought to maintain cordial relations with Russia. Expressing his hesitation to impose sanctions, Prodi stated that 'we should discuss what a sanction is and the consequences of sanctions'.[56] A former spokesman for EU External Relations indirectly explained Prodi's wavering stance by characterising him as a person who did not use 'strong words; he was a man of fine analysis, [who] was always trying to find constructive ways'.[57] On the other hand, there was friction between the Finnish EU Council Presidency and the EU Commissioner for External Relations, Chris Patten, over their respective stances on Russia. The Presidency was clearly nervous about the barrage of public criticism Patten intended to direct towards Russia during the first Foreign Policy Dialogue Meeting with Russian foreign minister Ivanov. According to a former EU External Relations spokesman who was present at the meeting, Patten, who was known for his high profile on human rights, was encouraged by the Commission to use a 'moderate tone'.[58] This incident offered a 'foretaste that there [were] things we like to [state] internally and things you should say when you speak officially about EU–Russia relations'.[59] The spokesman's reference to the discrepancy between the EU's official and unofficial political discourse with or about Russia reflected the EU's strong intent to maintain cordial relations with Moscow. Behind closed doors, the rhetoric employed by the EU was less diplomatic.

A brief moment of unity emerged within the EU which resulted in publication of the European Council's 'Declaration on Chechnya', demonstrating an uncompromising stance on the conflict. This declaration, launched at the Council summit in Helsinki on 10 and 11 December, focused on three main issues. First, it strongly criticised the 'intense bombardments' of Chechen cities and the 'threat levelled at the residents of Grozny as well as the treatment of the internally displaced persons [as] totally unacceptable'.[60] Russia's fight against terrorism in Chechnya was 'in contradiction with the basic principles of humanitarian law, the commitments of Russia as made within the OSCE as well as its obligations as a member of the Council of Europe'.[61]

Second, the declaration threatened political sanctions against Russia. It warned that it would review the implementation of the EU's Common Strategy on Russia which had established objectives for developing an EU–Russian 'partnership'.[62] It would be difficult to predict the results of such a review. Additionally, it proposed that 'some of the [EU–Russian] PCAs' provisions should be suspended and trade provisions applied strictly'.[63] However, the declaration failed to confirm whether these intended sanctions had already been approved by the European Commission.

Third, the declaration reaffirmed the EU's normative ambitions in its relations with Russia. It expressed its willingness to 'accompany Russia in its transition towards a modern and democratic state', but at the same time, it warned that 'Russia must live up to its obligations *if* the strategic partnership [was] to be developed'.[64] In an obvious allusion to the severity of the impact of the war on EU–Russia relations, the declaration on Chechnya stated that the 'EU [did] not want Russia to isolate herself from Europe'.[65]

At the summit, the EU struggled to balance public expectations of a robust stance with the need to preserve relations with Russia. Patten claimed that the EU had 'bent over backwards to try to be understanding and reasonable, but public

36   *Overcoming the 'Chechnya Irritant'*

opinion would not expect us to go on as though it were business as usual'.[66] Like Patten, the Finnish Prime Minister Lipponen, speaking on behalf of the EU Council Presidency now took a stronger line than he had in October while reiterating the Council's declaration. Referring to the negative repercussions of the Chechen War for EU–Russia relations, he warned that it was 'really up to Russia if they isolate[d] themselves. It was not us that were isolating Russia'.[67]

The controversy about the proposal to suspend certain accords of the PCA resulted in a major clash within the EU. At the EU heads of state and government meeting a few weeks after the European Council summit in Helsinki, both Schroeder and Chirac argued in favour of suspension.[68] The European Council would have the right to put parts of the PCA on hold by 'unilaterally suspending its application', even though article four stated that its provisions could only be amended if the EU and Russia were both willing to do so.[69] This proposed sanction was belittled by Patten, the Commissioner for EU External Relations, who characterised it as a 'meaningless gesture'.[70] As a result of this discrepancy, it came as no surprise that neither the PCA's provisions nor the Common Strategy were reviewed.

Putin's election – 'a fresh start' (January–October 2000)

The nature of the EU–Russia conflict over Chechnya transformed on the eve of the new millennium when Yeltsin announced his resignation and Prime Minister Vladimir Putin became president. The changing Russian leadership fostered the development of EU–Russia relations in two ways. First, Western leaders considered establishment of a personal rapport with Putin as key to improving EU–Russia relations. Second, his election on 26 March consolidated his power.[71] Putin's presidency seemed to provide an opportunity to overcome the instability which marked the Yeltsin era by increasing the possibility of the renewal of political and economic reforms.

Solana was one of the first EU officials to react to Putin's rise to power. In an article published in *Kommersant* about two months before Putin's election – an obvious attempt to appeal to Russian public opinion – Solana stated that the EU had to address the situation in Chechnya without endangering EU–Russia relations. Praising the 'strengthening of democracy in Russia', Solana declared that he was 'certain that the impending presidential election [would] confirm the irreversibility of Russia's changes'.[72] Solana stated that Russia was the EU's 'most important partner ... in the field of economic and politics'.[73] He therefore encouraged the development of plans to strengthen the PCA. Considering that at the European Council summit in Helsinki less than two months previously the possibility of suspending some of the PCA provisions had been discussed, Solana's statement was extraordinary. At the height of the Chechen War, he celebrated the EU and Russia as having 'common values' and affirmed that 'in the UN and the OSCE [the EU and Russia] act together'.[74] Given his positive stance at a time when Russia was not respecting the values those organisations sought to uphold, it was not surprising that his article made only a fleeting reference to

Overcoming the 'Chechnya Irritant'   37

the Chechen conflict. He declared that it was important to 'discuss and respond to a problem like this constructively and in a manner of mutual respect'.[75] He concluded his article by stating that the EU and Russia shared 'foundations of democracy, security, respect for international norms and the market economy'.[76]

While Solana was seeking to establish cordial relations with Russia, friction within the EU concerning the response to the Chechen conflict became evident. Maintaining a hard-line stance, the European Commission reduced aid to Russia in the Technical Assistance to the Commonwealth of Independent States (TACIS) programme from €130 million to €40 million in retaliation for humanitarian abuses in Chechnya.[77]

The effect of these sanctions was limited. According to a former spokesman for EU External Relations, the scope of the measure was:

> fairly limited in as much as it referred to the decision not to commit new funds, but the ongoing projects were not stopped.... If you look at the history of sanctions, this was not a real sanction, it was a freezing of new programmes. Real sanctions are visa bans, travel bans, freezing of assets and trade blockades. They tend to be taken towards smaller countries, it [is not the case that the EU] has a strong record on this with the big partners, except the arms embargo with regard to China.[78]

The Chechen War was not the only occasion on which the EU hesitated over the imposition of sanctions against Russia. About 13 years later, when EU–Russia relations were shaken by the Ukraine crisis, the EU failed once again to take a coherent position on the imposition of restrictive measures against Russia. A group of prominent European officials and heads of state sought to pursue appeasement with Russia, which prevented them from speaking out in favour of imposing sanctions. The EU's internal struggles regarding the imposition of sanctions are assessed in Chapter 7.

As well as the Commission, which was trying to avoid jeopardising relations with Russia, several prominent European political leaders attempted a balancing act with Russia.[79] Two months after the EU member states requested a freeze on part of the EU's financial aid to Russia, Tony Blair sought to establish cordial relations with Putin. He declared that the best way of ending the war was by 'engaging' with Russia instead of 'isolating' it.[80] In an attempt to urge European politicians to refrain from condemning Russia's war in Chechnya, Blair stated that 'it was important to realise that Chechnya isn't Kosovo.... The Russians have been subjected to really severe terrorist attacks'.[81]

In a similar vein to Blair, the German chancellor Gerhard Schroeder perceived Putin's election on 26 March as a window of opportunity in EU–Russia relations. He asserted that a 'constructive fresh start' was possible because of Russia's internal political changes.[82] In a telegram congratulating Putin on his success in the elections, Schroeder reminded him that 'great expectations are connected with your appointment to this high position – expectations of a strong, democratic, peaceful and open Russia, a country that realizes its international

38 Overcoming the 'Chechnya Irritant'

responsibility and shall become an active participant in every European process'.[83] However, Schroeder's vision of Russia as an integral partner in every European process lacked detail about the nature of Russia's role in Europe. His vision did not recognise the implications of the RMTS and the Foreign Policy Concept which revealed the Kremlin's disavowal of closer association with the EU and declaration of 'sovereign democracy' as two of the guiding principles of Russian foreign policy which characterised the Putin era.

Regardless of Russia's abstention from closer integration with the EU, its relations with Europe were nurtured by pragmatic European politicians. Having reminded Putin to 'really use the chance provided by his office to take a decisive step in reform and modernisation through to democracy and market economy', Fischer, the German foreign minister, expressed his intention to maintain business-like relations with Moscow.[84] He declared that

> [Berlin] clearly condemned the war ... and called for a political solution. By this war, Russia is in danger of destabilising the whole region, but also its internal development. Nevertheless we must not reduce our relations with Russia to Chechnya. Russia is too important for us.[85]

Unlike Fischer, Schroeder and Blair, the European Council summit in Lisbon, which took place two days prior to Putin's election, urged Russia for a political solution.[86] The fact that this was merely a repetition of the Council's previously expressed stance towards Russia demonstrated the EU's limited ability to coerce Russia during the Chechen War.

Shift of struggle over Chechnya to the Parliamentary Assembly of the Council of Europe (PACE)

As the EU's criticism of the Chechen War was muted, the arena of struggle shifted to PACE. Since November 1999, this non-EU institution, which was responsible for upholding democracy in Europe, had adopted a series of resolutions denouncing the Chechen War and urging Russia not to violate human rights.[87] About a fortnight after Putin's electoral success, on 6 April, PACE imposed a ground-breaking resolution suspending the Russian delegation's voting rights.[88] In comparison to earlier resolutions, Russia was now compelled to provide evidence of improvements of the situation in Chechnya.[89] Another sign of the PACE's seriousness concerning the sanction was the fact that it called on the Committee of Ministers of the Council of Europe to suspend Russia if it failed to comply with the human rights body's demand for a ceasefire.[90] David Russel-Johnston, PACE's president, justified the suspension of Russia's voting rights, arguing that Russia had violated its commitments as a member state of the Council of Europe. He declared that

> Russia is a civilized European state, a member of the Council of Europe and as such expected and obliged to abide by higher standards of conduct. No

Overcoming the 'Chechnya Irritant' 39

acts of its adversary, brutal as they may be, can serve as a justification for its own violation of the rules it has committed itself to respect.[91]

PACE's Russian delegation was outraged by the suspension of Russia's voting rights and walked out of the hall.[92] Before leaving, Dmitri Rogozin, the head of the delegation, mockingly declared: 'We [the Russian delegation] wish you [the Council of Europe] well. Good bye'.[93]

A week later Duma deputies still criticised PACE's voting ban as 'insulting' and as an 'infringements on rights'.[94] They announced that cooperation with PACE would only be possible after a 'revision of its discriminatory decision'.[95] The vice chairman of the Duma, Vladimir Zhirinovsky, who was known for his demagogic statements, criticised PACE's resolution. Justifying Russia's conduct in Chechnya as a means of combating terrorism, he declared to the Council of Europe that 'Russia was protecting you, preventing terrorists from getting from the Caucasus to Europe, and you are censuring us'.[96]

Meanwhile Russian Foreign Minister Igor Ivanov had accused PACE's deputies of relying on information from Chechen terrorists.[97] He condemned the imposed voting ban as a 'serious mistake, [because it] would play into the hands of international terrorism and those who would like to derail the difficult process of the restoration of peace in Chechnya'.[98] In an attempt to justify Russia's actions in Chechnya, Ivanov declared that there 'were certain parallels' between the conflict in Chechnya and the Kosovo war. Posing as a defender of Europe, Ivanov stated that as in Chechnya, 'members of extremist circles, who act[ed] under nationalist or separatist slogans, [were] trying to destabilize the situation and achieve the disintegration of sovereign states'.[99] Simultaneously, he belittled the assembly's impact on foreign policy by stating that it had 'not played a significant role in European affairs'.[100]

The day after the announcement of the voting ban, prominent European officials controversially went to great lengths to distance the EU from PACE in order to avoid affront to Russia. Javier Solana, known for his cordial relations with Russia during the Chechen War, stressed at a news conference in Moscow that the Council of Europe was an independent organisation and not a part of the EU.[101] He assured the Russian leadership that the EU would not impose further sanctions against Russia over Chechnya. The EU, he declared, was 'pragmatic' and 'need[ed] a permanent dialogue with Russia'.[102] Solana's emphasis on pragmatism was reflected in a meeting he and the chairman of the Portuguese European Council Presidency had with Putin in the Kremlin.[103] The agenda of the meeting was the preparation for the forthcoming EU–Russia summit and also a ministerial level meeting to be held in Luxembourg.[104]

The same day, the Portuguese foreign minister, Jaime Gama, speaking on behalf of the European Council Presidency, tried to diminish the significance of PACE's action. He stated that the ban was 'not yet a final decision. It [was] only a recommendation at the moment. I hope that by the time we do take a final decision, Russia will have created favourable conditions for quite a different view'.[105] Gama maintained this accommodating line in a meeting with Putin and Solana.

40   *Overcoming the 'Chechnya Irritant'*

He declared that the 'EU intend[ed] to continue building constructive relations with Russia despite disagreements with Russia on certain issues'.[106] Gama promised that the EU 'would not make a global confrontation with Russia over Chechnya'.[107]

Foreign Minister Igor Ivanov welcomed Gama's efforts to distance the EU from PACE. Ivanov expressed obvious satisfaction that PACE's 'recommendations' had 'nothing to do with the EU anyway'.[108] Portugal's stance had a lasting impact on the Russian leaders. After a meeting between Gama, Ivanov and Putin, seven months after PACE announced its sanction, Russian Foreign Ministry sources were quoted by Interfax as appreciating that 'Lisbon [did] not press us even over Chechnya.... It underst[ood] how ... painful this issue [was] for Moscow'.[109]

Putin made what seemed at first sight to be a significant concession by fulfilling the Council of Europe's request to create a human rights office in Chechnya in May 2000. Putin appointed the diplomat Vladimir Kalamanov as his representative to monitor human rights. Kalamonov's office sought to enhance the judicial system, giving legal advice to people in detention and presenting evidence of Russia's human rights violations, but did not have the power to investigate complaints or initiate criminal proceedings.[110] The EU Council of Ministers 'acknowledged the efforts made by the Russian authorities' for having agreed to let experts from the Council of Europe work in Mr Kalamanov's office'.[111]

Nine months after the establishment of the office, its limited capacity to ameliorate the situation on the ground became evident. Experts from the Council of Europe discovered that the responses of Russian prosecutors to complaints lodged by Kalamanov's office were either unsatisfactory or nonexistent. From 429 applications submitted to the civilian prosecutor, only 169 replies were received.[112] Kalamanov himself acknowledged that his role was ambiguous by stating he was 'like a clown in the circus [having] no formal powers, but everyone can [both] see and hear me'.[113] His statement and the constrained responsiveness to the submitted complaints suggested that the creation of this office had been rather a formality instead of offering an institutional framework suitable to address human rights violations.

'A new course in EU–Russia relations'

Despite the Chechen War, a group of prominent European leaders began to adopt a more accommodating stance towards Russia. The most obvious manifestation of the EU's sidelining of the war was the European Council's decision to reconsider the sanctions imposed against Russia. Whereas Russian policymakers were grateful to the EU for its cooperation, the European and Russian human rights community became increasingly critical of the European leaders who had shifted their positions on Russia.

Despite France's original outspoken opposition to the Chechen War, Foreign Minister Hubert Védrine and Finance Minister Laurent Fabius now sought to dismiss condemnations about France's continuing engagement with Russia in

Overcoming the 'Chechnya Irritant' 41

the run-up to the next EU–Russia summit. They hailed Russia as a guarantor for security and stability. They stated that achievement of security in Europe '[was] unlikely to happen if poverty, misrule and instability prosper[ed] in Russia. The ills of an unstable Russia [might] also spill over into Europe'.[114] Fabius and Védrine sought to reconcile the EU's role as a defender of European values with its geopolitical interests in maintaining relations with Russia, despite its human rights violations in Chechnya:

> In standing to help Russia, the EU does not have to turn a blind eye to Russia's misbehaviour in Chechnya. Contrary to what some critics say, there is no contradiction between long-term and short-term objectives – between the imperatives of European values and the necessities of European geopolitical interests. Our fundamental disapproval of the way Russia has so far dealt with the painful Chechen problem, and our equally fundamental willingness to help Russia, are two sides of the same coin.[115]

In what could be considered to be an attempt to encourage more Western leaders to follow the example of Védrine and Fabius, the Russian Foreign Minister Ivanov advanced two arguments to convince the West to change course in its relations with Russia. First, Ivanov sought to persuade Western leaders that Russia and the West faced the same enemy, namely terrorism, by reminding European politicians about the dangers of terrorism in Southeast Europe. He declared that 'not only will the situation in the Balkans be destabilized again, but the metastases of extremism will begin to spread to all Western European countries'.[116] Second, Ivanov portrayed Russia as a victim of terrorism that was seeking solidarity. He stated that

> [t]he anti-terrorist operation in the North Caucasus was a forced and, it must be said, belated response to the terrorist challenge. It was not a war against the Chechen people or against Islam, as some would like to portray it. [T]housands of mercenaries, trained in Chechnya, [were] preparing to spread extremist ideas across the world.[117]

He encouraged the West to 'lead an honest and constructive dialogue with Russia [instead] of launching calls for its punishment and moreover to excommunicate Russia from Europe'.[118]

In what could be considered a response to Ivanov, the European Commission president, Prodi, attempted to reorient EU–Russia relations prior to the upcoming summit in Moscow on 29 May. Prodi declared that 'Russia and the EU were important economic partners, no matter what', emphasising that the 'Chechen issue would not be a main topic at the summit'.[119] He declared that '[w]e must seize with both hands the extraordinary opportunity to open a comprehensive dialogue'.[120] On the day of the summit, Prodi declared that the EU–Russian partnership

42 Overcoming the 'Chechnya Irritant'

is sufficiently solid to weather very real, even acute disagreements. This is what leads me to share with you a few thoughts on what is termed the Chechnya irritant in our relations. [W]e have never challenged Russia's right or even duty to fight terrorism and uphold its territorial integrity.... [We] have consistently raised our strong concerns over what is, in our view, the disproportionate use of force, the immense suffering of civilians ... the humanitarian problems, which have resulted from this operation. We would have betrayed our most important shared values if we would not have reacted then.[121]

Despite the fact that Prodi requested the Russian government to 'resolutely carry out what it ha[d] offered' to terminate the Chechen War, he stressed their significance as partners. He boasted that the EU and Russia were like 'whiskey and soda' because they complemented one another.[122] Prodi emphasised the partners' 'enormous potential for economic cooperation'.[123] The summit's joint statement reflected Prodi's moderate stance and showed that the Chechen War had been sidelined. According to the statement, the EU expressed its 'well known concerns' and welcomed the 'intention of the Russian leadership to reach a political solution'.[124] At the same time, it demonstrated the interest of EU leaders and Putin in the 'progressive development of relations'.[125]

Prodi's surprisingly positive stance towards Russia at the summit was received with gratitude by Putin. He declared that the 'fundamental positions upon which Europe [was] uniting were also the basis of [Russia's] policies'.[126] Like Putin, the Russian Prime Minister Mikhail Kasyanov appreciated the EU's 'improved understanding' that 'the Russian leadership [was] paying increased attention to the situation in Chechnya'.[127]

In addition to the positive atmosphere of the summit, the European Council declaration of 19 and 20 June symbolised the reversal of the EU stance on Russia at its previous summit in December 1999. The declaration suggested reconsidering the sanctions imposed previously. The European Council invited the European Commission to 'review [the situation about TACIS and other instruments] in July, [at the General Affairs Council meeting] and take the necessary decisions'.[128] The declaration expressed the European Council's intention to establish a 'strong and healthy [EU–Russian] partnership' which 'required an open dialogue based on trust'.[129]

Representatives of the Russian human rights community condemned the West's cordiality with Russia despite the continuing Chechen War. Sergey Kovalev, a Duma deputy, member of the Russian delegation to PACE and a human rights advocate, called for a hardened stance on Russia's conduct in Chechnya by proposing that 'actions to expel Russia from the Council of Europe should be taken'.[130] Denouncing Russia as the 'main criminal in the North Caucasus', he indirectly belittled PACE's ban on Russian voting rights stating that when 'talking about sanctions against a state it [was] senseless to whip the servile, slavish State Duma Deputies'.[131]

Along with Kovalev's objections, a petition signed by 500 European and Russian intellectuals and politicians condemned the EU's stance on Russia. First, the petition, which was launched a month prior to the EU–Russia summit by philosophers André Glucksmann of France and Josep Ramoneda of Spain, criticised politicians' inaction, double standards and their silence concerning Chechnya. The signatories criticised the fact that Western politicians had 'condemned the former Serbian president Slobodan Milosevic for his actions, while giving Putin the honour of having tea with the Queen of England during his state visit to Britain' in April 2000.[132] Glucksmann considered the extraordinarily positive stance of the leaders towards Putin to be disproportionate to the scope of Russia's military operation in Chechnya, especially considering that the situation in Grozny was 'worse than in Sarajevo'.[133] Second, the signatories condemned EU plans for the launch of the EU–Russia Energy Dialogue. The signatories expressed their 'fear [that] the short-term calculations, swallowed the martyrdom of a people and celebrate[d] the grand energy deal which [the European Commission's president] Prodi had negotiated'.[134] Condemning the morality of the anticipated energy deal, the signatories asked rhetorically whether 'the trade of blood against gas, would ... be the last word of European civilisation'.[135] Addressing French President Jacques Chirac, who chaired the European Council Presidency and hosted the EU–Russia summit in October 2000 at which the Energy Dialogue was signed, they urged him to 'publicly and distinctively' remind Putin to respect international human rights conventions.[136]

Three days before this summit, the Russian non-governmental organisation Memorial and the International Federation for Human Rights joined the chorus of criticism and condemned the cooperative EU stance on Russia. These human rights organisations agreed that Putin should be prosecuted for crimes against humanity in Chechnya.[137] The EU position towards Russia also provoked criticism from the acting director of the European and Central Asia division of Human Rights Watch, who urged the EU to act 'if it want[ed] to retain its credibility on human rights issues'.[138] Despite these condemnations, as demonstrated in the following section, pragmatism proved stronger than moral conscience.

The EU's pragmatism – cooperation in energy policy (October 2000–April 2001)

Despite the wave of protest against the carnage in Chechnya, neither European politicians nor the leadership of the French European Council Presidency held back from developing cordial relations with Russia. The EU–Russia summit in Paris on 30 October coincided with the publication of an article in *Le Monde* which acknowledged that the Chechen War had hindered the 'normal' development of French-Russian relations, but stressed that a dialogue between these countries was 'normal and desirable'.[139] It stated that 'every sulkiness has to have an end, especially between two state powers which are essential for the balance of power in Europe'.[140]

44 *Overcoming the 'Chechnya Irritant'*

Silence regarding the condemnation of human rights abuses in Chechnya was also shaped by the launch of the EU–Russia Energy Dialogue at their summit. Prior to the Dialogue's establishment, the PCA referred to energy policy. It stated that 'cooperation in energy policy takes place within the principle of market economy and the European Energy Charter'.[141] According to the Vice Premier of the Russian government, Victor Khristenko, the Energy Dialogue aimed to ensure the long-term security of Europe's energy supply.[142] To emphasise the significance of the Dialogue, Jukka Valtasaari, Secretary of State of the Finnish Ministry of Foreign Affairs, declared that EU demand for gas would increase from 40 per cent to 70 per cent in the next 20 years.[143] As well as energy security, the Dialogue also aimed to achieve energy saving, rationalisation of production, transport infrastructure and opportunities for European investment in the Russian energy sector.[144] It had become institutionalised through the establishment of a Commission studying ways to 'bolster long-term energy cooperation and modernise Russia's dilapidated energy and industrial sectors'.[145]

A conciliatory approach towards Russia was adopted both by PACE and the EU. After the summit, Chirac wanted to write 'a new page in French-Russian relations'.[146] Chirac assured the Russians that bilateral relations had never been at risk of cooling and that the 'kind [French-Russian] relationship' would be preserved in all circumstances.[147] Bearing in mind that Chirac had been a strong proponent of suspending some of the provisions of the PCA, these statements demonstrate his change of heart. Chirac's sudden cordial attitude towards Russia was criticised by former EU Commissioner for External Relations Chris Patten. He lambasted Chirac's posturing over suspension of PCA provisions as the

> high water mark for [his] insignificant stand for human rights in Russia. Within weeks he was cosying up to Putin and never looked back. And within weeks as well, my officials and I at the European Commission were being hectored for being uncooperative with Russia.[148]

Putin embraced Chirac's changed attitude. He hailed the summit as the 'political zenith of the permanent dialogue between Russia and the EU'.[149]

No less surprising was PACE's sudden cordial approach, which was reflected in its decision to restore Russia's voting rights on 27 January 2001. The chairman of PACE, Lord Russell-Johnston, stressed that it was important that the Council of Europe did not condemn the atrocities committed in Chechnya, but instead assisted the Russian authorities in 'solving a difficult situation'.[150]

The assembly's decision evoked widespread criticism from the Russian human rights community. Human rights activist and member of the Russian delegation to PACE Sergey Kovalev condemned the restoration of Russia's voting rights as an 'intrigue'.[151] He accused the Council of Europe of having based the reports concerning positive developments in Chechnya on 'false facts'.[152] According to Kovalev, 'the artillery bombings had stopped, but evidence of constructive progress had been manufactured by the Council of Europe's president

Overcoming the 'Chechnya Irritant' 45

... to "cite at least some positive developments" to avoid jeopardis[ing] relations with Russia'.[153] Kovalev claimed that the Council of Europe was applying double standards by 'regularly betray[ing] its own concept of justice'.[154] He declared that the Council of Europe was putting 'zero pressure on countries violating its rules. Violators g[o]t accustomed to this and eventually realise that this chattering in PACE mean[t] nothing'.[155] Eventually the 'chattering' was replaced by silence both in PACE and in the EU. The silence was shaped by the attacks of 11 September.

Silence about Chechnya in the aftermath of 9/11

The terrorist attack against the US on 11 September was the nail in the coffin of EU condemnation of Russia's war in Chechnya. The atrocities had two significant repercussions for Russia's relations with the West. On the one hand, the attacks lent plausibility to the Kremlin's argument that Russia's conduct in Chechnya was part of the international struggle against terrorism. On the other hand, it made Russia an ally of the West in the 'global war against terror', offering its support to the US government. Putin had been among the first heads of state to express his condolences to US President George W. Bush after the terrorist attacks.

The special envoy for human rights in Chechnya, Vladimir Kalamanov, noted the West's changing attitude towards Chechnya in the aftermath of 9/11. He pointed out that Russian human rights envoys to PACE and the Committee of Ministers of the Council of Europe had 'detected a significant shift in the attitude to our actions in the Chechen republic'.[156] His view was shared by the Russian Foreign Minister Igor Ivanov, who declared in a meeting with Alexander Vershbow, the US ambassador to Russia, that 9/11 had influenced the 'way of thinking ... of the West generally' in their 'understanding of the need for greater solidarity in the face of new threats'.[157]

The events of 9/11 were used as an opportunity by Russia to cast the Kremlin's military operation in Chechnya as part of the global fight against terrorism. The Russian Defence Minister Sergei Ivanov declared that Moscow 'had been struggling against terrorism for many years, not only in Chechnya'.[158] The crowning gesture symbolising Russia's alliance with the US in the struggle against terrorism came when he announced the Russian government's preparedness to provide financial, military and technical assistance to the US operation in Afghanistan.[159] About a fortnight after 9/11, Putin's speech before the German Parliament emphasised the need for joint efforts in the struggle against international terrorism. Putin stressed that 'terrorism, national hatred, separatism and religious extremism [had] the same roots everywhere and [brought] about the same poisonous fruits'.[160] Therefore, the 'measures to fight these problems should also be universal'.[161]

Schroeder was receptive to the Russian president's interpretation of the Chechen War as two days later, he declared that the conflict must be reassessed in light of the attacks against the US: 'concerning Chechnya there will be and

46   *Overcoming the 'Chechnya Irritant'*

must be a more differentiated opinion in world opinion'.[162] However, he did not explain how this should be achieved. Schroeder's changed stance on the Chechen War was well received by Putin, who stated 'the more I get to know him, the more surprised I am. I did not ask him to modify his position in the way he did.'[163]

EU–Russian cooperation in the struggle against international terrorism was demonstrated in a joint statement released at the summit on 3 October 2001. According to this statement, EU–Russia relations should 'take advantage of the momentum which has built up in order to intensify cooperation and strategic partnership'.[164]

Conclusion

The shift from EU–Russian confrontation over the Chechen War to cooperation was influenced by three factors. The first factor was internal division in the EU. The European Council reduced aid to Russia. However, other restrictive measures such as reviewing the EU's Common Strategy towards Russia and freezing part of the PCA were not imposed. The surprisingly positive stance taken by the Finnish and Portuguese European Council Presidencies and European Commission President Prodi on Russia during the Chechen War undermined the EU's ability to give a strong, unified response to Russia's conduct in Chechnya.

Internal division in the EU over its reaction to the Chechen War, together with the Kremlin's push for greater autonomy in its foreign policy, severely diminished the EU's ability to exert pressure on Russia. The change in Russian foreign policy was reflected in the RMTS which rejected the idea of integration with the EU. Instead, the strategy declared that Russia's foreign policy was focused on the former Soviet space where it aimed to become a 'leading power' shaping interstate political and economic relations. This heralded a significant shift in Russian foreign policy from Yeltsin's lament in February that same year that Russia was not a member state of the EU. This reversal contributed to the shift from confrontation to cooperation during the Chechen War: the EU's attempt to promote its own values in relations with Russia was limited by both Russia's reluctance to absorb these values and its repudiation of EU membership.

Due to the EU's complex system of governance, individual leaders could separate their opinions from those of the EU institutions that were outspoken against Russia's human rights abuses in Chechnya. This was not the only moment when the EU's internal division undermined its ability to develop a unitary and affirmative policy towards Russia. This was the case during the Italian European Council Presidency when at an EU–Russia summit Berlusconi declared himself as wanting to be Putin's advocate in the Chechen War. His declaration openly contradicted the EU's stance. The repercussions of this rift within the EU for EU–Russia relations will be examined in the following chapter.

The second factor which transformed EU–Russia relations was the EU's prioritisation of economic and political benefits over humanitarian concerns. Putin's rise to power was regarded by European politicians like Solana, Schroeder,

Overcoming the 'Chechnya Irritant'   47

Blair, Prodi and the heads of states holding the rotating European Council Presidencies as a chance to seek to establish rapprochement between Brussels and Moscow. Cooperation in energy policy, manifested in the launch of the EU–Russian Energy Dialogue, together with internal divergence on the Chechen War, contributed to the EU leadership's muted criticism of human rights violations in Chechnya. The EU took a pragmatic line because it anticipated an increase in the demand for energy following EU enlargement in 2004. Russia's energy resources created the need for an expanding EU to engage with Russia in order to safeguard the security of the energy supply.

The third factor contributing to the transformation from confrontation to cooperation was the terrorist attacks of 9/11. It lent plausibility to the Russian government's interpretation of the Chechen War as part of the 'global war against terrorism'. At the same time, the attacks enabled President Putin to present himself as the West's ally in the struggle against terrorism. In turn, the West's condemnation of human rights abuses in Chechnya became muted.

Within a year of 9/11, EU–Russia relations were characterised by acrimonious clashes between diplomats over the continuing conflict in Chechnya and repercussions of the EU's eastern enlargement.

Notes

1   The notion 'Chechnya Irritant' was used in a speech delivered on 29 May 2000 at the EU–Russia summit by the European Commission President Romano Prodi. See Prodi (2000a).
2   Forsberg and Herd (2005).
3   European Parliament (1999a).
4   Ibid. Section J. 4; Ibid. Section J. 5.
5   Ibid. Section C.
6   Zolotov (1999).
7   *Le Monde* (1999).
8   Bohlen (1999).
9   Lloyd (1999).
10   Ibid.
11   Patten (2006), p. 217.
12   Ibid.
13   Ibid.
14   European Council (1999c).
15   Ibid.
16   The Delegation of the European Union to Russia (1999a). For a more detailed comparison of the EU's Common Strategy on Russia with Russia's Medium Term Strategy see: Haukkala (2010), pp. 92–110.
17   Isachenkov (1999).
18   European Council (1999b).
19   Ibid. §5.1.
20   Ibid.
21   Webber (2000), p. 86.
22   European Council (1999b).
23   Haukkala (2008), p. 325.
24   European Council (1999b).
25   Ministry of Foreign Affairs of the Russian Federation (2000).

48 *Overcoming the 'Chechnya Irritant'*

26 Ibid.
27 Haukkala (2010), p. 102.
28 Ibid.
29 Ibid. p. 103.
30 Surkov (2008), p. 21.
31 Ibid.
32 European Parliament (1999c).
33 BBC Monitoring Former Soviet Union – Political. Supplied by BBC Worldwide Monitoring. Source: ITAR-TASS news agency, Moscow. Russia rejects European Parliament's Chechen charges. 23 November 1999.
34 Ibid.
35 European Commission (1999).
36 Solana (1999). Javier Solana addresses the European Parliament. 17 November 1999. Retrieved 20 April 2009 from: www.european-security.com/index.php?id=2218
37 OSCE (1999a). Speech by Mr Romano Prodi to the OSCE summit. 19 November 1999. Retrieved 20 April 2009 from: www.lex.unict.it/cde/documenti/rel_ester/98_99/prodi18_11_99en.htm.
38 Ibid.
39 Bollaert and Biagala (1999).
40 Gulyi (1999).
41 BBC Monitoring Europe – Political. Supplied by BBC Worldwide Monitoring. Source: Deutschlandfunkradio, Cologne. EU security chief says Chechnya war unreasonable. 19 November 1999.
42 Ibid.
43 The Kremlin (1999).
44 Ibid.
45 Ibid.
46 OSCE (1999b).
47 *Die Welt* (1999).
48 Ibid.
49 BBC Monitoring Former Soviet Union – Political. Supplied by BBC Worldwide Monitoring. Source: Russian Public TV. Russian PM says there will be no pause in Chechen operation. 21 November 1999.
50 Deutsche Presse Agentur (1999a).
51 Deutsche Presse Agentur (1999b).
52 *Der Spiegel* (1999); Blome (1999).
53 Agence France Presse (1999a).
54 Ibid.
55 Agence France Presse (1999b); Rouach (1999).
56 Deutsche Presse Agentur (1999c).
57 Interview with a former spokesman for EU External Relations, Directorate General for External Relations, European Commission. Interview conducted on 23 June 2010 at the European Commission in Brussels.
58 Ibid.
59 Ibid.
60 European Parliament (1999). Helsinki European Council 10 and 11 December 1999. Presidency Conclusions. Declaration on Chechnya. Retrieved 26 June 2009 from: www.europarl.europa.eu/summits/hel1_en.htm
61 Ibid.
62 Ibid.; The Delegation of the European Union to Russia (1999b).
63 European Parliament (1999b).
64 Ibid. Emphasis added.
65 Ibid.

Overcoming the 'Chechnya Irritant' 49

66 AFX (1999).
67 Ibid.
68 Patten (2006), p. 217.
69 European Commission (1997); Interview with a former spokesman for EU External Relations in the Directorate General for External Relations, European Commission. Interview conducted on 23 June 2010 at the European Commission.
70 Patten (2006), p. 217.
71 Deutsche Presse Agentur (2000a).
72 *Kommersant* (2000).
73 Ibid.
74 Ibid.
75 Ibid.
76 Ibid.
77 Deutsche Presse Agentur (2000b).
78 Interview with a former spokesman for EU External Relations, European Commission. Interview conducted on 23 June 2010 at the European Commission in Brussels.
79 Deutsche Presse Agentur (2000c).
80 BBC News (2000).
81 Traynor and White (2000).
82 Deutsche Presse Agentur (2000d).
83 BBC Monitoring Former Soviet Union. Source: RIA news agency. German chancellor congratulates Putin with victory in elections. 27 March 2000.
84 Deutsche Presse Agentur (2000d).
85 BBC Monitoring Europe – Political. Supplied by BBC Worldwide Monitoring. 'Europe facing the next big bang, we are working on it' – German minister. *Die Zeit*. 24 March 2000.
86 European Council (2000b).
87 For details of the resolutions see: PACE (2000).
88 PACE (2001).
89 Ibid.
90 Francis (2008), p. 323.
91 Russell-Johnston (2000).
92 BBC Monitoring Former Soviet Union – Political. Supplied by BBC Worldwide Monitoring. Source: Ekho Moskvy. Leader of Russian delegation to PACE condemns Yabloko for breaking rank. 7 April 2000.
93 Ibid.
94 Black (2004), p. 44; BBC Summary of World Broadcasts. Source: Interfax. Duma adopts 'toned down resolution on PACE'. 14 April 2000.
95 BBC Monitoring Former Soviet Union. Source: ITAR-TASS. Russian lower house decides to shun PACE until voting rights reinstated. 12 April 2000.
96 Prokofyev (2000).
97 BBC Summary of World Broadcasts. Source: NTV Moscow. Ivanov says PACE move will hurt dialogue. 8 April 2000.
98 BBC Monitoring Former Soviet Union – Political. Supplied by BBC Worldwide Monitoring. Russian FM downplays PACE decision, Says it has nothing to do with EU. 7 April 2000; BBC Monitoring Former Soviet Union Political. Supplied by BBC Worldwide Monitoring. Source: Russian Public TV. Russian foreign minister hopes to continue work with PACE: 8 April 2000.
99 BBC Summary of World Broadcasts. Ivanov likens Chechen Rebels to Kosovo 'Extremists'. Source: Interfax news agency. 10 April 2000.
100 BBC Monitoring Former Soviet Union – Political. Supplied by BBC Worldwide Monitoring. Source: Russian Public TV. Russian foreign minister hopes to continue work with PACE: 8 April 2000.

50 *Overcoming the 'Chechnya Irritant'*

101 BBC Monitoring Former Soviet Union – Political. Supplied by BBC Worldwide Monitoring. Source: Interfax. EU envoy questions legitimacy of Kremlin's spokesman's statements on Chechnya. 7 April 2000.
102 Deutsche Presse Agentur (2000e).
103 The Kremlin (2000).
104 BBC Monitoring Former Soviet Union – Political. Supplied by BBC Worldwide Monitoring. Source: Interfax. EU envoy questions legitimacy of Kremlin's spokesman's statements on Chechnya. 7 April 2000.
105 BBC Summary of World Broadcasts. No Plans to Change Chechen Policy to Suit PACE. Source: Russia TV, Moscow. 10 April 2000.
106 BBC Monitoring Former Soviet Union – Political. Supplied by BBC Worldwide Monitoring. Source: Interfax news agency. EU, Russia to continue constructive relations despite differences-EU troika. 7 April 2000.
107 Deutsche Presse Agentur (2000f).
108 BBC Monitoring Former Soviet Union – Political. Supplied by BBC Worldwide Monitoring. Russian FM downplays PACE decision, says it has to do with EU. 7 April 2000.
109 Interfax (2000).
110 Gilligan (2010), p. 169.
111 The Delegation of the European Union to Russia (2000a).
112 Ibid. p. 170.
113 Kalamanov quoted in Gilligan (2010), p. 171.
114 United Press International (2000); Védrine (2000).
115 Ibid. For more information on the French government's change of stance see Haukkala (2010), p. 123.
116 Ivanov (2000a).
117 Ibid.
118 Ivanov (2000b).
119 *Vechernyaya Moskva* (2000).
120 Prodi, R. (2000a).
121 Prodi, R. (2000b).
122 Portanski (2000). See also: Chudodeev (2000).
123 *Le Monde* (2000a).
124 The Delegation of the European Union to Russia (2000b).
125 *European Voice* (2000).
126 Russian Public TV (2000); *Le Monde* (2000a).
127 BBC Summary of World Broadcasts. Source: ITAR-TASS news agency. PM says European worry about Chechen problem exaggerated. 31 May 2000.
128 European Council (2000a).
129 Ibid.
130 BBC Monitoring Former Soviet Union – Political. Supplied by BBC Worldwide Monitoring. Source: Interfax. Russian Duma human rights envoy says violations continuing in Chechnya. 28 September 2000.
131 Ibid.
132 Bollaert and Lacroix (2000).
133 Ibid.
134 Shihab (2000).
135 Ibid.
136 Ibid.
137 Nougayrède (2000).
138 Human Rights Watch (2000).
139 *Le Monde* (2000b).
140 Ibid.
141 The Delegation of the European Union to Russia (1997).

Overcoming the 'Chechnya Irritant' 51

142 *RIA Novosti* (2000).
143 *Novye Izvestia* (1999).
144 European Commission (2004).
145 Associated Press (2000).
146 *Le Figaro* (2000).
147 De Barcochez (2000).
148 Patten (2006), p. 217.
149 BBC Monitoring Former Soviet Union – Political. Supplied by BBC Worldwide Monitoring. Source: Interfax News Agency. Putin praises Russia–EU Summit in Paris. 30 October 2000.
150 BBC Monitoring former Soviet Union – Political. Supplied by BBC World Wide Monitoring. Source: Radio Russia, Moscow. PACE head says Council of Europe should provide help to Russia in Chechnya. 27 January 2001.
151 BBC Summary of World Broadcasts. Source: Ekho Moskvy news agency. Moscow. Human rights champion blasts PACE, says no real improvement in Chechnya. 29 January 2001.
152 Ibid.
153 Ibid.
154 Ibid.
155 Ibid.
156 BBC Monitoring Former Soviet Union. Source: NTV Moscow. EU attitude to Russian policy on Chechnya shifting, says human rights envoy. 3 October 2001.
157 Ministry of Foreign Affairs of the Russian Federation (2002).
158 Interfax (2001).
159 BBC Monitoring Former Soviet Union – Political. Supplied by BBC Worldwide Monitoring. Source: gazeta.ru website. Russian website predicts Russia's direct action in Afghan operation. 24 September 2001.
160 Putin (2001).
161 Ibid.
162 Erlanger (2001).
163 BBC Monitoring Europe – Political. Supplied by BBC Worldwide Monitoring. Source: Deutschlandfunkradio Cologne. Putin surprised by Germany's softer line on Chechnya. 26 September 2001.
164 Joint statement on international terrorism – see The Delegation of the European Union to Russia (2001), p. 5.

Bibliography

AFX. (1999). European focus. EU summit: leaders threaten to suspend trade links, condemn Russia. 10 December 1999.
Agence France Presse. (1999a). M. Védrine demande à la Russie de retirer son ultimatum. 9 December 1999.
Agence France Presse. (1999b). Tchétchénie: le message devra être 'plus net' à Helsinki selon Védrine. 9 December 1999.
Associated Press. (2000). World Stream. With Europe–Putin EU–Russian Commission set up to study energy cooperation. 30 October 2000.
BBC Monitoring Europe – Political. Supplied by BBC Worldwide Monitoring. Source: Deutschlandfunkradio, Cologne. EU security chief says Chechnya war unreasonable. 19 November 1999.
BBC Monitoring Europe – Political. Supplied by BBC Worldwide Monitoring. 'Europe facing the next big bang, we are working on it' – German minister. *Die Zeit*. 24 March 2000.

52 *Overcoming the 'Chechnya Irritant'*

BBC Monitoring Europe – Political. Supplied by BBC Worldwide Monitoring. Source: Deutschlandfunkradio Cologne. Putin surprised by Germany's softer line on Chechnya. 26 September 2001.

BBC Monitoring Former Soviet Union. Source: RIA news agency. German chancellor congratulates Putin with victory in elections. 27 March 2000.

BBC Monitoring Former Soviet Union. Source: ITAR-TASS. Russian lower house decides to shun PACE until voting rights reinstated. 12 April 2000.

BBC Monitoring Former Soviet Union. Source: NTV Moscow. EU attitude to Russian policy on Chechnya shifting, says human rights envoy. 3 October 2001.

BBC Monitoring Former Soviet Union – Political. Supplied by BBC Worldwide Monitoring. Source: Russian Public TV. Russian PM says there will be no pause in Chechen operation. 21 November 1999.

BBC Monitoring Former Soviet Union – Political. Supplied by BBC Worldwide Monitoring. Source: ITAR-TASS news agency, Moscow. Russia rejects European Parliament's Chechen charges. 23 November 1999.

BBC Monitoring Former Soviet Union – Political. Supplied by BBC Worldwide Monitoring. Source: Ekho Moskvy. Leader of Russian delegation to PACE condemns Yabloko for breaking rank. 7 April 2000.

BBC Monitoring Former Soviet Union – Political. Supplied by BBC Worldwide Monitoring. Russian FM downplays PACE decision, says it has nothing to do with EU. 7 April 2000.

BBC Monitoring Former Soviet Union – Political. Supplied by BBC Worldwide Monitoring. Source: Interfax news agency. EU, Russia to continue constructive relations despite differences-EU troika. 7 April 2000.

BBC Monitoring Former Soviet Union – Political. Supplied by BBC Worldwide Monitoring. Source: Interfax. EU envoy questions legitimacy of Kremlin's spokesman's statements on Chechnya. 7 April 2000.

BBC Monitoring Former Soviet Union – Political. Supplied by BBC Worldwide Monitoring. Source: Russian Public TV. Russian foreign minister hopes to continue work with PACE. 8 April 2000.

BBC Monitoring Former Soviet Union – Political. Supplied by BBC Worldwide Monitoring. Source: Interfax. Russian Duma human rights envoy says violations continuing in Chechnya. 28 September 2000.

BBC Monitoring Former Soviet Union – Political. Supplied by BBC Worldwide Monitoring. Source: Interfax news agency. Putin praises Russia–EU Summit in Paris. 30 October 2000.

BBC Monitoring Former Soviet Union – Political. Supplied by BBC World Wide Monitoring. Source: Radio Russia, Moscow. PACE head says Council of Europe should provide help to Russia in Chechnya. 27 January 2001.

BBC Monitoring Former Soviet Union – Political. Supplied by BBC Worldwide Monitoring. Source: gazeta.ru website. Russian website predicts Russia's direct action in Afghan operation. 24 September 2001.

BBC News. (2000). Blair calls for Chechnya probe. 11 March 2000. Retrieved 30 November 2009 from: http://news.bbc.co.uk/1/hi/world/europe/673978.stm.

BBC Summary of World Broadcasts. Source: NTV Moscow. Ivanov says PACE move will hurt dialogue. 8 April 2000.

BBC Summary of World Broadcasts. Ivanov likens Chechen Rebels to Kosovo 'Extremists'. Source: Interfax news agency. 10 April 2000.

BBC Summary of World Broadcasts. No Plans to Change Chechen Policy to Suit PACE. Source: Russia TV, Moscow. 10 April 2000.

Overcoming the 'Chechnya Irritant' 53

BBC Summary of World Broadcasts. Source: Interfax. Duma adopts 'toned down resolution on PACE'. 14 April 2000.

BBC Summary of World Broadcasts. Source: ITAR-TASS news agency. PM says European worry about Chechen problem exaggerated. 31 May 2000.

Black, L. (2004). *Vladimir Putin and the New World Order. Looking East. Looking West.* Oxford: Rowman and Littlefield.

Blome, N. (1999). Grosny's Schatten ueber Helsinki: der EU Gipfel in Finnland zwischen Verurteilung und Einbindung Russlands. *Die Welt.* 11 December 1999.

Bohlen, C. (1999). Blast in Chechen capital unleashes new wave of refugees. *New York Times.* 23 October 1999.

Bollaert, B and Biagala, E. (1999). Le sommet de l'OSCE s'est achevé hier à Istanbul; la Russie a évité l'isolement. *Le Figaro.* 20 November 1999.

Bollaert, B. and Lacroix, A. (2000). Idées. La série du 'Figaro' sur le paysage intellectuel français: André Glucksmann: 'Le silence effrayant des politiques'. *Le Figaro.* 21 September 2000.

Chudodeev, A. (2000). Moskve predlagaiut pereimi na viski c codovoi. *Segodnya.* 30 May 2000.

De Barcochez, L. (2000). Russie. Vladimir Poutine et Jacques Chirac veulent développer un partenariat stratégique; Convergence euro-russe sur la Tchétchénie. *Le Figaro.* 31 October 2000.

Der Spiegel. (1999). Tschetschenien. Fischer verurteilt russischen ‚Akt der Barbarei.' 8 December 1999.

Deutsche Presse Agentur. (1999a). Roundup: Thousands in Grozny unaware of Russian ultimatum. 7 December 1999.

Deutsche Presse Agentur. (1999b). Germany warns consequences if Russia carries out ultimatum. 8 December 1999.

Deutsche Presse Agentur. (1999c). Prodi: EU summit may discuss possible sanctions against Russia. 8 December 1999.

Deutsche Presse Agentur. (2000a). Putin elected Russian president, succeeding Yeltsin. 27 March 2000.

Deutsche Presse Agentur. (2000b). EU plans suspension 90 million euros in aid, stops more trade preferences for Moscow. 24 January 2000.

Deutsche Presse Agentur. (2000c). Germany says lift Serbian sanctions, no EU moves planned against Russia. 24 January 2000.

Deutsche Presse Agentur. (2000d). Putin win offers fresh start to German–Russian ties, says Schroeder. 27 March 2000.

Deutsche Presse Agentur. (2000e). No new EU sanctions against Russia, Solana says. 8 April 2000.

Deutsche Presse Agentur. (2000f). Russia angered by Council of Europe expulsion move. 7 April 2000.

Die Welt. (1999). OSZE einigt sich auf Sicherheitscharta. Nach zaehen Verhandlungen stimmt Russland politischer Loesung in Tschetschenien zu. 19 November 1999.

Erlanger, S. (2001). Schroeder urges milder view of Moscow role in Chechnya. *New York Times.* 25 September 2001.

European Commission. (1997). Agreement on partnership and cooperation establishing a partnership between the European Communities and their Member States, of one part, and the Russian Federation, of the other part. Official Journal L 327 , 28/11/1997 P. 0003 – 0069. Retrieved 27 October 2015 from: http://trade.ec.europa.eu/doclib/docs/2003/november/tradoc_114138.pdf

54 *Overcoming the 'Chechnya Irritant'*

European Commission. (1999). Rapid. The Rt. Hon Christopher Patten Member of the European Commission responsible for External Relations Declaration on Chechnya European Parliament Strasbourg. 17 November 1999. SPEECH/99/166. Press release.

European Commission. (2004). Communication from the Commission to the Council and the European Parliament. The Energy Dialogue between the European Union and the Russian Federation between 2000 and 2004. p. 2. Brussels, 13.12.2004. COM (2004). 777 final. Retrieved 20 November 2009 from: www.ec.europa.eu/energy/russia/reference_texts/doc/2004_0777_en.pdf

European Council. (1999a). Common Strategy of the European Union on Russia. 4 June 1999. Retrieved 30 March 2009 from: http://trade.ec.europa.eu/doclib/docs/2003/november/tradoc_114137.pdf

European Council. (1999b) Russia's response to the Common Strategy of the European Union of 4 June 1999 on Russia. (1999/414/CFSP) §1.8. Retrieved 27 April 2004 from: http://europa.eu.int/comm/external_relations/russain_medium_term_strategy

European Council. (1999c). EU–Russia Summit. Helsinki, 22 October 1999. Joint Statement. Retrieved 30 November 2009 from: www.consilium.europa.eu/ueDocs/cms_Data/docs/pressData/en/er/12119.en.html

European Council. (2000a). Santa Maria de Feira European Council. 19 and 20 June 2000. Retrieved 3 June 2009 from: www.europarl.europa.eu/summits/feil_en.htm?textMode=on

European Council. (2000b). Lisbon European Council. March 23 and 24 2000. Retrieved 28 June 2009 from: www.europarl.europa.eu/summits/lis1_en.htm?redirected=1#4

European Parliament. (1999). Helsinki European Council 10 and 11 December 1999. Presidency Conclusions. Declaration on Chechnya. Retrieved 26 June 2009 from: www. europarl.europa.eu/summits/hel2_en.htm

European Voice. (2000). EU–Russia summit. 31 May 2000. Retrieved 2 December 2009 from: www.europeanvoice.com/article/imported/29-may-eu-russia-summit/40811.aspx

Forsberg, T. and Herd, G.P. (2005). The EU, Human Rights, and the Russo-Chechen Conflict. *Political Science Quarterly*. 120(3): 455–478.

Francis, C. (2008). 'Selective Affinities': The reactions of the Council of Europe and the European Union to the Second Armed Conflict in Chechnya (1999–2006). *Europe–Asia Studies*. 60(2): 317–338.

Gilligan, E. (2010). *Terror in Chechnya. Russia and the tragedy of civilians in war.* Princeton and Oxford: Princeton University Press.

Gulyi, S. (1999). Russia and the US agree to disagree. Boris Yeltsin refused to sign the Charter for European Security. *Novye Izvestia.* 19 November 1999.

Haukkala, H. (2008). The EU's Common Strategy on Russia. *European Foreign Affairs Review* 13(3): 317–331.

Haukkala, H. (2010). *The EU–Russia Strategic Partnership. The limits of post-sovereignty in international relations.* London and New York: Routledge.

Human Rights Watch. (2000). Inside the Hell of 'Chernokozovo'. *Moscow Times.* 26 October 2000.

Interfax. (2000). Portuguese foreign minister arrives in Moscow. 9 November 2000.

Interfax. (2001). Russian defence minister says Chechnya, Afghanistan branches of one tree. 24 September 2001.

Isachenkov, V. (1999). Yeltsin meets with German, EU leaders. Associated Press. 18 February 1999.

Ivanov, I. (2000a). Russia, Europe at the Turn of the Century. *International Affairs* (Moscow). 46(2): 1–11.

Ivanov, I. (2000b). Tchétchénie. Nous lançons un appel à nos amis occidentaux pour qu'ils évaluent objectivement la situation; En finir avec le terrorisme. *Le Figaro.* 12 May 2000.

Overcoming the 'Chechnya Irritant' 55

Kommersant. (2000). ES vidit v Rossii partnera. 14 January 2000.

Le Figaro. (2000). Vladimir Poutine à Paris: le nouveau souffle franco-russe. 31 October 2000.

Le Monde. (1999). Après les changements politiques en France et en Allemagne, il fallait réapprendre à travailler ensemble. 28 October 1999.

Le Monde. (2000a). L'élargissement vers l'Est et le conflit tchétchène au menu du sommet entre Moscou et l'UE. 30 May 2000.

Le Monde. (2000b). Parler avec M. Poutine. 30 October 2000.

Lloyd, A. (1999). Chechen wolf at bay as missiles strike Grozny. *The Times.* 22 October 1999.

Ministry of Foreign Affairs of the Russian Federation. (2000). The Foreign Policy Concept of the Russian Federation. Approved by the President of the Russian Federation. V. Putin. 28 June 2000.

Ministry of Foreign Affairs of the Russian Federation (2002). 'Round the World with Igor Ivanov'. Russian Minister of Foreign Affairs Igor Ivanov Interview with the Newspaper *Rossiskaya Gazeta*, 30 December 2002. Information and Press Department. Retrieved 15 March 2010 from: www.mid.ru/BRP_4.NSF/f68cd37b84711611c3256f6d00541094/f1d2 6efd6c1f412d43256c9f00546849?OpenDocument

Nougayrède, N. (2000). Plusieurs ONG dénoncent les crimes de guerre russes en Tchétchénie. *Le Monde.* 28 October 2000.

Novye Izvestia. (1999). Roccia i ES: vmecte v novoe ctoletie. 22 October 1999.

Novye Izvestia. (2000). Ne razlei voda. 30 May 2000.

OSCE. (1999a). Speech by Mr Romano Prodi to the OSCE summit. 19 November 1999. Retrieved 20 April 2009 from: www.lex.unict.it/cde/documenti/rel_ester/98_99/ prodi18_11_99en.htm.

OSCE. (1999b). Istanbul Summit 1999. Istanbul Document. Charter for European Security. Retrieved 2 February 2010 from: www.osce.org/documents/mcs/1999/11/4050_en.pdf

PACE. (2000). Recommendation 1465 2000. Conflict in the Chechen Republic. Retrieved July 30 2009 from: http://assembly.coe.int/Main.asp?link=/Documents/AdoptedText/ ta00/EREC1456.htm

PACE. (2001). 'Credentials of the Delegation of the Russian Federation', Resolution 1241, 25 January 2001. Retrieved 30 July 2009 from: http://assembly.coe.int/Mainf. asp?link=/Documents/AdoptedText/ta01/ERES1241.htm.

Patten, C. (2006). Neighbourhood Watch. In *Cousins and Strangers. America, Britain and Europe in a new century.* New York: Henry Holt and Company.

Portanski, A. (2000). Rossia i EC ponimaiut drug druga s poluslova. *Vremya MN.* 30 May 2000.

Prodi, R. (2000a). Comment and Analysis: Moscow's mandate for change: Romano Prodi finds much to be optimistic about in Vladimir Putin's Russia-given the right programme of reform. *Financial Times.* 26 May 2000.

Prodi, R. (2000b). Speech by Romano Prodi. President of the European Commission, Maly Manege, Moscow. 29 May 2000. Retrieved 24 June 2009 from: www.delrus.ec. europa.eu/en/images/pText_pict/241/sum12.doc

Prokofyev, V. (2000). Strasbourg: The Chechnya syndrome. *Trud.* 7 April 2000.

Putin, V. (2001). Wladimir Putin, Praesident der Russischen Foederation. Wortprotokoll der Rede am 25. September 2001 vor dem Deutschen Bundestag. 25 September 2001. Retrieved 18 May 2009 from: www.bundestag.de/geschichte/gastredner/putin/putin_ wort.html.

Rouach, H. (2009). Sanctions contre la Russie: un arsenal limite, une efficacité douteuse. Agence France Presse. 9 December.

56 Overcoming the 'Chechnya Irritant'

Russell-Johnston, D. (2000). Human Rights for the Chechens, too. *New York Times*. 14 April 2000.

RIA Novosti. (2000). The forthcoming Russia–EU summit will be another major step in their fuel and energy dialogue. 30 October 2000.

Russian Public TV. (2000). Putin tells EU delegation that Russia is a European country. 31 May 2000.

Shihab, S. (2000). A Paris il faut parler de la Tchétchénie avec M. Poutine, car le silence tue. *Le Monde*. 28 October 2000.

Solana, J. (1999). Javier Solana addresses the European Parliament. 17 November 1999. Retrieved 20 April 2009 from: www.european-security.com/index.php?id=2218

Surkov, V. (2008). Russian Political Culture. The view from Utopia. *Russian Politics and Law*. 46(5): 10–26.

The Delegation of the European Union to Russia. (1997). Partnership and Cooperation Agreement. EU and Russia. Retrieved 24 June 2009 from: www.delrus.ec.europa.eu/en/p_243.htm

The Delegation of the European Union to Russia. (1999a). The Russian Federation's Middle Term Strategy towards the EU (2000–2010). Retrieved 18 November 2009 from: www.delrus.ec.europa.eu/en/p_245.htm

The Delegation of the European Union to Russia. (1999b). Common Strategy of the European Union on Russia. 4 June 1999. Retrieved 26 June 2009 from: www.delrus.ec.europa.eu/en/p_244.htm

The Delegation of the European Union to Russia. (2000a). Conclusions on Russia/Chechnya by the EU Council of Ministers. Recent press releases and speeches. 10 April 2000. Retrieved 3 June 2009 from: www.delrus.ec.europa.eu/news_509.htm

The Delegation of the European Union to Russia. (2000b). EU–Russia Summit. Moscow. 29 May 2000. Retrieved 2 December 2009 from: www.delrus.ec.europa.eu/en/images/pText_pict/241/sum11.doc

The Delegation of the European Union to Russia. (2001). Joint Statement. EU–Russia Summit. Press Release. 3 October 2001. Retrieved 2 December 2011 from: www.consilium.europa.eu/uedocs/cms_data/docs/pressdata/en/er/12423.en1.doc.html

The Kremlin. (1999). Press conference with Vladimir Lukin, chairman of the State Duma Committee for International Affairs. News Broadcast. 22 November 1999.

The Kremlin. (2000). Vladimir Putin met with Jaime Gama, foreign minister of Portugal, current holder of the European Union presidency, and Javier Solana, Secretary-General of the EU Council. Press release. 7 April 2000. Retrieved 5 November 2015 from: http://en.kremlin.ru/events/president/news/37495

Traynor, I. and White, M. (2000). Blair courts outrage with Putin visit. *The Guardian*. 11 March 2000.

United Press International. (2000). French ministers want closer EU–Russia ties. 25 April 2000.

Uzelac, A. (2001). Terror may be that binds. *Moscow Times*. 13 September 2001.

Vechernyaya Moskva. (2000). Partnerstvo RF i ES ukrepitsia. 13 April 2000.

Védrine, H. (2000). Comment and Analysis: How Russia can be helped to help itself. Laurent Fabius and Hubert Védrine set out a framework for a constructive new relationship between the EU and Moscow. *Financial Times*. 25 April 2000.

Webber, M. (2000). *Russia and Europe. Conflict or cooperation?* Basingstoke, UK: Palgrave Macmillan.

Zolotov Jr., A. (1999). Talks fail, invading Chechnya in cards. *Moscow Times*. 30 September 1999.

3 Russia and the politics of EU eastern enlargement

From 2002 to 2004, the process of eastern enlargement of the EU transformed EU–Russia relations. The admission of ten new member states from Central and Eastern Europe on 1 May 2004 did not only make the EU and Russia neighbours, but it confronted them with a new set of fundamental challenges. For both sides, relations with each other rose on their list of diplomatic priorities. Both competed for influence in the former Soviet space.

This chapter argues that this transformation in EU–Russia relations was determined by the EU's increasing influence in the post-Soviet space as a result of its eastern enlargement. For the first time since 1999, EU external policies encroached on the former Soviet space (the absorption of the Baltic republics as new member states) and impinged on the lives of Russian citizens. By ignoring Russian protests and admitting Lithuania and Poland to the Schengen zone, the EU impeded the ability of Russian citizens to travel between the Russian mainland and the Kaliningrad enclave. As a result of Kaliningrad's enclosure within EU territory, the European Commission introduced visas for Russian citizens to regulate travel. The introduction of visas sparked a harsh reaction from the Kremlin.

But as this chapter demonstrates, the EU's initial assertiveness was undermined by the Italian European Council Presidency's chairman Silvio Berlusconi in 2003. Berlusconi's declaration that he would be Putin's advocate concerning the Chechen War was in total contradiction to the EU's outspokenly critical stance towards continuing Russian human rights violations in the north Caucasian republic. His statement resulted in a spectacular clash in the EU and provoked a significant redesign of EU–Russia relations.

No less problematic for the evolution of EU–Russia relations in the run-up to EU eastern enlargement were the EU's intentions of exporting some of its values through the development of the ENP, which Russia was invited to join. The much-vaunted ENP, which proposed a set of integrative policies and standards for neighbouring states excluded from the 2004 EU enlargement, was vigorously rejected by Russia. The reason for this repudiation was twofold. First, the fact that the ENP encouraged its members to implement economic and political reforms in return for closer integration with the EU was not appealing to Russian politicians. The Kremlin's ambition was to maintain political autonomy and

58 *Russia and EU eastern enlargement*

gradually increase state control, as reflected in the aftermath of a terrorist attack on a school in Beslan in the North Caucasus which is discussed further in this chapter. As a result of these internal developments in Russia, a normative gap developed between the EU and Moscow. Second, as that the ENP had been established for countries that were less economically privileged than those of the EU, the Kremlin regarded the EU's offer to include Russia in the ENP as an affront to Russia's status as a 'great power'.

The dispute over Kaliningrad

The major stumbling block in EU preparations for its eastern enlargement was the confrontation over the Russian enclave Kaliningrad, which became enclosed within EU territory with the accession of Poland and Lithuania. This prospect resulted in acrimonious clashes between European and Russian diplomats and politicians over transit regulations for Russians travelling to and from the enclave. The EU proposal to introduce visas for Russians travelling to and from Kaliningrad as well as preparations for the EU's eastward expansion were perceived by the Kremlin as an encroachment of the former Soviet space.

Emerging tensions regarding Kaliningrad stemmed from divergent concerns regarding the enclave. Policy makers in Brussels were concerned about negative repercussions for the internal security of the EU of enclosing Kaliningrad within EU territory. This concern was aggravated by the fact that, in comparison to other parts of the former Soviet Union, the Russian enclave was a major haven of organised crime, high HIV rates, poverty and underdevelopment.[1] The enclave's impoverishment and economic depression was partly caused by the withdrawal of parts of the military from Kaliningrad, which had been the headquarters of the Soviet Baltic fleet.[2] The EU's fears about Kaliningrad were articulated by Chris Patten, Commissioner for EU External Relations, in an article in the *Guardian* entitled 'Russia's hell-hole enclave: There is a centre of organised crime in the middle of Europe'.[3]

In contrast, Russia had long-standing concerns about the impact on Kaliningrad of the EU's enlargement. The RMTS discussed the 'ambivalent impact of the European Union's expansion on the terms of its cooperation with Russia and on the Russian interests, to strive for achieving the best advantages of such expansion' while 'preventing, eliminating or setting off possible negative consequences'.[4] These views were reiterated by Vladimir Yegorov, the governor of Kaliningrad, who stated that the EU intended to make a 'closed tin' out of Kaliningrad, which would be a 'disaster that impeded the region'.[5]

The Kremlin's dissatisfaction with EU expansion had also been expressed in the Foreign Policy Concept of the Russian Federation in June 2000. In a section on regional priorities, it referred to 'concrete problems, primarily the problem of an adequate respect for the interests of the Russian side in the process of the EU's expansion', which 'will be dealt with on the basis of the [RMTS]'.[6] According to the strategy, negative repercussions of EU eastern enlargement should be 'prevented or eliminated'.[7] Although the strategy did not outline

Russia and EU eastern enlargement 59

specific measures to minimise such repercussions, it can be asserted that EU expansion was a source of friction in relations with Russia.

Dmitry Rogozin, chairman of the Duma's Committee for International Affairs, attempted to create countermeasures to make the EU more sensitive to Russian concerns about Kaliningrad. Rogozin insisted that Russia could not accept the EU proposals and stated that the problem 'cannot and must not be resolved' in the framework of the EU–Russia summit on 29 May 2002, but should be addressed by direct contact between Russia and the 15 EU member states instead. The so-called '15 plus one procedure' was intended to strengthen EU–Russia cooperation.[8] Instead of having to deal with the EU troika, which consisted of the past, current and future European Council Presidencies, Rogozin suggested negotiating with each of the EU member states directly. Rogozin intended 'to have free discussions without a fixed EU position which one EU voice was reading out'.[9] Obviously perceiving that this could undermine the EU's ability to maintain a coherent policy towards Russia and would give the Kremlin an opportunity to apply a 'divide and rule policy' among EU member states, the European Commission rejected the proposal.[10]

Unwilling to compromise, the EU reiterated its stance on Kaliningrad. At the EU–Russia summit in Moscow on 29 May, European Commission President Romano Prodi declared that the EU member states were bound to abide by visa regulations.[11] However, when it came to economic matters, Prodi's tone was more moderate. He stressed that the economies of the EU and Russia 'complement[ed] each other; [they could] be compared to vodka and a good snack'.[12] Prodi, who had made himself known for his accommodating stance during the second Chechen War as demonstrated in Chapter 2, was not willing to jeopardise long-term economic relations with Russia.

For Putin, the future development of EU–Russia relations was directly linked to the Kaliningrad dispute. He declared that 'one can say without exaggeration that the way in which our relation with the [EU] develop[ed] [would] depend on the resolution of the Kaliningrad issue'.[13] Putin criticised the solutions put to the Kremlin by the EU which 'in essence just mean one thing – the right of Russian people to freedom of contact with their relatives within Russia will depend on the decision of some other state'.[14]

The opposing positions of the EU and Russia meant that the summit, which had been the first opportunity to resolve the Kaliningrad question, was unsuccessful. The joint statement issued after the summit simply reiterated that that the Schengen rules applied[15] and contained general statements about addressing common challenges such as international terrorism and improving cooperation in the spheres of foreign and security policy.[16] According to the joint statement, EU enlargement would 'open new prospects' for EU–Russia relations, but might simultaneously 'create new problems in the sphere of trade, economic cooperation and human contacts'.[17]

A sign of the severity of the dispute over the Russian enclave was a declaration issued less than a month after the summit by Aleksandr Bespalov, chairman of the General Council of Russia's ruling party Edinaya Rossiya. Accusing the

60 *Russia and EU eastern enlargement*

EU of double standards, he declared that EU representatives 'always talked about Chechnya, though many of them had apparently no idea where [it] [was] located. And we shall talk to them about Kaliningrad'.[18] In an obvious allusion to the EU as an upholder of democracy and human rights, he continued 'if they really support democratic principles, they should demonstrate that in the case of Kaliningrad'.[19] Bespalov criticised the EU for referring to Chechnya in the context of human rights abuses while failing to acknowledge that from Russia's point of view, the imposition of visas for transit to and from Russia's enclave was a human rights violation.

Criticism of the EU increased sharply following *Edinaya Rossiya*'s declaration. Rogozin, chairman of the Duma Committee for International Affairs, condemned the European Parliament's stance on Chechnya after it published yet another resolution urging Russia to negotiate a political solution to the conflict. Rogozin stated that 'we [saw] no flexibility from the European Parliament on the Kaliningrad issue, but we [did] see how aggressive it [was] on the Chechen issue'.[20]

The scope of the conflict over Kaliningrad widened, including critical deliberations about the EU among Russian diplomats. In a major Russian journal on international affairs, Vladimir Chizhov, the Russian deputy foreign minister and Russia's permanent representative to the EU, condemned the European Commission's imposition of visas. In a clear reference to EU pretensions as a promoter of values in its foreign policy, Chizhov asked: 'how does the EU's perceived image as an advocate of human rights and freedoms square with its refusal to discuss the sheer possibility of retaining visa-free travel procedure for Russians ... citing the 'inviolability' of the Schengen ... bed?'[21] This reference to the Schengen Agreement, signed by Belgium, the Netherlands, Luxembourg, and France as well as Germany, resulted in the 'gradual abolition of [border] controls at the common frontiers'.[22] Chizhov accused the EU of double standards in liberalising travel in the Schengen zone through the abolition of internal borders, but simultaneously building 'an increasingly impenetrable wall ... along [the EU's] external borders.'[23]

Taking a similar line to Chizhov, Rogozin condemned the EU for discriminating against Russia on human rights. Rogozin's anti-EU rhetoric and his reputation as an aggressive defender of Russia's national interest had certainly influenced Putin to appoint him as his special envoy for problems related to Kaliningrad.[24] Rogozin's appointment aimed at ensuring the 'Russian Federation's right to remain within its own borders regardless of the fact that somebody has decided to expand ... and the right to protect the rights of Russian citizens to the full'.[25] Soon after his appointment he started a public relations offensive against the EU. At a plenary session of PACE, Rogozin denounced the EU's introduction of visas for Russians travelling to and from Kaliningrad as a 'flagrant violation of fundamental acts and conventions on human liberties and rights'.[26] He added that the EU's reluctance to seek to negotiate a political solution was evidence of the fact that it sought to undermine Russia's sovereignty while seeking to alienate the enclave.[27] Rogozin declared that it was 'obvious

Russia and EU eastern enlargement 61

that the lies and slander', which were spread in Western Europe and depicted the Kaliningrad region as a criminal area, were 'spread deliberately ... to justify the discriminatory steps being taken against this region'.[28] Rogozin equated the resolution of the Kaliningrad issue with an improvement of EU–Russia relations. He declared that the goal of the Russians was to convince the European Commission that '[Kaliningrad was] a test for Russia–EU relations that [would] show how we [would] be able to protect Russia's interest and speed up its integration with the European community'.[29]

In September Rogozin used a meeting with the Commissioner for EU External Relations, Chris Patten, and Guenther Verheugen, the Commissioner for Enlargement, as an opportunity to influence the drafting of a European Commission document on Kaliningrad. He requested the adoption of a 'scheme of free transit' for Russians from Russia to Kaliningrad before Poland and Lithuania signed up fully to the Schengen Agreement. Rogozin also criticised Lithuania for holding talks with the EU on becoming a member of the Schengen zone because this was an indication that Vilnius had 'handed over part of its sovereignty and its right to tackle the visa issue to Brussels. Now Russia ha[d] to deal with the EU', which suggests that Russian policy makers would have preferred to deal with this issue by engaging directly with Lithuania instead of with Brussels.[30] The reasons for Russia's preference for bilateral discussions with Vilnius are difficult to discern. One hypothesis might be that bilateral negotiations with the Lithuanian government might have increased the Kremlin's potential bargaining power instead of having to abide by the EU approach towards the regulation of transit to and from Kaliningrad.

The dispute threatened to derail the impending EU–Russia summit in November. Rogozin warned that his failure to convince Verheugen and Patten to make concessions in favour of Russia's position would result in Russian representatives facing a 'stonewall EU response' at the summit.[31] In Moscow he told journalists that he might have to advise Putin to boycott the summit if insufficient progress was made on the issue by then.[32] One indication of the strength of feeling on the issue was that Vladimir Lukin, vice chairman of the Duma and a liberal from the pro-European Yabloko Party, urged that 'Russia should end its relations with every EU agency' unless the EU made concessions concerning transit to and from Kaliningrad.[33]

A breakthrough in the negotiating process came on September 18 when the European Commission proposed special transit arrangements to facilitate transit through EU territory for residents of the enclave after eastern enlargement. When unveiling the plan, Prodi declared that the EU had 'to take Russian concerns into consideration without undermining the relations with our future member states'.[34] He suggested introducing a special, multi-entry transit document, which became known as the Kaliningrad pass. Even though this pass, which would be granted by consulates, was not technically a visa, it would operate like one.[35]

Rogozin welcomed the Kaliningrad pass as a 'starting point' but sought to achieve further concessions by exploiting the EU's rotating European Council

62   *Russia and EU eastern enlargement*

Presidency.[36] He declared that a decision 'need[ed] to be taken during Denmark's [European Council] presidency ... before that chair pass[ed] on to Greece'.[37] Lars Grønbjerg, a former national expert in the Russia Unit at the European Commission Directorate General for External Relations, explained that Danish public opinion in favour of safeguarding Lithuanian sovereignty would make it impossible to negotiate further concessions between the EU and Russia over Kaliningrad under the Danish Presidency.[38] Denmark identified with Lithuania as it had also experienced domination and occupation by a more powerful adjacent state, and the Danish Prime Minister was in danger of losing votes if he was seen to be undermining Lithuanian sovereignty.[39] Grønbjerg stated that had the European Council Presidency been held by another member state like Portugal, for instance, 'it would not have been a vote gaining issue' and it would have had more flexibility in seeking a resolution on Kaliningrad.

Obstacles to the resolution of the Kaliningrad dispute

The attempt to resolve the issues over Kaliningrad during the Danish European Council Presidency was overshadowed by two events. First, there was a siege in Moscow's Dubrovka Theatre on 23 October in which 115 hostages were killed by anaesthetic gas.[40] The EU faced difficulties in responding to the siege. A declaration on the hostage crisis, written on behalf of the Danish European Council Presidency, had been, according to its author, 'very vague because like the Russian public at the time, we did not really know what had happened and who did what'.[41]

The second event was the announcement that the World Chechen Congress would take place in Copenhagen less than a fortnight before the EU–Russia summit. The Congress was organised by a Danish non-governmental organisation (NGO), the Centre for Holocaust and Genocide Studies, and Akhmed Zakayev, the European representative of the former president of Chechnya, Aslan Maskhadov, and took place on 28 October.[42] About 100 Russian and Chechen human rights activists participated in the conference.

The Congress threatened to jeopardise the planned EU–Russia summit chaired by the Danish European Council Presidency. The Kremlin was outraged and accused the Danish government of supporting terrorists in Chechnya. Putin stated that the Danish president had used the Congress as a 'cover to raise money for Chechen rebels', whom he held responsible for the siege in Moscow's Dubrovka Theatre.[43] In a protest note to Lars Vissing, the Danish ambassador to Russia, the Russian deputy foreign minister Valery Loschchinin accused the Danish government of 'solidarising with the Chechen terrorists' and stressed that it had 'acted at the detriment of Russia's interests, [which] was fraught with the gravest consequences for the bilateral relations'.[44]

The Danish Ministry of Foreign Affairs did not know that the conference was taking place until it read an announcement on the website of the Russian Foreign Ministry that Putin would not attend the EU–Russia summit, unless Denmark prohibited the Congress.[45] In a meeting with Nikolai Bordyuzha, the Russian

Russia and EU eastern enlargement 63

ambassador to Denmark, the head of the Danish Foreign Ministry tried to explain that he could not be held responsible for the people who had been invited by the Danish NGO which organised the Congress.[46] But it was too late for explanations. The Kremlin perceived the Congress as a provocation because Putin was on a state visit to Denmark. The fact that the conference coincided with Russia's mourning for the victims of the hostage crisis in the Dubrovka Theatre exacerbated already strained EU–Russian relations.[47] Sergey Yastrzhembsky, Putin's presidential aide and special envoy for EU–Russia relations, declared that the Kremlin had been 'deeply outraged' by the Danish government's decision to hold the Congress while Russia grieved for the victims. He criticised the Danish government's decision as 'sacrilegious and cynical'.[48]

The magnitude of the crisis became evident when the Danish European Council Presidency offered a concession. To avoid confrontations, the Danish Foreign Minister, Per Stig Moeller and the Danish Prime Minister Anders Fogh Rasmussen, chairing the European Council Presidency, decided to hold the EU–Russia summit in Brussels instead of in Copenhagen.[49] Rasmussen was apologetic and 'regretted' that the Danish government could not fulfil the Kremlin's request to cancel the Chechen Congress because the Danish constitution included the right to freedom of speech and assembly.[50]

Despite these obstacles, negotiations on a resolution to the Kaliningrad dispute gained momentum. After a meeting in Brussels on 5 November with the Commissioners for EU External Relations, Enlargement, and Justice and Home Affairs, as well as a member of the Danish Foreign Ministry representing the Danish European Council Presidency, Rogozin elaborated on the Russian proposal for a resolution of the Kaliningrad question.[51] The European Commission proposed the so-called Facilitated Transit Documents (FTDs), enabling Russian citizens to travel between Kaliningrad and Russia by rail without visas.[52] FTDs were available for Russian citizens who travelled frequently and directly between the Russian mainland and the enclave.[53] The Russian Foreign Ministry criticised the FTDs as substitute visas, which would be issued to a 'limited, very vague category of Russians'.[54] Rogozin's objections to the FTDs were reflected in his statement that the proposal would need to be 'polished' by including road travel in addition to travel by train. The Russians would then accept this 'surrogate visa regime'.[55]

The partners reached a compromise concerning Kaliningrad at the EU–Russia summit. The summit's joint statement outlined arrangements for the transit of persons and goods to and from Kaliningrad by implementing the necessary laws for creating FTDs.[56] According to the statement, the EU would introduce the legislation to establish FTDs by 1 July 2003. There were two types of time-limited FTDs: One which would allow Russians multiple entries through direct transit by all forms of transport; the other enabled Russians to undertake single return trips by train through Lithuania.[57]

Despite the EU–Russian compromise on Kaliningrad, the press conference highlighted the vast gap between EU and Russian perceptions of politics and civility. It was shown that the partners' joint statement on terrorism declared that

64 *Russia and EU eastern enlargement*

the EU and Russia were 'united' in the 'war against terrorism'. The statement was political rhetoric rather than pragmatism. Putin's perception that the 'struggle against international terrorism' was marked by 'religious extremists and international terrorists, [who] planned to set up a caliphate throughout the world; ... Chechnya was just the first stage of their plan'.[58] According to Putin, both terrorists and extremists were determined to kill all non-Muslims. In his answer to a question from a journalist of *Le Monde*, Putin radically suggested that:

> If you [were] determined to become a complete Islamic radical and [were] ready to undergo circumcision, then I invite you to Moscow. We have experts in this sphere as well.[59]

The Danish Prime Minister Rasmussen, who chaired the summit, listened to Putin's remark in embarrassed silence. After the controversy over the World Chechen Congress he obviously sought to avoid further confrontation with Putin.[60] At the press conference, Jonathan Faull, a European Commission spokesman, criticised Putin's remark as 'entirely inappropriate'.[61] A former spokesman for EU External Relations stated that the European Commission's reaction to Putin's comment was 'shock and disbelief'.[62]

The Danish European Council Presidency's accommodating stance towards Putin's remark was perceived by the press as a way of avoiding jeopardising the EU–Russian resolution of the Kaliningrad issue. A day after the summit, the Commissioner for EU External Relations Chris Patten defended the Danish European Council Presidency against these allegations.[63] He stated that at six of the ten EU–Russia summits at which the Chechnya conflict had been discussed, 'no presidency had raised Chechnya as comprehensively and vigorously as the Danish presidency'.[64] Patten's statement demonstrates that the member states chairing the rotating European Council Presidencies set priorities on their agenda differently. This agenda setting is likely to be determined by endogenous and exogenous factors. It lies beyond the scope of this research to elucidate the main motivations for determining the Council Presidencies' agendas. This agenda setting also has an impact on the EU's relations with Russia. The most significant illustration of the Council Presidency's impact on EU–Russia relations is discussed later in the chapter following an examination of the ENP. The following section sheds light on some fundamental discrepancies between Brussels and Moscow which gradually developed into major sources of confrontation in the 'strategic partnership'.

The European Neighbourhood Policy (ENP)

The EU's enlargement created a division between insiders (newly acceded member states) and outsiders (states which had not qualified for membership). Aiming at decreasing this division, the European Commission published the communication *Wider Europe – Neighbourhood: A New Framework for Relations with our Eastern and Southern Neighbours* on 11 March 2003. It proposed developing a 'zone of prosperity and a friendly neighbourhood – a 'ring of friends' – with whom the EU enjoy[ed] close, peaceful and cooperative relations ... in return for concrete progress demonstrating shared values and effective implementation of political, economic and institutional reform'.[65] *Wider Europe – Neighbourhood*, which became known as the ENP from May 2004, sought to enhance integration through values such as democracy, human rights and the rule of law, the extension of the EU's internal market, and the promotion of the free movement of persons, capital, goods and services.[66] Countries in the Mediterranean such as Algeria, Egypt, Israel, Jordan, Lebanon, Libya, Morocco, Syria, Tunisia and Palestine, as well as Eastern Europe, became members.[67] Within the framework of this policy, the EU intended to 'socialise' these countries by 'stimulating common values and cooperation'.[68] It was in this context that Tom Casier referred to 'political conditionality' as one of the underlying principles of the ENP, meaning that it was a 'foreign policy instrument [giving] incentives to a third country to comply with certain rules or norms. Certain conditions are imposed [to achieve this objective] and the targeted country is rewarded or sanctioned in case of (non-)fulfilment'.[69]

The fluctuating relationship between the EU and Russia over the period 2002 to 2004 deteriorated when Russia rejected the European Commission's invitation to join the ENP. Russia's decision defeated one of the major purposes of this policy, namely the 'active transference' of some of the EU's 'norms and values'.[70] As a consequence of Russia's rejection of ENP membership, the EU did not have the leverage to export some of its values in its relations with Russia. As a result, a normative gap developed between the EU and Russia, which contributed to the deterioration of their relations. The increasing gap between the values the EU sought to uphold in its relations with Moscow and Russia's political reality was a source of increasing strain in the further evolution of EU–Russia diplomatic relations. Furthermore, the fact that the EU attempted to transfer its values through integrating former Soviet satellite states became an additional source of friction, which culminated in the strategic partnership's existential crisis.

Russia's rejection of its inclusion in the ENP prevented the EU from making use of what Ian Manners, the pioneer of the concept of normative power, called 'informational diffusion', namely the export of EU norms through new policy initiatives implemented by the EU.[71] According to Hiski Haukkala, Russia's rejection of the EU's offer exempted Russia from the 'tough conditionality to which it would have been bound in [this policy]' and thus prevented the EU from trying to obtain concessions from Russia.[72] He argued that Russia's recent policies indicated that the ENP, and with it the EU's normative power, was in danger of 'serious erosion'.[73] Due to the difficulty of fulfilling the EU's normative ambitions in its relations with Russia, a normative gap between the EU and Russia emerged, which in addition to the EU's inability to create a coherent policy towards Russia, contributed to the alienation between the 'strategic partners' in 2003 and 2004. A prominent example of the EU's inability to develop a coherent policy towards Russia is examined in the following section.

66 *Russia and EU eastern enlargement*

The Russian deputy foreign minister and permanent representative to the EU Vladimir Chizhov had two major objections to Russia's ENP membership. First, he regarded the EU's offer of accession to this policy as an affront given that the ENP had been launched for countries whose economic performance was less strong than Russia's. Chizhov stated that the ENP was an 'attempt to reduce to the least [lowest] common denominator ... states that are entirely different in their level of development and ... have different objectives with respect to the EU itself- objectives that are oftentimes incompatible with one another'.[74] In this way, Chizhov referred to the fact that the European Commission had launched the ENP for countries with a 'history of autocratic and non-democratic governance[,] poor record in protecting human rights and freedom of the individual'.[75] He emphasised that the Russian government was insulted by the EU's offer to include Russia as an ENP member state when he stated that

> Russia [was] a large self-sufficient country with its own views on European and Euro-Atlantic integration. In contrast to some smaller Eastern European or South Caucasus countries striving for EU membership, Russia [was] neither a subject nor an object of the [ENP].[76]

In this way, Chizhov outwardly rejected the EU's pretensions as an upholder of values. Given that 'sovereign democracy', the doctrine of the Putin era, emphasised autonomy, among other aspects, which was also reflected in the RMTS, Chizhov's intransigence to Russia's adoption of the EU's self-imposed values in the ENP framework was not surprising.

Second, Chizhov publicly justified the Russian government's rejection of its ENP membership when he declared that the Kremlin perceived this policy as an attempt by the EU to create an integrative political project with states belonging to the former Soviet space at the detriment of Russia's interests in the region. He warned that the ENP would create dividing lines within Europe – 'limitrophes on Russia's Western borders'.[77] Chizhov stated that Russia sought to avoid making the former Soviet states an 'arena of rivalry for forces pursuing their various interests, as it [was] a matter of guaranteeing Russia's national security and defending its political and economic interests, and ultimately European security'.[78] In this way Chizhov emphasised the Kremlin's intention to 'make full use of its dominant position' in the former Soviet states.[79] These issues mentioned by Chizhov were the first indications of the simmering tensions between the EU and Russia over the post-Soviet space, which culminated in a political crisis between the EU and Russia after the Orange Revolution in Ukraine in 2004. An assessment of the evolution of this crisis will be at the core of the following chapter.

The Berlusconi crisis

The initial assertiveness the EU had displayed in its relations with Russia when dictating transit regulations for Kaliningrad and the offer of ENP membership

Russia and EU eastern enlargement   67

was severely undermined during the Italian chairmanship of the European Council Presidency (July to December 2003). During this period, internal fragmentation of the EU significantly undermined EU–Russia relations. A rift between the Presidency, the European Commission and the Parliament was caused by Berlusconi's announcement of his wish to be Putin's 'advocate' concerning the Chechen War. This was not the first time that a prominent European politician had declared himself an advocate for Russia. In 1999, the German chancellor Gerhard Schroeder stated that he wanted to be Russia's advocate in negotiations with the IMF concerning the repayment of Russia's foreign debts in the aftermath of the economic crisis of 1998. Schroeder's statement marked the beginning of EU–Russian diplomatic cooperation, which culminated in the resolution of the Kosovo crisis.

Paradoxically, Berlusconi's statement had the reverse effect. It revealed two characteristics of the EU's foreign policy towards Russia. First, it demonstrated that internal divisions between EU institutions undermined its ability to adopt a coherent policy towards Russia. Second, as a consequence, the EU had become aware of the necessity of reviewing its policy towards Russia. In a historic communication, the European Commission called on the European Council to make drastic changes to EU–Russia relations seeking to both fulfil the EU's interests in this 'strategic partnership' and to present a firmer line in its relations with Russia.

About a week prior to the EU–Russia summit on 6 November, an EU delegation led by Italy's foreign minister Franco Frattini gave a foretaste of the Italian European Council Presidency's pro-Russian stance. Frattini declared that this summit would become the 'ground for consolidating relations'.[80] In a meeting with Javier Solana, the European Commissioner for EU enlargement Guenther Verheugen, and the Russian Foreign Minister Igor Ivanov, Frattini was extraordinarily sympathetic to Russian concerns.[81] Frattini vowed that the EU would continue to support Russia in the struggle against international terrorism.[82] It was a stance that was welcomed by Ivanov, who declared that the Russian leadership was 'satisfied with the development of EU–Russian cooperation'.[83]

Despite the cordial relations between Frattini and Ivanov, EU–Russian cooperation was undermined by the first signs of division between the Italian European Council Presidency and the European Commission. This fragmentation was reflected in a contradiction between the differing perspectives of Frattini and the Commission on the Khodorkovsky affair. Frattini declared that the arrest of Mikhail Khodorkovsky, the CEO of the Russian oil company Yukos, on charges of tax evasion in October 2013, was Russia's internal affair.[84] Thus, Frattini made clear that the Italian European Council Presidency would not interfere in the Kremlin's resolution of the affair. The European Commission, on the other hand, issued a statement in which it called on Putin to clarify issues related to the Khodorkovsky case as well as the rule of law in Russia. The statement declared that the 'Commission will recall the need for fair, non-discriminatory and proportional application of the law by Russian authorities'.[85]

The EU's internal divergence was aggravated at the press conference after the EU–Russia summit in Rome on 6 November. Berlusconi's remarks on the

68   *Russia and EU eastern enlargement*

Chechen War triggered a spectacular clash between the European Council Presidency and the European Commission. When journalists grilled Putin on the war in Chechnya, Berlusconi, who had made himself known as a political ally of Putin, condemned their questions as 'Western lies and fairytales' and addressed himself to Putin: 'let me be your advocate in this one'.[86] Berlusconi defended the Russian authorities' conduct in Chechnya. He stated that 'in Chechnya there has been terrorist activity that had produced many attacks against Russian citizens and there had never been an equivalent response from the Russian Federation'.[87] He added that the 'truth was that there were often distortions in the press, in Italy as abroad. It is the same thing [with] Chechnya and the Yukos story'.[88]

By seeking to defend Russia's conduct in Chechnya, Berlusconi contradicted the European Commission's stance on this war. A Commission official criticised Berlusconi for having undermined the Commission's position on the Chechen War. The official asked rhetorically 'what the point of [the Commission's posturing on human rights in Chechnya] [was] if the president of the Council then contradict[ed] them'.[89] Berlusconi's remarks were not the only issues on which he publicly contradicted the EU position at the press conference. His statement that 'we [were] completely interested in the abolition of the visa regime' between the EU and Russia also contradicted the recently adopted regulation of transit to and from Kaliningrad.[90]

The European Commission spokesman Reijo Kemppinen sought to distance the Commission from the Council Presidency's stance on Chechnya and the Khodorkovsky affair. Four days after Berlusconi announced that he would be Putin's advocate, Kemppinen described his remarks as 'personal' and declared that the European Commission 'did not share the view of Prime Minister Berlusconi when it [came] to [either] the situation of Yukos [or] the present or past situation in Chechnya'.[91] The Commissioner for EU External Relations, Chris Patten, condemned Berlusconi's statement as 'unbelievable'.[92]

Berlusconi's remarks resulted in an unusual rift between the Commission and the European Council Presidency. Some European diplomats commented that it was 'very rare' for the Commission to publicly rebuke the member state in charge of the Presidency.[93] One diplomat was quoted as saying that the Berlusconi incident 'looked bad for the pivotal role between the European Commission and the Presidency ... just as we face[d] EU enlargement'.[94]

The Russian Foreign Minister Ivanov was gloating over the EU's lack of unity in its foreign policy. After Berlusconi's statement at the Rome summit, Ivanov acknowledged that 'there [was] the EU position and the position of individual states, which [did] not always coincide fully'.[95] Ivanov was aware that he and other Russian politicians could exploit the internal friction in the EU to Russia's advantage. This issue was raised in a European Parliament report discussed later in this section.

The clash between the European Council Presidency and the European Commission over Berlusconi's remark was reflected in a confrontation between Berlusconi and the Commission's President Romano Prodi. According to a former spokesman for EU External Relations, who was present at the press

Russia and EU eastern enlargement 69

conference, Berlusconi and Prodi openly opposed each other.[96] Berlusconi's aides downplayed the incident and stated that

> if the Commission and President Prodi had something contrary to say to Prime Minister Berlusconi's remarks about the Yukos or the Chechen controversies, they could have done so freely during the course of the entire meeting with President Putin or [at] the long and animated press conference afterwards.[97]

The rift caused by Berlusconi's statement highlighted the EU's weakness as a diplomatic actor, which was exacerbated by the EU's rotating European Council Presidencies. The Swedish foreign minister, Leila Freivalds, referred to the potential abuse of the position of a politician chairing the Presidency. She stated:

> the incident with Berlusconi show[ed] how vital it [was] for the person speaking as a representative of the EU to indeed represent the EU. It [was] unacceptable and several of us have protested. I hope all the EU member states [would] do it, showing that it [did] not confirm with the EU opinion.... [T]his incident affirm[ed] the need to change the present system of presidency.[98]

As well as inconsistency in EU foreign policy towards Russia, friction between 'old' and 'new' EU member states over their approach to Russia also led to increasing tension in EU relations with Russia. This issue is discussed further in Chapter 5.

A day after the summit, the European Parliament initiated a series of condemnations of Berlusconi's remark. Pat Cox, the speaker for the European Parliament, 'issued an appeal' to Berlusconi in which he urged him to make amendments to the summit's conclusion and to explain why the joint statement did not contain any references to Chechnya.[99] Cox declared that the summit's conclusion was 'not at all to [his] liking' because it failed to address human and political rights in Chechnya.[100] The European Parliament proposed a radical reorientation of the EU's policy on Russia. A report from the Committee on Foreign Affairs, Human Rights, Security and Defence, written by Bastiaan Beelder, a Dutch member of the European Parliament, and issued on 19 November 2003, aimed to 'set a new tone in the discussion' of the EU's policy towards Russia.[101] It identified three major problems in EU–Russia relations: lack of progress, the European Commission's stance towards Chechnya, and the EU's fragmentation concerning its policy towards Russia.[102] The Beelder report proposed measures to prevent the lack of unity from further undermining its relations with Russia. It contended that the 'lack of coordination on the EU side' enabled Russia to take advantage of the EU's internal division. Attempting to prevent this in the future, the report advised the European Council to 'refrain from actions which could weaken the EU's ability to exert influence' in its relations with Russia.[103] The report used Berlusconi's statement, which

70   *Russia and EU eastern enlargement*

'went straight against well-established and fully-motivated EU positions' on Chechnya, to exemplify the EU's fragmentation.[104]

Apart from blaming the European Council, this report held the European Commission partly responsible for the EU's lack of a coherent policy towards Russia. The report criticised the Commission's response to the second Chechen War as 'soft' as it had reduced the financial contribution to Russia in the framework of the TACIS programme, instead of freezing the funds Russia continued to receive during the conflict. The reduction of the TACIS fund contributions to Russia as a consequence of the Chechen War was discussed in Chapter 2. The report stated that the Commission's failure to impose sanctions resulted in a 'two track approach', namely the EU's continuous condemnation of human rights abuses in Chechnya, while developing economic relations with Russia 'with a view not least to influence the Russian action in Chechnya'.[105] According to the report, the Commission's 'soft reaction' was also demonstrated by the moderate tone of the European signatories in the joint statement of the EU–Russia summit of 31 May 2003. The report lamented that the signatories were 'fighting [to have] a few words [on Chechnya] included' in the statement and then '[were] content [to have] achieved that, although the text basically endorsed the Russian position and ignored [the EU's]'.[106]

The European Commission was even more outspoken on the need to re-examine EU–Russia relations than the European Parliament. In its communication of 9 February 2004, the European Commission instigated a review aimed at establishing a 'more coherent and effective approach to relations with Russia reflecting the views of the EU 25'.[107] The communication identified a 'need for increased EU coordination and coherence across all areas of EU activity [aiming to send] clear, unambiguous messages to Russia'.[108] It stated that the EU needed to establish an 'effective, realistic, balanced and consistent approach ... and [had] to improve the functioning of existing structures of cooperation' in its relations with Russia. However, it did not specify how these objectives should be achieved.

The communication outlined three issues in EU–Russia relations, which would need to be addressed in order to ameliorate the relationship. The first was the EU's inability to promote its interests with Russia. The communication stated that the EU should 'make full use of its influence with Russia to promote and defend EU interests [vigorously].... The EU need[ed] to define realistic common positions, which [could] be used to present a firm EU line to Russian interlocutors'.[109] This proposal is crucial in seeking to address one of the fundamental difficulties in the EU's relations with Russia. However, the European Commission did not specify how the EU intended to both promote and defend its interests in relations with Russia. As a result, the EU's objectives in its policy with Moscow were not achieved. This omission severely hampered EU–Russia relations and was reflected in a second review on EU–Russia relations which was issued in 2008 and will be analysed in Chapter 6. The second issue was the promotion of values in the relationship. According to the communication, the EU needed to stress that its partnership with Russia was founded on 'shared

Russia and EU eastern enlargement 71

values' and 'common interests'.[110] This implied 'discussing frankly Russian practices that run counter to universal and European values, such as democracy and human rights in Chechnya'. The communication declared that these 'frank discussions' would 'enhance the EU's credibility' and 'contribute to a more substantive forward-looking partnership with Russia'.[111] Although these proposals are legitimate but would require the development of principles to guide relations between the EU and Russia in order to prevent the sort of friction that built up within the EU during the second Chechen War, as discussed in Chapter 2. The third issue mentioned in the Commission's communication was the lack of a strong EU stance in negotiations with Russia. The communication stated that the EU could achieve a firmer negotiating position in relations with Moscow by continuing to 'give priority to substance over form'.[112] The need to 'agree [on] key objectives and clear positions' on issues such as the ratification of the Kyoto protocol, facilitating human aid delivery, the ratification of border agreements with Latvia and Estonia, the extension of the PCA, and Russia's refusal of energy sector reform was an extension of the Commission's second perceived issue, namely the need for 'frank discussion'.[113] This last concern regarding the establishment of 'clear positions' on the aforementioned areas, was likely to be undermined by divergence among EU member states over some of these aspects. Chapter 5 demonstrates that the renewal of the PCA was another major contentious area exacerbated by internal friction between EU member states over the development of EU relations with Russia.

Seeking to prevent incidents such as Berlusconi's announcement in the future, the European Commission recommended improving the structure for EU–Russian cooperation. It suggested that the EU–Russian Permanent Partnership Council, 'the main working body of EU–Russia relations' where consultations take place among both foreign and other ministers, should be set up in a troika format, comprising the past, current and future European Council Presidencies.[114] The Commission aimed to promote policy coherence in EU relations with Russia by preparing a list of EU policy priorities at the beginning of each presidency.[115] However, it remains doubtful whether this approach would prevent problems in EU–Russian diplomatic relations such as the Berlusconi incident in the long term.

The European Commission communication was a historic and unique document, which proposed a set of guidelines intended to improve internal cohesion in the EU following the Berlusconi incident. The European Commission recommended that the EU should prepare guidance for the biannual summits several months in advance. In this way, the EU could 'clearly determine positions for the EU beyond which it would not go'.[116] However, because of potential divergence between EU institutions, setting a joint agenda could prove difficult. A note prepared on the expected issues on the agenda of the upcoming EU–Russia summit needed to be approved by the European Council, the Committee of Permanent Representatives and the European Council's working party on Eastern Europe and Central Asia. At the same time, the European Commission also prepared a document outlining the EU position on additional unresolved issues between the EU and Russia.[117] Despite the proposed measures, it remained very

72 Russia and EU eastern enlargement

difficult for the EU to 'determine positions beyond which the EU would not go' because of Russia's increasingly affirmative and independent foreign policy, which hampered the development of a streamlined EU policy towards Russia. The tragic Beslan massacre, which resulted in increased power in the Kremlin, tested EU strategies for relations with Moscow to their limits and called their effectiveness into question.

The growing normative gap between the EU and Russia after Beslan

A massacre in Beslan in North Ossetia on 1 September 2004 served as a pretext for curtailing democracy in Russia. This challenge was exacerbated by the EU's inability to implement its normative agenda in its policy with Russia. The resulting divergence over the importance of norms and values contributed to the rift between these 'strategic partners' in the aftermath of the Beslan massacre. As Russian families celebrated the beginning of the new school year, Chechen terrorists took about 1,100 children and adults as hostages to put pressure on the Kremlin to end human rights abuses in Chechnya.[118] The situation deteriorated when Russian security forces stormed the building and fighting began, costing the lives of 334 hostages.[119] After the massacre, Putin portrayed Russia as a victim of international terrorism: 'Our country, formerly protected by the most powerful defence system ... overnight found itself defenceless'.[120] He denounced the attack in Beslan as an act of international terrorism and held al-Qaeda responsible for terrorist activities in Chechnya and for the school hostage crisis. He claimed that the reforms launched in the aftermath of the massacre, including the direct appointment of regional leaders by Putin rather than by election, would strengthen the Russian state.[121]

The signs of increasing authoritarianism and the curtailing of democracy in the aftermath of the Beslan massacre made it difficult for the EU to respond. According to Lars Grønbjerg, a former national expert seconded to the Russia Unit at the European Commission Directorate General for External Relations, it was 'difficult' for the EU to condemn certain of Putin's announced reforms such as the direct appointment of governors. This was because governors were not always elected in some EU countries, for example, the appointment of prefects in France. He explained that it was difficult for the EU to respond because 'due to the complexity of democracy, it [was] not possible to say that one isolated component [was] right or wrong – the totality count[ed]'.[122]

The first reaction to the massacre from the Dutch European Council Presidency resulted in a clash with the Russian Ministry of Foreign Affairs. Two days after the massacre, the Dutch Foreign Minister Bernard Bot published a statement on behalf of the Dutch European Council Presidency, in which he declared that 'to better understand what happened at the school, we would like to learn more details from the Russian authorities so we can help each other to combat terrorism in any form'.[123] When the Russian First Deputy Minister of Foreign Affairs, Valery Loshchinin, criticised Bot's statement as 'inappropriate, odious'

Russia and EU eastern enlargement 73

and 'offensive', it became evident that the Beslan massacre was a sensitive topic for Russian politicians, which should not be touched upon by the West.[124]

Putin's intention to enhance the power of the Kremlin deepened the rift between the EU and Russia. On 13 September, about a fortnight after the massacre, Putin gave a speech in which he outlined his intention to strengthen the Kremlin's powers. He stressed that

> when a man [was] born, some disease-causing germs, some virus appear almost immediately in his organism endangering his health. But if the organism [grew] strong and powerful then its immunity suppresse[d] all these disease-causing germs.... As soon as the organism weaken[ed], they all flare up in a life-threatening disease. This [was] the way it happened with us.... We need[ed] to revitalize the entire organism of Russian statehood and the political system.[125]

Two days later, the Commissioner for EU External Relations Chris Patten spoke out about the Kremlin's implementation of reforms. He hoped that the Russian government would not conclude that the sole solution to terrorism 'was to increase the power of the Kremlin. Frankly, there [was] not much good history on the side of that proposition'.[126] At the same time, Patten emphasised the need for the EU to adopt a unitary stance when addressing the Chechen War. According to Patten, the EU should discuss the situation in Chechnya with Russia in a

> consistent, intelligent way that [did] not risk changing from presidency to presidency and that underst[ood] the complex nature of ethnic conflict in the Caucasus.... [W]e and our Russian partners need[ed] urgently to come to a shared understanding of this point.[127]

Patten's reference to the EU's lack of a unified stance regarding Chechnya had already undermined the EU's development of a coercive foreign policy towards Russia in 2000, as was demonstrated in Chapter 2 of this book. Even though Patten acknowledged that this was not the right moment to 'read Russia lectures about Chechnya [because] [t]his [was] a time of grief and shock', he stressed that a 'long-lasting resolution' of the Chechen War depended on the 'pursuit of far-sighted, humane and resolute policies in Moscow'.[128]

Three weeks after the Beslan massacre, certain prominent European opinion makers joined the chorus of criticism. In a letter to European heads of state and government and to NATO, 114 scholars, public intellectuals, academics and former politicians, among whom were the former Swedish Prime Minister Carl Bildt, the former President of the Czech Republic Vaclav Havel and the French philosopher André Glucksmann, condemned Putin for having 'systematically undercut the freedom and independence of the press and arbitrarily imprisoned both real and imagined political rivals'.[129] The latter point could be understood as an allusion to Khodorkovsky's imprisonment in 2003. The signatories condemned the West for having remained 'silent and [for having] restrained its

74 *Russia and EU eastern enlargement*

criticism in the belief that President Putin's step in the wrong direction was temporary'.[130] They concluded by stressing that: 'We must speak the truth about what [was] happening in Russia. We owe it to the victims of Beslan and the tens of thousands democrats who [were] still fighting to preserve democracy and human freedom in their country'.[131]

The opinion makers' call for a hardened stance by the West in its policy on Russia was reciprocated by the Dutch European Council Presidency. In a speech given at the meeting of the EU–Russian ministerial troika on 19 October, the Dutch Foreign Minister Bernard Bot, speaking on behalf of the European Council Presidency, acknowledged that the conflicting perceptions of the EU and Russia about the importance of norms and values undermined their relationship.[132] Bot contradicted the point of view held by a Russian parliamentarian who stated on a visit to the EU that 'too much democracy can be bad for you'.[133] According to Bot, democracy and the rule of law should complement each other as far as the EU was concerned, but the Russian politicians condemned the EU for being 'difficult to understand, for being bureaucratic and arrogant'.[134] About a month later, the European Parliament supported Bot's condemnations. It criticised the 'weakening of the hope for real "common values"' in a resolution on the EU–Russia summit in The Hague in November 2004.[135] The resolution expressed concern about the 'further accumulation of powers by the central government in Moscow such as the appointment of Supreme Court judges, governors and mayors of large towns'.[136] The European Parliament's disappointed hopes concerning common values with Russia, combined with the centralisation of power in the Kremlin, demonstrated the divergence between the values the EU aspired to uphold in its relations with Moscow and Russia's domestic political reality. Both this discrepancy and the EU's ability to gain prominence in the post-Soviet space were the reasons for the deterioration of EU–Russia relations between 1999 and 2015.

The EU's response to Russia's increasing authoritarianism was undermined by prominent political leaders who sought to maintain cordial relations with Russia. Less than three months after the Beslan massacre, the German chancellor Gerhard Schroeder characterised Putin as a 'flawless democrat'.[137] Schroeder emphasised that he was convinced that the Russian president would 'transform Russia into a fair democracy'.[138] He stated that Putin's attempt to reform Russia was challenging to the EU but that he had tried to tackle situations in contrast to the Russian state's previous failure to deal with crises.[139]

Conclusion

This chapter demonstrates that between 2002 and 2004, the EU's initial assertiveness in its relations with Russia was soon undermined by internal division. When Kaliningrad became enclosed in EU territory after the accession of Poland and Lithuania to the EU, the European Commission imposed visas for Russians travelling to and from the enclave. It was the first time in EU–Russia relations since 1999 that an EU policy had had a direct impact on Russian citizens. Its

Russia and EU eastern enlargement 75

repercussions became evident when various Russian diplomats denounced the introduction of visas as against the free movement of persons. After acrimonious clashes between European and Russian diplomats, the Russian government had to accept European Commission transit regulations.

In 2003, several months after the EU adopted a visa policy for Kaliningrad, EU foreign policy towards Russia was undermined by the chairman of the European Council Presidency, Berlusconi. His announcement that he wanted to be Putin's 'advocate' concerning Chechnya was in direct contradiction to the EU's position on Chechnya and severely hampered the EU's external relations with Russia. EU reactions to Berlusconi's extraordinary support for Putin's war in Chechnya revealed the EU's fragile political cohesion in its relations with Russia. Seeking to prevent further similar incidents, the European Commission outlined guidelines intended to both restore cohesion in the EU's policy towards Russia and to prevent the European Council Presidency from contradicting the EU's stance in the future. The Berlusconi incident showed that the EU as an actor can be susceptible to an individual, who chairs the European Council Presidency.

In addition, an increasing normative gap between the EU and Russia contributed to transformation of the partnership. Differences concerning the significance of values in EU–Russia relations were demonstrated by the Russian government's rejection of the EU's offer to make Russia a member of the ENP. The Kremlin was not willing to undertake political and economic reforms to become part of an integrated Europe. Instead, as reflected in both the Russian Foreign Policy Concept and the RMTS, the Kremlin sought to maintain autonomy in its domestic and foreign policies. As the Kremlin did not aspire to adopt EU values, the EU was unable to influence Russia not to curb democracy in the aftermath of the Beslan tragedy. Consequently, the EU and Russia drifted apart. However, the increasing normative divergence between Brussels and Moscow was not the only reason for this development – a multitude of factors, including the EU's increasing influence in the post-Soviet space, also contributed to the deterioration of EU–Russia relations. This chapter examined the first indications of an increasing EU–Russian confrontation over the post-Soviet space. The confrontation intensified, culminating in the first political crisis between the partners since 1999 over the EU's interference in Ukrainian domestic politics. The following chapter assesses the confrontation between the EU and Russia over the EU's role in resolving the Orange Revolution in Ukraine.

Notes

1 Interview with a former spokesman for EU External Relations working at the Directorate General for EU External Relations at the European Commission. Interview conducted at the European Commission on 23 June 2010.
2 Bainbridge (2002), p. 342.
3 Patten (2001).
4 European Commission (1999).
5 BBC Summary of World Broadcasts. EU rules might shut off Russian exclave from the rest of Russia. 28 May 2002.

76 *Russia and EU eastern enlargement*

6 Ministry of Foreign Affairs of the Russian Federation (2000).

7 Ibid.

8 BBC Summary of World Broadcasts. Source: Interfax news agency (2002). Russian MPs blame EU for not listening to Moscow's proposals on Kaliningrad. 29 May 2002.

9 Interview with Lars Grønbjerg. He is a former seconded national expert at the unit for EU relations with Russia at the Directorate General for EU External Relations at the European Commission Conducted on 23 June 2010 at DG RELEX, European Commission in Brussels.

10 Ibid.

11 BBC Summary of World Broadcasts. Source: ITAR-TASS news agency. EC chairman outlines European Union relations with Russia. 29 May 2002.

12 BBC Summary of World Broadcasts. Source: ITAR-TASS news agency. Russia, Ukraine, not to join the EU in the foreseeable future, EU chief says. 29 May 2002.

13 BBC Summary World Broadcasts. Source: Interfax news agency. Putin critical of EU lack of understanding on Russian exclave. 29 May 2002.

14 BBC Summary of World Broadcasts. Source: Radio Mayak Russia. Russian president calls for special status for Kaliningrad region. 29 May 2002.

15 The Delegation of the European Union to Russia (2002a).

16 Ibid.

17 Ibid.

18 BBC Summary of World Broadcasts. Source: BNS news agency. Russia: Pro-Putin party official makes tough statement on Kaliningrad issue. 25 June 2002.

19 Ibid.

20 BBC Summary of World Broadcasts. Source: Interfax. Russian top MP opposes EU visit to Chechnya. 8 July 2002.

21 Chizhov (2003), p. 12.

22 Bainbridge (2002), p. 457; BBC Summary of World Broadcasts. Source: ITAR-TASS. Russian officials details latest talks with Europe over Kaliningrad. 4 September 2002.

23 Chizhov (2003), p. 12.

24 BBC Summary of World Broadcasts. Source: Interfax news agency. Putin appoints special envoy to deal with problems concerning the Kaliningrad region. 13 July 2002.

25 BBC Summary of World Broadcasts. Source: Ekho Moskvy. Putin envoy cautiously optimistic about EU talks on Kaliningrad. 22 July 2002.

26 BBC Summary of World Broadcasts. Source: *Nezavisimaya Gazeta*. Putin aide unlikely to derail diplomatic approach on enclave. 16 July 2002.

27 Ibid.

28 BBC Summary of World Broadcasts. Source: Interfax news agency, Moscow. Russian envoy complains of unfair attitude to westernmost region. 15 August 2002.

29 Ibid.

30 BBC Summary of World Broadcasts. Source: Interfax news agency, Moscow. Russian envoy complains of unfair attitude to westernmost region. 15 August 2002.

31 Europolitics (2002).

32 Ibid.

33 Osborne (2002a).

34 Black (2002).

35 Castle (2002).

36 Ibid.

37 BBC Summary of World Broadcasts. Source: BNS news agency, Kaliningrad. Russian envoy says Kaliningrad issue needs solution under Danish EU presidency. 14 October 2002.

Russia and EU eastern enlargement 77

38 Interview with Lars Grønbjerg. From 1995 until 1998 Mr Grønbjerg was a former Deputy Head of Mission of Denmark to Russia. He was chief adviser on EU–Russia affairs in the Danish Ministry of Foreign Affairs from 2005 until 2008. The interview was conducted at the European Commission in Brussels on 16 June 2010.
39 Schumacher (1996), Berichte Nr. 4.
40 McGrory and Shepherd (2002); *Moscow Times* (2002).
41 Interview with Lars Grønbjerg. Interview conducted via email on 4 March 2011.
42 BBC Summary of World Broadcast. Source: Russian Public TV (ORT). Putin aide slams Danes for allowing Chechen Congress on day of mourning. 28 October 2002.
43 BBC Monitoring Europe – Political. Supplied by BBC Worldwide Monitoring. Source: Danmarks Radio P1 Copenhagen. Danish Foreign Minister moves EU–Russia meeting to Brussels. 28 October 2002; Osborne (2002b).
44 ITAR-TASS (2002a).
45 Interview with Lars Grønbjerg. The interview was conducted at the European Commission in Brussels on 23 June 2010.
46 Ibid.
47 Ibid.
48 BBC Summary of World Broadcasts. Source: Russian Public TV (ORT). Putin aide slams Danes for allowing to Chechen Congress on day of mourning. 28 October 2002.
49 Interview with Lars Grønbjerg. The interview was conducted at the European Commission on 23 June 2010.
50 BBC Summary of World Broadcasts. Source: Danmarks Radio website. Danish premier criticises Russia over Chechen congress. 11 November 2002; Associated Press Worldstream (2002).
51 BBC Summary of World Broadcast. Source: Interfax news agency. Russian envoy notes 'certain progress' on Kaliningrad. 6 November 2002.
52 ITAR-TASS (2002b).
53 Holtom (2005), p. 45.
54 Ibid.
55 Ibid.
56 The Delegation of the European Union to Russia (2002b).
57 Ibid.
58 The Delegation of the European Union to Russia (2002c); BBC Monitoring Former Soviet Union – Political. Supplied by BBC Worldwide Monitoring. Source: Interfax News Agency. Putin warns against terrorists, welcomes results of the EU–Russia summit. 11 November 2002.
59 Wines (2002).
60 Fuller (2002).
61 Ibid.
62 Interview with a former spokesman for EU External Relations. Interview conducted at European Commission on 23 June 2010.
63 European Commission (2002).
64 Ibid.; Sciolino (2002).
65 European Commission (2003).
66 Panebianco (2006), p. 134.
67 Casier (2007), pp. 73–94.
68 Ibid.; For a detailed overview of the significance of the ENP see: Dannreuther (2006).
69 Casier (2007), pp. 73–94.
70 Haukkala (2008c), p. 1602.
71 Manners (2002), p. 244.
72 Haukkala (2008b), p. 37.

78 *Russia and EU eastern enlargement*

73 Ibid.
74 Chizhov quoted in Haukkala (2008a), p. 43.
75 Ibid.; Commission of the European Communities (2003), p. 7.
76 Haukkala (2008b), p. 38.
77 Chizhov quoted in Roberts (2007).
78 Chizhov (2004).
79 Casier (2007).
80 BBC Summary of World Broadcasts. Source: ITAR-TASS. Italian minister praises strategic EU–Russia partnership. 28 October 2003.
81 BBC Summary of World Broadcasts. Source: ITAR-TASS. Europe will not let Yukos affair affect relations with Russia-Italian Prime Minister. 28 October 2003; BBC Summary of World Broadcast. Foreign minister looks forward to successful Russia–EU summit in Rome. 28 October 2003.
82 BBC Summary of World Broadcasts. Source: ITAR-TASS. Europe will not let Yukos affair affect relations with Russia-Italian Prime Minister. 28 October 2003.
83 BBC Summary of World Broadcasts. Foreign minister looks forward to successful Russia–EU summit in Rome. 28 October 2003.
84 Thapar (2003).
85 Nicholson (2003).
86 Ibid.
87 Castle (2003).
88 Ibid.
89 Ibid.
90 BBC Summary of World Broadcasts. Source: ITAR-TASS. Russian, Italian, EU leaders detail results of discussion at summit. 6 November 2003.
91 McGregor (2003); Owen (2003).
92 Owen (2003).
93 Ibid.
94 Ibid.
95 BBC Summary of World Broadcasts. Source: ITAR-TASS. EU leaders 'appreciate' Putin's frankness- Russian foreign minister. 7 November 2003.
96 Interview with a former spokesman of EU External Relations, DG RELEX, European Commission. Interview conducted at the European Commission in Brussels on June 23
97 Castle (2003).
98 Baltic News Service (2003).
99 BBC Summary of World Broadcasts. Source: Corriere della Sera. European parliament head urges Italian premier, EU chief to end polemics. 11 November 2003.
100 Ibid.
101 European Parliament (2004a).
102 Ibid.
103 Ibid.
104 Ibid.
105 Ibid.
106 Ibid.
107 European Commission (2004).
108 Ibid.
109 Ibid.
110 Ibid.
111 Ibid.
112 Ibid.
113 Ibid.
114 Permanent Mission of the Russian Federation to the European Union (nd); European Commission (2004).

Russia and EU eastern enlargement 79

115 European Commission (2004).
116 Ibid.
117 Email interview with Lars Grønbjerg. Conducted on 17 July 2012.
118 Politkovskaya (2004), p. 286.
119 Lucas (2008), p. 68.
120 Speech by Vladimir Putin quoted in Lucas (2008), p. 69.
121 CNN.com (2004).
122 Email interview with Lars Grønbjerg. Interview conducted on 16 October 2010.
123 European Report (2004).
124 Ibid.; Loshchinin quoted in Lynch (2005); BBC Summary of World Broadcasts. Source: Interfax news agency. Dutch minister's siege utterances an 'outrage' – Russian deputy foreign minister. 4 September 2004.
125 Lynch (2005), p. 153.
126 European Parliament (2004b).
127 Ibid.
128 Ibid.
129 Erler (2004).
130 Ibid.
131 Ibid.
132 Bot (2004).
133 Ibid.
134 Ibid.
135 European Parliament (2004c).
136 Ibid.
137 *Wirtschaftswoche* (2004).
138 Ibid.
139 *Sueddeutsche Zeitung* (2004).

Bibliography

Associated Press Worldstream. (2002). Prime minister expects more criticism when Danes rule whether to extradite senior Chechen. 5 November 2002.

Bainbridge, T. (2002). *The Penguin Companion to European Union.* Third edition. London: Penguin Books.

Baltic News Service. (2003). Swedish Foreign Minister says Russia has no say over the EU. 14 November 2003.

BBC Monitoring Europe – Political. Supplied by BBC Worldwide Monitoring. Source: Denmark's radio P1Copenhagen. Danish Foreign Minister moves EU–Russia meeting to Brussels. 28 October 2002.

BBC Monitoring Former Soviet Union – Political. Supplied by BBC Worldwide Monitoring. Source: Interfax news agency. Putin warns against terrorists, welcomes results of EU–Russia summit. 11 November 2002.

BBC Monitoring Former Soviet Union – Political. Supplied by BBC Worldwide Monitoring. Source: Ekho Moskvy news agency, Moscow. Independent Russian radio slams Kremlin stubbornness on Chechnya. 28 October 2002.

BBC Summary of World Broadcasts. EU rules might shut off Russian exclave from the rest of Russia. 28 May 2002.

BBC Summary of World Broadcasts. Source: Interfax news agency. Putin critical of EU lack of understanding on Russian exclave. 29 May 2002.

BBC Summary of World Broadcasts. Source: Radio Mayak Russia. Russian president calls for special status for Kaliningrad region. 29 May 2002.

80　*Russia and EU eastern enlargement*

BBC Summary of World Broadcasts. Source: ITAR-TASS news agency. Russia, Ukraine, not to join the EU in the foreseeable future, EU chief says. 29 May 2002.

BBC Summary of World Broadcasts. Source: Interfax news agency. Russian MPs blame EU for not listening to Moscow's proposals on Kaliningrad. 29 May 2002.

BBC Summary of World Broadcasts. Source: ITAR-TASS. EC chairman outlines European Union relations with Russia. 29 May 2002.

BBC Summary of World Broadcasts. Source: BNS news agency. Russia: Pro-Putin party official makes tough statement on Kaliningrad issue. 25 June 2002.

BBC Summary of World Broadcasts. Source: Interfax. Russian top MP opposes EU visit to Chechnya. 8 July 2002.

BBC Summary of World Broadcasts. Source: Interfax news agency. Putin appoints special envoy to deal with problems concerning the Kaliningrad region. 13 July 2002.

BBC Summary of World Broadcasts. Source: *Nezavisimaya Gazeta*. Putin aide unlikely to derail diplomatic approach on enclave. 16 July 2002.

BBC Summary of World Broadcasts. Source: Interfax news agency, Moscow. Russian envoy complains of unfair attitude to westernmost region. 15 August 2002.

BBC Summary of World Broadcasts. Source: ITAR-TASS. Russian officials details latest talks with Europe over Kaliningrad. 4 September 2002.

BBC Summary of World Broadcasts. Source: BNS news agency, Kaliningrad. Russian envoy says Kaliningrad issue needs solution under Danish EU presidency. 14 October 2002.

BBC Summary of World Broadcasts. Source: Russian Public TV (ORT). Putin aide slams Danes for allowing to Chechen Congress on day of mourning. 28 October 2002.

BBC Summary of World Broadcast. Source: Interfax news agency. Russian envoy notes 'certain progress' on Kaliningrad. 6 November 2002.

BBC Summary of World Broadcasts. Source: Danmarks Radio website. Danish premier criticises Russia over Chechen congress. 11 November 2002.

BBC Summary of World Broadcasts. Source: ITAR-TASS. Europe will not let Yukos affair affect relations with Russia-Italian Prime Minister. 28 October 2003.

BBC Summary of World Broadcasts. Source: ITAR-TASS. Italian minister praises strategic EU–Russia partnership. 28 October 2003.

BBC Summary of World Broadcast. Foreign minister looks forward to successful Russia–EU summit in Rome. 28 October 2003.

BBC Summary of World Broadcasts. Source: ITAR-TASS. Russian, Italian, EU leaders detail results of discussion at summit. 6 November 2003.

BBC Summary of World Broadcasts. Source: ITAR-TASS. EU leaders 'appreciate' Putin's frankness- Russian foreign minister. 7 November 2003.

BBC Summary of World Broadcasts. Source: Corriere della Sera. European parliament head urges Italian premier, EU chief to end polemics. 11 November 2003.

BBC Summary of World Broadcasts. Source: Interfax news agency. Dutch minister's siege utterances an 'outrage' – Russian deputy foreign minister. 4 September 2004.

Black, I. (2002). Russia welcomes EU's offer of Kaliningrad pass. *Guardian*. 19 September 2002.

Bot, B. (2004). Why Russia and the EU need one another. WPS Russian Media Monitoring Agency. 19 October 2004.

Casier, T. (2007). The clash of integration processes? The shadow effect of the enlarged EU on its Eastern neighbours. In Malfielt. K., Verpoest, L. and Vinokurov, E. (eds) *The CIS, the EU and Russia. The challenges of integration.* Studies in Central and Eastern Europe. Basingstoke, UK: Palgrave Macmillan. pp. 73–94.

Russia and EU eastern enlargement 81

Castle, S. (2002). Prodi offers deal to end stand-off over Russian enclave. *Independent*. 19 September 2002.

Castle, S. (2003). Berlusconi causes new EU rift with Chechnya remarks. *Independent*. 8 November 2003.

Chizhov, V.A. (2003). From St Petersburg to Rome. *International Affairs (Moscow)*. 49(5): 8–16.

Chizhov, V.A. (2004). European Union: A partnership strategy. *International Affairs (Moscow)*. 50(6): 79–87.

CNN.com. (2004). Putin: Children's safety paramount. 2 September 2004.

Dannreuther, R. (2006). Developing the alternative to enlargement: The European Neighbourhood Policy. *European Foreign Affairs Review* 11: 183–2001.

Erler, G. (2004). Open letter to the heads of state and government of the European Union and NATO. 28 September 2004. Retrieved 13 September 2010 from: www.gernot-erler.de/cms/upload/Texte/Offener_Brief.pdf

European Commission. (1999). Russia's response to the Common Strategy of the European Union of 4 June 1999 on Russia. (1999/414/CFSP). Section 5. Securing the Russian interests in an expanded European Union. EU External Relations.

European Commission. (2002). Commissioner for External Relations at the European Parliament Development Committee 12 November 2002. Declaration as regards the EU–Russia summit and the situation in Chechnya. Retrieved 3 March 2011 from: http://europa.eu/rapid/pressReleasesAction.do?reference=IP/02/1655&format=HTML&aged=1&language=EN&guiLanguage=en

European Commission. (2003). Wider Europe- Neighbourhood: A New Framework for Relations with our Eastern and Southern Neighbours. Communication from the Commission to the Council and the European Parliament. 11 March 2003. COM (2003)104 final. Retrieved 11 January 2011 from: www.ec.europa.eu/world/enp/pdf/com03_104_en.pdf

European Commission. (2004). Communication from the Commission to the Council and the European Parliament on relations with Russia. COM (2004) 106 final. 9 February 2004.

European Parliament (2004a). Session Document. Report with a proposal for a European Parliament recommendation to the Council on EU–Russia relations. (2003/2230 INI) Committee on Foreign Affairs, Human Rights, Common Security and Defence Policy. Rapporteur: Bastiaan Beelder. Final A5–0053/2004. 2 February 2004. Retrieved 13 March 2011 from: www.europarl.europa.eu/sides/getDoc.do?pubRef=-//EP//NONSGML+REPORT+A5-2004-0053+0+DOC+PDF+V0//EN

European Parliament. (2004b). Commissioner Patten's speech on the tragedy in Beslan and the fight against terrorism. Speech given in the European Parliament. Summary. 15 September 2004. Retrieved 11 December 2010 from: www.eu-un.europa.eu/articles/en/article_3808_en.htm

European Parliament (2004c). European Parliament resolution on the EU–Russia summit held in The Hague on 25 November 2004. Retrieved 13 March 2011 from: http://eurlex.europa.eu/LexUriServ/LexUriServ.do?uri=OJ:C:2005:226E:0224:0226:EN:PDF

European Report. (2004). CFSP: EU ponders anti-terrorist policy. European Information Service. 8 September 2004.

Europolitics. (2002). EU enlargement. Kaliningrad cuts deeper into EU–Russia relations. 6 September 2002. Retrieved 3 March 2011 from: www.europolitics.info/eu-enlargement-kaliningrad-cuts-deeper-into-eu-russia-relations-artr189564-44.html

82 *Russia and EU eastern enlargement*

Fuller, M. (2002). EU reaches pact with Russians on enclave; but Kaliningrad deal is upstaged by Putin's Chechnya warnings. *International Herald Tribune*. 12 November 2002.

Haukkala, H. (2008a). Russian Reactions to the European Neighbourhood Policy. *Problems of Post-Communism*. 55(5): 40–48.

Haukkala, H. (2008b). The Russia Challenge to EU Normative Power. The case of European Neighbourhood Policy. *The International Spectator*. 43(2): 35–47.

Haukkala, H. (2008c). The European Union as a Regional Normative Hegemon: The case of European Neighbourhood Policy. *Europe–Asia Studies*. 60(9). November 2008. pp. 1601–1622.

Holtom, P. (2005). The Kaliningrad Test in EU–Russia Relations. *Perspectives on European Politics and Society*. 6(1): 31–54.

ITAR-TASS. (2002a) Russian reaction to 'World Chechen Congress' in Denmark. 28 October 2002.

ITAR-TASS. (2002b). Putin's envoy hails Kaliningrad agreement as great success for Russia. 12 November 2002.

Lucas, E. (2008). *The New Cold War. How the Kremlin menaces both Russia and the West*. London: Bloomsbury.

Lynch, D. (2005). 'The Enemy is at the Gate': Russia after Beslan. *International Affairs* 81(1): 141–161.

Manners, I. (2002). Normative Power: A contradiction in terms? *Journal of Common Market Studies*. 40(2): 235–58.

McGregor, C. (2003). Berlusconi defends Putin's Yukos line. *St Petersburg Times*. 13 November 2003.

McGrory, D. and Shepherd, R. (2002). Mystery gas kills 115 hostages. *The Times*. 28 October 2002.

Ministry of Foreign Affairs of the Russian Federation. (2000). The Foreign Policy Concept of the Russian Federation. Approved by the President of the Russian Federation. V. Putin. 28 June 2000.

Moscow Times. (2002). Maskhadov denies backing the attack. 28 October 2002.

Nicholson, A. (2003). President flies into firestorm in Rome. *Moscow Times*. 5 November 2003.

Osborne, A. (2002a). Cold front over Kaliningrad: Russians warn EU that its visa plan for the enclave's citizens could put relation back in the freezer. *Guardian*. 7 September 2002.

Osborne, A. (2002b). Moscow siege: row over Chechen meeting threatens EU relations with Russia. *Guardian*. 29 October 2002.

Owen, R. (2003). Berlusconi and Brussels fall out over Chechnya. *The Times*. 10 November 2003.

Panebianco, S. (2006). Promoting human rights and democracy in European Union relations with Russia and China. In Lucarelli, S. and Manners, I. *Values and Principles in EU Foreign Policy*. Routledge.

Patten, C. (2001). Russia's hell-hole enclave. *Guardian*. 7 April 2001. Retrieved 8 August 2010 from: www.guardian.co.uk/world/2001/apr/07/russia.politics

Permanent Mission of the Russian Federation to the European Union Retrieved 13 May 2015 from: www.russianmission.eu/en/permanent-partnership-council.

Politkovskaya, A. (2004). *Putin's Russia.* London: The Harvill Press.

Roberts, C.A. (2007). Russia and the European Union: The sources and limits of 'special relationships'. Strategic Studies Institute. US. Army War College Retrieved 8 March 2011 from: http://se2.isn.ch/serviceengine/Files/RESSpecNet/32227/ipublicationdocument_singledocument/F401D30F-0ABB-4C85-BEB4-C9BF3B2BB7B9/en/Russia_EU_Sources_Limits.pdf.

Schumacher, T. (1996). Die Haltung der skandinavischen Staaten zum Unabhaengigkeitsprozess der baltischen Laender 1989–1991. *Berliner Interuniversitäre Arbeitsgruppe Baltische Staaten Berichte*, 4.

Sciolino, E. (2002). Putin unleashes his fury against Chechen guerrillas. *New York Times*. 12 November 2002.

Sueddeutsche Zeitung. (2004). Schroeder stellt sich hinter Putin- Ich habe nicht die Absicht die Russlandpolitik zu ändern. 2 October 2004. Retrieved 21 September 2010 from: http://sueddeutsche.de/politik/schroeder-stellt-sich-hinter-putin-ich-habe-nicht-die-absicht-die-russland-politik-zu-aendern-1.297629

Thapar, N. (2003). Yukos plans Khodorkovsky human rights appeal. *The Business*. 9 November 2003.

The Delegation of the European Union to Russia. (2002a). EU–Russia Summit. Moscow, 29 May 2002. Press release. Retrieved 2 December 2009 from: www.delrus.ec.europa.eu/en/images/pText_pict/237/sum51.doc

The Delegation of the European Union to Russia. (2002b). Joint statement of the European Union and the Russian Federation on transit between the Kaliningrad region and the rest of the Russian Federation. Russia–EU summit. Brussels 11 November 2002. Retrieved 6 August 2010 from: www.delrus.ec.europa.eu/en/images/pText.../sum%20jointst.doc

The Delegation of the European Union to Russia. (2002c). Joint statement on the fight against terrorism. Russia–EU summit. Brussels 11 November 2002. Retrieved 6 August 2010 from: www.delrus.ec.europa.eu/en/images/pText_pict/235/sum62.doc

Wines, M. (2002). Why Putin boils over: Chechnya is his personal war. *New York Times*. 13 November 2002.

Wirtschaftswoche. (2004). Schroeder haelt Putin fuer einen lupenreinen Demokraten. 22 November 2004. Retrieved 7 December 2010 from: www.wiwo.de/unternehmen-maerkte/schroeder-haelt-putin-fuer-lupenreinen-demokraten-368600/

4 The threat to EU–Russia relations of EU enlargement in the Orange Revolution

Ukraine's Orange Revolution was the first major political crisis between the EU and Russia. Although the struggle between revolutionaries and the incumbent regime took place on many levels, one of the central issues of contention was whether Ukraine's future lay with the EU or with Russia. The Kremlin went to extraordinary lengths to persuade Ukrainians to choose the latter, with President Putin himself staking his reputation on a high profile visit to Kiev during the last week of the Ukrainian presidential election campaign. The EU's position was more cautious, but when the Ukrainian opposition instigated mass protests over electoral fraud, European diplomats conducted their most aggressive intervention yet in the affairs of the former Soviet space. In the process, they provided the catalyst for the negotiations that ultimately ensured victory for the pro-EU candidate, Viktor Yushchenko. The result was a drastic transformation of Russian perceptions of the EU. Barely five years since they embraced the EU as the acceptable face of the West during the Kosovo crisis, Russian policymakers and key Kremlin officials conceived the EU as an enemy – a threat not only to the stability of the post-Soviet space but also to the semi-authoritarian regime that was forming in Russia.

This chapter argues that the open confrontation between the EU and Russia during the Ukrainian revolution was shaped by the EU's capacity to interfere in the affairs of Ukraine, a state which had barely registered in EU diplomacy since its emergence from the break-up of the Soviet Union. The aim of this chapter is twofold. On the one hand, it seeks to examine why the EU was able to play such a significant role in the outcome of the Orange Revolution. The effective intervention of the EU in the revolutionary crisis was made possible by three developments. First, the new EU member states, Poland and Lithuania, provided essential political impetus, leadership and local contacts. Second, the prospect of EU enlargement was a lure for the pro-Western Ukrainian elite. Their wish for accession to the EU destroyed the Russian policymakers' plans of creating an integrated economic project with countries in the former Soviet space. Third, the EU benefited from the utter ineptitude of Russia's intervention in the Ukrainian presidential election, which compromised Victor Yanukovich, its favoured candidate, making him appear to be a Russian puppet.

Enlarged EU and the Orange Revolution   85

On the other hand, this chapter analyses the reasons why the EU's interference in Ukraine precipitated a crisis in EU–Russia relations. The Kremlin perceived EU meddling in Ukraine as jeopardising Moscow's close ties with Kiev. This perception was strengthened three months after the Ukrainian revolution by EU interference in the political turmoil following a revolution in Kyrgyzstan. This revolution raised concerns in Russian policy-making circles about the emergence of a pattern of upheavals in the former Soviet space that might weaken Russia's grip on the region. As a consequence, the Kremlin became hostile towards what it saw as EU interference in the former Soviet space.

The road to confrontation

The struggle between the EU and Russia over the Orange Revolution can be traced back to the Ukrainian presidential election campaign. The Ukrainian opposition led by Victor Yushchenko made integration with the EU a centrepiece of their campaign. They offered voters a choice between Brussels and Moscow by making an emotional appeal for Ukraine's future in Europe. For a long time relations with Ukraine had not been important to the EU and were thus not a reason for conflict between the EU and Russia. However, after the EU's eastern enlargement in May 2004, Ukraine became the EU's immediate neighbour, which changed its perspective on Kiev. More importantly, Ukraine was significant as a transit country for Russian gas and oil to Europe.

The establishment of close relations with the EU was not the centrepiece of Victor Yanukovich's election campaign. The pro-Russian candidate, who was strongly supported by the Kremlin, made integration with Russia the key element in his political programme. His pro-Russian stance was also exemplified by his aspirations for Ukraine's membership in the Single Economic Space (SES), a free trade zone between Russia, Belarus, Ukraine and Kazakhstan. The potential creation of the SES became a major bone of contention in the EU–Russian contest over Ukraine. In April 2004 Guenther Verheugen, the EU Commissioner for Enlargement, called on Russian policy-making circles to repeal the SES if it wanted to maintain good relations with the EU.[1]

Yushchenko, in contrast, made a calculated effort to fashion himself as the pro-European candidate. In an article he published in the Western media on 10 September he advanced a three-point case for his aspirations for Ukraine's EU membership. First, he criticised the EU for excluding Ukraine from Europe. He declared that since the EU's eastern enlargement, Ukrainians had been feeling isolated as they 'were anxious about European integration halting at our western frontier and in fact creating a new dividing line'.[2] He added that 'we in the East are subject of a European policy, the very jargon of which jars our ears precisely because we always considered ourselves part of Europe, and not just "neighbours"'. Second, he declared that Europe was divided into two spheres of influence in which Ukraine would fall under Putin's spell. Yushchenko warned that there had emerged the 'threat of a new bipolar Europe ... with centres in Brussels and Moscow'.[3] He referred to the increasing tensions concerning Ukraine's

86   *Enlarged EU and the Orange Revolution*

political future by stating that the presidential election would be the 'climax in the struggle between a European and a non-European choice for Ukraine'.[4] Third, he stated that the Ukrainian opposition was an upholder of European values. He emphasised his admiration for the values the EU represented by stating that he and his supporters would strive for a Ukraine that would be an 'integral part of a truly united Europe – a Europe without any divisive lines. This Ukraine will not only propagate European values, but transmit them beyond its borders'.[5] In what was an obvious criticism of the planned SES, Yushchenko declared that Ukraine's transmission of European values 'would halt attempts at creating an "alternative Europe" in the East'.[6]

Three weeks later, in an apparent riposte to Yushchenko, Yanukovich made a very different case in the same newspaper. He advanced two arguments. First, he stressed that Ukraine's EU membership was not the centrepiece in his election campaign, declaring that Kiev had ceased urging Brussels for Ukraine's accession to the EU. Instead he suggested developing relations between Ukraine and the EU through two- to three-year agreements addressing specific issues such as trade. He explained his opposition to Ukraine's integration with the EU by emphasising the country's historical ties with Russia. He stressed that Ukraine

> has always been an 'alternative Europe' with our own faith, history and homeland.... One cannot achieve acknowledgement in the [European circle] unless one has historical memory and human persistence in upholding one's own national interests.... This is why there is no choice for us between the [EU] and Russia. We are tied to Russia by culture and by blood.[7]

Second, he contended that Ukraine's integration with Europe should at the same time enhance economic cooperation between Ukraine and Russia.[8]

The Kremlin made no secret of its support for Victor Yanukovich. Its political involvement in the election had already become evident in the summer of 2004 when Russian 'political technologists' went to Kiev.[9] Gleb Pavlovsky, a key Kremlin strategist and adviser, arranged meetings of Russian politicians and industrialists with their Ukrainian counterparts at a think tank in Kiev, the 'Russian Club'.[10] One critic of the Russian Club denounced it as having merely been a front for 'legalised interference by Moscow figures' in the Ukrainian election to support Yanukovich.[11]

President Putin's involvement in Yanukovich's campaign was marked by two major strategies. First, on 26 October, five days before the first round of the elections, Putin travelled to Ukraine to participate in celebrations for the sixtieth anniversary of Kiev's liberation from German fascist invaders in November 1944. Second, Putin praised Yanukovich for his achievements in an interview broadcast on all major Ukrainian national channels in an interactive TV show entitled 'Vladimir Putin Live'.[12] About 80,000 questions from spectators had been sent to the broadcasting company.[13] Putin's efforts to support Yanukovich seemed to have borne fruit when he achieved slightly better results in the first round of the polls than his opponent Yushchenko.[14]

Enlarged EU and the Orange Revolution   87

The Kremlin's reasons for supporting Yanukovich were Ukraine's economic ties with Russia as well as the vital role it played for Russia's regional integration. On 23 February 2003, the outgoing president of Ukraine Leonid Kuchma, his Belarusian counterpart Alexander Lukashenko, the Kazakh president Nursultan Nazarbayev and Putin had agreed on a draft to establish an agreement on the creation of a free trade zone.[15] At a summit in Astana in September 2004 they signed documents establishing the SES, which encompassed a trade policy in individual areas, the coordination of trade laws and the creation of an interstate independent commission aimed at regulating trade and tariffs.[16] The SES was a driving force for the Kremlin's effort to consolidate Russian influence over the post-Soviet space.

Kuchma used the summit in Astana as an opportunity to send a message to voters in the upcoming presidential election about the benefits Ukraine would gain from the creation of the SES. He declared that Ukraine would become an 'influential regional economic structure'.[17] Kuchma announced the SES as an alternative to Ukraine's accession to the EU. He mentioned his reservations regarding Ukraine's EU membership when explaining that he did not mind that the EU did not consider Ukraine as a possible member. He stated that because of the EU enlargement in May 2004, it was not prepared for Ukraine's accession. He emphasised his point of view that the EU was likely to be overwhelmed by the enlargement when he declared 'God help Europe deal with ten member states, chew over Romania and Bulgaria with Turkey at the doorstep'.[18]

There were diverging motivations among the Russian political elite regarding the launch of the SES. On the one hand, Putin referred to the economic benefits which might be created by the SES by likening this free trade area to the EU. According to Putin, the SES was a way of improving the living standards of its member states so that that they would be better off in comparison to the 'average statistical European citizen'.[19] He predicted that about ten to 12 years after the establishment of the SES, its member states would create a 'single financial system following the example of the [EU]'.[20]

The Kremlin's political adviser Gleb Pavlovsky, on the other hand, emphasised the political leverage the SES could bring to Russia's relations with the EU. Envisaging the SES as a counterweight to the EU, he claimed that it would enable Russia to become a stronger negotiating partner in its relations with Brussels. According to Pavlovsky, facing a 'leading troika' of Russia, Ukraine and Kazakhstan, the

> EU will no longer dictate [to] us.... Now it speaks to us like this: 'Why didn't you implement Brussels decree 735? Implement it urgently'. [After the creation of the SES, it] will then have to negotiate with us about genuine integration ... because it will be negotiations of the strong. We will always lose in negotiations of the weak.[21]

Pavlovsky's reference to the EU's dictatorial approach in its relations with Russia exemplifies his perception of the tendency of the EU to communicate its

88   *Enlarged EU and the Orange Revolution*

principles of governance to Russia in a patronising manner. The Kremlin did not feel inclined to adopt either values or principles which were forced upon it by the EU. Instead, the Kremlin sought to maintain autonomy in its domestic and foreign policy, as clearly demonstrated in both its RMTS and in the Foreign Policy Concept. Both documents disavow any intention of Russia developing closer association or integration with the EU. This distancing in Russian foreign policy was a first indicator of the shift from courtship to confrontation in EU–Russia relations after 1999. Back then, President Yeltsin and Prime Minister Chernomyrdin regretted that Russia was not an EU member state (see Chapters 2 and 3).[22]

The implementation of the SES was a major issue during the Ukrainian presidential election campaign. This became evident during a TV debate between Yushchenko and Yanukovich which took place on 15 September, about two months prior to the first round of the election. Yanukovich emphasised his support for the free trade zone by stating that it was 'our prospect and we are working on it ... it was a step into the future, a step towards us having an opportunity to maintain the level of the economy that we have'.[23] In comparison to Yanukovich, Yushchenko was strongly opposed to the creation of the SES as he preferred to see Ukraine's future aligned with the EU. He disapproved of Ukrainian policymakers under the Kuchma regime for letting themselves be torn between the EU and Russia. He criticised Ukrainian politicians for

> rushing to Brussels to swear loyalty to the EU and European values. Then shortly before the heating season, the same crowd rushes to Moscow where they say they want nothing to do with Europe, complain that we are not wanted there and swear loyalty to the [SES].[24]

Confrontation over the Ukrainian presidential election

EU–Russia relations were affected by the transformation of the Ukrainian election campaign into a contest between a pro-EU and a pro-Russian candidate. Putin's request for the postponement of the EU–Russia summit, due to take place on 11 November in The Hague, was widely perceived as a sign of increasing strain in relations between Brussels and Moscow.[25] The Russian Foreign Minister Sergei Lavrov acknowledged that Putin's request to reschedule the summit to 25 November had been 'interpreted as virtually a crisis [between the EU and Russia and] as an indication that we [were] afraid to meet our counterparts'.[26] The European Commission's spokeswoman Emma Udwin sought to uphold diplomatic etiquette explaining that the pretext for the postponement was Putin's declaration that he preferred to discuss matters such as Russia's border conflicts with Estonia and Latvia and respect for the rules of law and democracy with the newly appointed members of the European Commission, who would begin their work after the former Portuguese Prime Minister José Manuel Barroso's appointment as president of the European Commission on 18 November.[27]

Enlarged EU and the Orange Revolution 89

Three weeks later, the elections transformed simmering tensions into a major international struggle. The fact that Yanukovich had gained more than 90 per cent of the votes in the eastern regions of Ukraine, which had a pro-Russian stance, made the opposition suspicious about the possibility of fraud.[28] The head of the Central Election Commission (CEC) Serhiy Kivalov, whose responsibility was to collect, count and announce the election results, had provided a team of Yanukovich's supporters with the necessary passwords to gain access to the computers in the CEC to manipulate the results.[29] This team had also organised 'busloads of voters' travelling throughout Ukraine to cast votes in several places.[30]

The Orange Revolution began with a massive protest on Kiev's Independence Square, the Maidan, on the night of 22 November. After Yanukovich had been announced as the winner of that round, the Democratic Initiatives Centre claimed in leaflets that the election had been won by Yushchenko with 54 per cent in comparison to 43 per cent of votes gained by Yanukovich.[31] In protest against the election's outcome, about 200,000 to 300,000 protestors assembled on the Maidan encircling public buildings.[32]

The likelihood that the EU would be forced to take a public stance was increased by international observers, who condemned the circumstances under which the election had taken place. On 22 November, prior to the announcement of the results of the second election round, the International Election Observation Mission, the OSCE Parliamentary Assembly, the European Parliament, PACE and NATO made a preliminary assessment of the conduct of the elections. These organisations concluded that the round had failed to meet a 'considerable number of [the] OSCE's, [and PACE's] commitments [for democratic elections].... Overall, state executive authorities and the Central Electoral Commission [in Ukraine] displayed a lack of will to conduct a genuine democratic election process'.[33]

The announcement of the results was greeted with harsh criticism from the European Council and the Commission. The Presidency's chairman, Dutch Prime Minister Jan Peter Balkenende, criticised the election for violating 'international criteria for a democratic election'.[34] Before the beginning of the EU–Russia summit, more EU officials joined the chorus of condemnation. The High Representative of the EU's CFSP and Secretary-General of the European Council, Javier Solana, declared that the EU was not going to accept the results of the 'fraudulent' elections.[35] Newly appointed European Commission President Barroso emphasised that it was the EU's 'duty to say that we are not happy with the way the elections occurred in Ukraine'.[36] He called for a 'serious, objective review' of the election results.[37]

The EU's stance provoked an angry public reaction from the Kremlin. On the eve of the EU–Russia summit, on 24 November, Putin's presidential aide and special envoy for EU–Russia relations, Sergey Yastrzhembsky, referred to a likely confrontation between the EU and Russia over the election in Ukraine. He warned that the 'danger would always exist when people [did] not listen to each other'.[38] He added that he hoped that the EU and Russia would 'listen to each

90   *Enlarged EU and the Orange Revolution*

other or at the very least understand each other's arguments'.[39] He urged the EU to talk to the Ukrainian government, but advocated caution as the election results had not yet been publicly announced.[40] In an obvious attempt to shift the focus away from Ukraine, Yastrzhembsky stressed that the Russian government would like to see progress concerning the safeguarding of rights of Russian-speaking minorities in Latvia and Estonia.[41]

A similar tone of hostility was evident in a statement made that day by the Russian Foreign Minister Sergei Lavrov. In what could be considered as a potential attempt to shift the EU's attention from uprisings in Kiev, Lavrov denounced the EU for 'not paying enough attention' to resolving the conflicts in Cyprus and in Kosovo.[42] He added that the situation in Kosovo in particular was an 'acute problem which threatens, if it is not settled, to seriously undermine not only [security in the] Balkans but also all European stability'.[43]

The already tense atmosphere on the eve of the EU–Russia summit in The Hague on 25 November was exacerbated by the presentation of a communiqué in which Putin congratulated Prime Minister Yanukovich on his success in the poll.[44] Putin responded to the Ukrainian Supreme Court's announcement of Yanukovich's success with 49.46 per cent of the vote, in comparison to 46.6 per cent for his opponent Yushchenko, by asserting that the Ukrainian people had cast a vote for 'stability, [for the] reinforcement of the state and the development of economic as well as political structures to establish good neighbourly relations with Russia'.[45] He asserted that Yanukovich's election would 'bring the Russian–Ukrainian strategic partnership to a new level'.[46] Putin also boasted that the election results had been 'transparent'.[47]

The situation at the summit reached the point of no return when the Dutch Prime Minister Balkenende contradicted Putin's congratulatory remarks. He stressed that the EU could not accept the election results.[48] Balkenende implicitly criticised Putin's involvement in Yanukovich's election campaign by asserting that 'Europe did not choose the political leaders in another country'.[49] At the dinner after the summit, a representative for the Dutch EU Presidency presented Putin with the OSCE's report containing evidence of 'massive electoral fraud' in Ukraine. Putin retaliated by declaring that 'if the elections in Ukraine had been fraudulent, then the elections in Kosovo and Afghanistan would have to be treated in the same manner'.[50]

While this confrontation was unfolding, Polish diplomats were laying the groundwork for a major EU intervention in the Ukrainian crisis. A delegation led by Jacek Kluchowski, adviser to the Polish Prime Minister, and Nicolaas Biegman, a representative of the Dutch EU Presidency, began talks with Ukrainian officials. Kuchma as well as Yushchenko had agreed to launch a round-table discussion with international mediators. Yanukovich, however, was reluctant to meet with representatives of the Polish government due to disagreements with Poland's former president Lech Walesa, who on his visit to Kiev, had aligned himself with Yushchenko's supporters.[51]

The press conference after the EU–Russia summit revealed the partners' fundamental differences over Ukraine. Balkenende emphasised that the EU and

Enlarged EU and the Orange Revolution   91

Russia had 'not been able to reach agreements on all points', adding that there remained a 'great deal to be done'.[52] In particular, he stated that the EU and Russia could not agree on security cooperation, which touched upon Russia's relations with Ukraine, Moldova, Belarus and the Caucasian Republics. He did not attempt to conceal the friction between Russia and the EU over Ukraine when he stated that the 'two sides' approaches differ'.[53] Putin's tone was blunter than Balkenende's. In an obvious criticism of the West's intervention in Ukraine he declared that he was 'deeply convinced that we had no moral right to push a big European state to any kind of disorder'.[54] He reiterated his opposition to the West's meddling in Ukraine by stressing that 'these elections do not need any affirmation from outside'.[55] Balkenende insisted on the EU's position. He stated that the election in Ukraine must be brought up in negotiations by stressing that the EU and Russia had to be 'honest to say that in order for a democracy to work, it required non-fraudulent elections'.[56]

The summit press release made an obvious effort to shift the focus from the clash over Ukraine to cooperation in EU–Russia relations. It merely stated that the EU and Russia had an 'exchange of views on the current developments in Ukraine'.[57] Instead, it emphasised the potential of the EU–Russian road maps aiming to create the Common Economic Space, the Common Space of Freedom, Security and Justice, the Common Space of External Security and the Common Space of Research, Education and Culture, whose establishment had been agreed at the EU–Russia summit in May 2003.[58] According to this statement, these spaces reflected the 'strategic nature of the partnership based on common values and shared interests'.[59] Furthermore, the signatories to the statement strongly upheld political rhetoric when they asserted that this summit had been a 'good basis' for 'closer cooperation' on the free movement of persons, the fulfilment of the long-term goal of visa-free travel between the EU and Russia, and border management.[60]

EU mediation efforts in Ukraine

Due to the intensifying political tensions in Ukraine, outgoing President Kuchma turned to the European Council Presidency for advice. Kuchma also asked his Polish counterpart, Aleksander Kwasniewski, for support in mediating a resolution.[61] Kwasniewski's role as mediator had been supported by the former German chancellor Gerhard Schroeder, his Austrian counterpart Wolfgang Schuessel, the Czech President Vaclav Klaus, and chairman of the European Council Presidency Prime Minister Balkenende. Kwasniewski's close relations with members of the Kuchma administration made him a useful mediator.[62] Kwasniewski explained that he had been asked by Kuchma as well as by the opposition to come to Ukraine as a negotiator.[63] He emphasised that he was going to Kiev as the Polish president but hoped that his mission would be supported by the EU.[64] Yushchenko mentioned that another reason why Kwasniewski was chosen as a mediator was the fact that at the time of the Orange Revolution, he was also the chairman of the Polish Presidency of

92   *Enlarged EU and the Orange Revolution*

the Council of Europe, the intergovernmental institution which is responsible for upholding democracy and human rights in Europe.[65] Yushchenko added that an international mediator was important as the opposing parties could not have 'achieve[d] effective talks on [their] own. Neither side [could].... That [was] why I was talking to Kwasniewski on the phone'.[66]

The EU's mediation mission to Kiev faced two major obstacles. First, the former Polish president, Lech Walesa, had attempted to mediate in the conflict, but clearly sided with the opposition. When he addressed the crowd in the Maidan on 25 November he expressed his sympathy for Yushchenko's supporters by declaring that he was 'profoundly certain that [the protests] lead to victory'.[67] Second, a senior official from the Ukrainian Foreign Ministry made an appeal to the German government to send Chancellor Schroeder as a mediator to Kiev, instead of the EU's High Representative for the CFSP, Solana. The senior official explained his proposal by stating that Solana's support of the accession of Poland, Hungary and the Czech Republic to NATO in contrast to his reluctance to back the Ukrainian government's aspirations for membership would be a point of contention.[68]

For the first time, a major diplomatic EU mission was led by two of the new member states. Kwasniewski and his Lithuanian counterpart Valdas Adamkus, spearheaded this mission to Kiev. The fact that Solana, who had at first been reluctant to participate in the mediation efforts, accompanied Kwasniewski and Adamkus, gave their diplomacy the character of an official EU mission.[69] On 24 and 25 November Kwasniewski, Adamkus and Solana went to Kiev to negotiate between Yushchenko and Yanukovich, seeking to avoid violence and to achieve a resolution of the political crisis.[70] The EU's representatives arrived at a significant moment when the opposition's protests were no longer gaining momentum and the authorities were considering declaring Yanukovich the winner.[71] Kwasniewski had arrived with a plan comprising four points: (1) defusing the conflict by verifying the election's outcome, (2) repeating the elections in constituencies where there had been evidence of election fraud, (3) refraining from the use of force, and (4) holding negotiations with the losing party in a round-table discussion.[72]

The EU's diplomatic mission sparked harsh criticism from Putin. He denounced the EU for having encouraged 'mayhem' on the streets of Ukraine.[73] In a more moderate tone than Putin, the Russian Foreign Minister Sergei Lavrov criticised 'attempts by certain governments to steer the situation in Ukraine away from a legal path'.[74] In particular, he denounced the EU's refusal to accept the election results by stating that

> certain European capitals are declaring that they did not recognise the election and that Ukraine has to be with the West. These declarations make one think that someone would very much like to draw up new border lines across Europe.[75]

He claimed that 'destabilising attempts to impose democracy from outside [would be] to the detriment of democratic values'.[76] He declared that Russia was

Enlarged EU and the Orange Revolution   93

not indifferent to developments in Ukraine and stressed that geographically speaking, it was close to the West but also to Russia. Lavrov warned that, as a consequence of the West's meddling in Ukraine, European leaders' attempts to 'isolate Russia [might] have fatal consequences for a united Europe'.[77]

The political crisis was resolved when the Ukrainian Supreme Court announced on 3 December that the results of the run-off were invalid and that a repeat of the elections would take place on 26 December. According to Kuchma, a meeting between Adamkus, the speaker of the Russian State Duma Boris Gryzlov, Solana, Kwasniewski, Yanukovich and Yushchenko in Kiev was the 'first attempt to draw political and legal ways out of this crisis'.[78] They stressed the need to refrain from the use of force, to unblock government buildings and to launch an expert group assessing changes to presidential election law.[79]

Meanwhile the Russian State Duma became the platform for harsher criticism of the EU's involvement in Ukrainian politics. The first speaker of the Duma, Lyubiv Sliska, condemned the EU's interference by likening it to an 'act of occupation' given that they had 'nothing to do whatsoever with the election process in Ukraine'.[80] She urged the EU to 'calm down and stop inciting any kind of provocation as regards Ukraine'.[81] In a more moderate tone, the chairman of the State Duma Committee on Foreign Affairs, Konstantin Kosachev, declared that he regarded the election in Ukraine to be the climax of the West's 'systematic tendency' during the last few years to support a 'pro-Western and hence anti-Russian [political leader]'.[82] In a resolution that coincided with the Supreme Court's decision to repeat the election, the Duma accused the EU of having carried out 'destructive interference in the development of the situation in Ukraine'.[83]

In response to the Duma's condemnations, Elmar Brok, the head of the Foreign Affairs Committee of the European Parliament, justified the EU's attempts to resolve the political crisis in Ukraine. He declared that because Ukraine and the EU had shared a border since the EU's eastern enlargement, it was in the EU's interest to have neighbours that were 'democratic and stable'.[84] Three weeks later, in a much less moderate tone, Kwasniewski explained the EU's motives for its diplomatic mission to Kiev. He acknowledged that 'Russia without Ukraine [was] a better solution than Russia with Ukraine'.[85]

Kwasniewski's stance sparked harsh criticism from Putin. He stated that 'if we interpret this as striving to limit Russia's ability to develop relations with its neighbours, then it means a desire to isolate [Russia]'.[86] This perception was exacerbated when the Kremlin's favoured candidate was defeated. The EU's diplomatic mission to Kiev and its call for repeated elections laid the groundwork for a third round of elections, which took place on 26 December. The pro-Western candidate Yushchenko won with 52 per cent of the vote against 44.2 per cent for Yanukovich.[87] Yushchenko was sworn in as president on 23 January.[88]

The triumph of the Orange Revolution did not only contribute to a crisis in EU–Russia relations, but had implications for Russian geopolitics as well. Russian policymakers regarded this revolution as a geopolitical catastrophe because it had shaken both Russia's diplomacy and its international order. The

94 *Enlarged EU and the Orange Revolution*

outcome of the revolution had destroyed the Kremlin's plan to establish the SES and was thus a defeat for Russian diplomacy. Due to the EU's intervention, the Kremlin's efforts to achieve closer integration with Ukraine by backing the pro-Russian candidate were fruitless. Fyodor Lukyanov, the foreign policy expert and editor of *Russia in Global Affairs*, acknowledged that the end of Kuchma's regime was Russia's 'biggest foreign policy defeat since the collapse of the Soviet Union'.[89]

The EU Commissioner for External Relations, Chris Patten, demonstrated that Ukraine had also become significant for EU foreign policy for two reasons. First, Ukraine began to play a crucial part in the EU's external relations after its eastern enlargement. Patten stated that Poland's accession to the EU in May 2004 'moved all of us closer – politically and economically, as well as geographically – to Ukraine'.[90] Second, according to Patten, the EU's 'shared neighbourhood' with Russia was likely to raise conflicts. He stressed that the 'main victims of our failure to develop a better and more balanced' relationship with Russia were 'its neighbours'.[91] Patten declared that the EU sought 'stable [and] well-off neighbours' but criticised Russia for seeking 'weak neighbours and a sphere of influence inhabited by dependent supplicants'.[92] He added that it would 'take vigilance to ensure that Ukraine [was] not now bullied off the democratic path it [had] chosen by political threats'.[93] Patten criticised the EU for 'conniving ... at policies and attitudes that will create a more dangerous neighbourhood for us all'.[94] Patten's perception of the potential threat posed to Ukraine by the EU and Russia's competing integrative projects with Kiev was accurate. Nine years after the Orange Revolution had shaken Ukrainian politics, a severe existential crisis emerged in Ukraine, which has put its future political orientation in serious question. At the same time, the EU and Russia's conflicting approaches regarding future integrative efforts with Kiev have cast doubt on the EU's diplomacy with Ukraine in the framework of the EaP and resulted in the most severe confrontation in EU–Russia relations since 1999. A close analysis of both the origins of the EU–Russian confrontation over Ukraine since 2013 and its repercussions for the future of the 'strategic partnership' is discussed in Chapter 7.

The second reason for Ukraine's increasing importance in EU foreign policy was the impact of the outcome of the Orange Revolution for EU external relations. Patten claimed that the revolution 'ma[d]e it difficult to hold the [EU's] neighbourhood line' with Ukraine in the framework of the ENP.[95] The need for the EU to establish a straightforward approach for Ukraine's integration with Europe became evident when Patten referred to a discussion with the Ukrainian Foreign Minister, who had already questioned the reasons for the lack of closer Ukrainian–EU integration five years prior to the Orange Revolution. Patten recalled that during a meeting in 1999 the Ukrainian Foreign Minister Borys Tarasyuk explicitly expressed his aspirations to enhance integration between Ukraine and the EU. He asked Patten 'what [was] so special about Turkey's European vocation and so deficient about Ukraine's'.[96] Patten, who was in favour of Turkey's accession to the EU, acknowledged in his memoirs that he

Enlarged EU and the Orange Revolution 95

'stumbled through an unconvincing answer'.[97] Patten's conversation with Tarasyuk regarding the future of Ukraine's relations with the EU demonstrated the EU's lack of a clear vision regarding its political relations with Kiev. An in-depth analysis of the repercussions of this lack of streamlined foreign policy with Ukraine is provided in Chapter 7.

The European Parliament's resolution of 13 January provided evidence supporting Patten's claim that the outcome of the Orange Revolution made it difficult for the EU to maintain Ukraine's integration with the EU solely in the framework of the ENP. This resolution reminded the EU's institutions as well as the member states to 'meet the expectations and hopes raised by the [EU's] close involvement in the peaceful Orange Revolution'.[98] It urged the European Commission, the European Council and the member states to consider 'other forms of association with Ukraine'.[99] In this way, the European Parliament intended to give Ukraine the prospect of EU membership. [100] Due to the fact that the Parliament has no authority to decide on the membership of a state in the EU, its call for 'other forms of association' with Kiev was merely an attempt to develop alternative integrative approaches.

Ten days later, in an obvious response to the European Parliament's resolution, Yushchenko reiterated that Ukraine's integration with the EU was the centrepiece of his presidency. He expressed his hopes of seeing Ukraine as a future member state of the EU. In a speech he gave at the European Parliament on 23 February 2005, Yushchenko acknowledged that Ukraine still 'had much to do to become a full member of the European family'.[101] He declared that Ukraine had to 'move beyond words and take action to develop democracy, the rule of law [and] freedom of the media' as well as to undertake measures to deal with corruption.[102] He stressed that Ukraine and the EU 'were all now united by values, history and aspirations.... European integration [was] the only path open for Ukraine'.[103] No less attracted to the prospect of Ukraine's membership of the EU was Ukrainian Foreign Minister Tarasyuk. In a speech given on 5 March he declared that Ukraine was an 'inseparable part of Europe'.[104] He complained that it would be both 'unfair' and 'unwise' for the EU to refuse to accept Ukraine as a member state.[105]

Seven months later Tarasyuk and Yushchenko's great expectations were disappointed by Verheugen, the EU Commissioner for Enlargement. He declared that even though the EU was reluctant not to offer to the Ukrainian government the prospect of membership, it hesitated to make commitments concerning a new cooperation agreement with Ukraine.[106] In an interview given on 3 September 2005 Verheugen explained that there would not be a fixed date for Ukraine's accession to the EU.[107] The EU Commissioner for External Relations, Patten, explained the EU's hesitation in making commitments to Ukraine's prospect of becoming an EU member state. He stated that the 'most worrying aspect of the 'No' vote in the French and Dutch referendums on the Draft Treaty establishing a Constitution for Europe was the evidence of opposition to the recent enlargement and of even greater antipathy to any future enlargement'.[108] The seemingly ajar door to Ukraine's EU membership remained a stumbling block in Ukraine's

96 *Enlarged EU and the Orange Revolution*

trilateral relations with the EU and Russia for a decade after the Orange Revolution. In May 2015, the EU stated that it would not consider further enlargement until 2020.[109] As demonstrated in the next section, the foundation for the troubled relations between Ukraine, the EU and Russia were laid after the Orange Revolution. The wider repercussions of the EU–Russian confrontation over Ukraine for both Kiev's relations with Moscow and the EU–Russian strategic partnership are discussed at length in Chapter 7.

Kremlin hostility towards the EU interference in the former Soviet space

Soon after the political crisis in Ukraine, a revolution in Kyrgyzstan was perceived by the Kremlin as a sign of the spread of revolution in the former Soviet space. The factors which triggered the revolution in Kyrgyzstan were comparable to those which brought about the Orange Revolution. As in Ukraine, the revolution was caused by allegations of election fraud. In addition, clan politics and accusations of nepotism against the president, Askar Akayev, were also factors.[110] The Kremlin was outraged by the EU's condemnation of the presidential election results in Kyrgyzstan and its 'crude' interference in the internal affairs of other countries.

The EU's reaction to the political crisis in Kyrgyzstan, which was prompted by the results of the election on 27 February 2005, increased tensions between Brussels and Moscow. On behalf of the EU, Javier Solana denounced the circumstances under which the election had taken place. He stated that they 'did [neither] conform to the OSCE's requirements [nor] to other international standards'.[111] According to Solana, 'outbreaks of violence had caused particular concern' and thus he emphasised that the crisis would need to be resolved by non-violent means.[112] A day later, Solana's criticism of the conduct of the election provoked an angry reaction from the Russian foreign minister, Lavrov. In a telephone conversation with Solana, Lavrov criticised his statement on Kyrgyzstan for 'contain[ing] incorrect assessments of the situation in [the country] and their underlying causes and [for being] "counter-productive"'.[113] In an article published in the journal *Russia in Global Affairs* Lavrov accused the EU of hypocrisy and of debasing the values it pretended to uphold to advance its geostrategic interests. He criticised the EU for having caused

> no less damage to the universality of democratic principles ... by attempts, under the banner of 'defending democracy' to interfere crudely in the internal affairs of other countries and exert political pressure on them. The[se attempts] merely discredit democratic values, turning them into small change for the attainment of selfish geostrategic interests.[114]

Lavrov's reference to 'attempts under the banner of defending democracy' in Kyrgyzstan was a criticism of the EU's pretensions to promote its values in a self-righteous way in some of the former Soviet satellite states, which the

Enlarged EU and the Orange Revolution   97

Kremlin perceived as belonging to its sole sphere of influence. Solana rejected Lavrov's condemnation. He declared that if the EU's statement on Kyrgyzstan and the 'region as a whole [had been] perceived as destabilizing, then this [was] probably the result of them being interpreted incorrectly'.[115]

The Kremlin struck back at European initiatives to promote democracy. It reinforced its strong opposition to any kind of foreign interference, such as the monitoring of elections during the Kyrgyz presidential election, by withholding its financial contribution to OSCE in March 2005. Aleksei Borodavkin, Russia's ambassador to OSCE, argued that it 'was not a financial problem [but one] of principle. [If] the parties expected us to pay a large amount into the OSCE's budget, then Russia's interests and concerns should also be taken into consideration'.[116] He criticised OSCE for applying double standards to human rights. In particular, he expressed his criticism by asking why 'the OSCE [did] not apply more pressure on Latvia to give full citizenship rights to the large Russian [speaking] minority'.[117] He added that Russians in Latvia had 'non-citizen status'.[118]

The EU rallied in support of OSCE. A confidential EU document presented to EU ambassadors urged its member states to support OSCE by contributing Russia's share to OSCE's budget.[119] According to the document, 'at the heart of the present crisis between the OSCE and Russia lies a more fundamental values gap. Russia's main problem with the OSCE concerns those things we most value in it – its monitoring of democracy and human rights'.[120] This gap, namely the discrepancy with mutually accepted values of both the EU and OSCE such as human rights, democracy and the rule of law, was rejected by the Kremlin. The EU's intention to develop and maintain shared values in its relations with Russia was rejected by the Kremlin, as demonstrated in Chapter 3 and discussed in Chapter 5. The Kremlin's emphasis on sovereignty and autonomy in its domestic and foreign policies was in utter contradiction to the influence of the EU's values in relations with Russia.

Russian policymakers began to see a pattern concerning the spread of revolutions in the post-Soviet space after the orange shock in Ukraine. In the March issue of the leading foreign policy journal *International Affairs*, the most influential policy adviser in the Duma and member of United Russia, Konstantin Kosachev, put forward three points about Russia's response to the 'coloured revolutions in the CIS' and about the EU's increasing influence in the region. First, after having acknowledged that he did not know how to react to the coloured revolutions in the former Soviet space, he declared that he was nervous about Russia's policy towards the CIS. He acknowledged that there was a 'lack of coordination among the various levels and branches of power, and a general lack of consistency'.[121] Second, Kosachev warned heads of state in the CIS of negative repercussions stemming from enhanced integration with the EU. In this way he sought to prevent the CIS countries from turning their foreign policy westwards. He criticised the EU for making false promises regarding some former Soviet satellite states' prospective EU membership. He rhetorically asked what needed to be done with those who were

98 *Enlarged EU and the Orange Revolution*

lured by the prospects of European integration and were enticed away, like a bride, from the parental home by a promise of marriage only to find that [it was] being put off on various pretexts and that the bride was first required to 'prove her right to marry'.[122]

According to Kosachev, if this situation occurred for a CIS state, it was a 'breach of promise on [the EU's side] ... a dastardly act with regard to the peoples of the seduced countries'.[123]

Kosachev criticised the assertiveness of some of the new EU member states in determining European foreign policy in the post-Soviet space. In this context, he referred to the EU's 'Balticisation process [which had] turned the EU into an aggressive organisation'.[124] This was an obvious reference to the Lithuanian President Valdas Adamkus and his Polish counterpart Kwasniewski, who had spearheaded the EU's intervention in the resolution of the Orange Revolution. Kosachev's use of the phrase 'aggressive organisation' was a harsh confirmation of the deterioration of EU–Russia relations since the Kosovo War in 1999. At the time of the Kosovo crisis, this perception of the EU by Russian policymakers would have been unthinkable. NATO, which had been bombing Yugoslavia, Russia's political ally, was at that time regarded in Russian policy-making circles as the 'aggressor', whereas the EU was a benign actor and the 'acceptable face of the West', with whom Russia had cooperated during the war to resolve this international crisis, as demonstrated in Chapter 1.

The extent of the crisis in EU–Russia relations became evident when the Russian Defence Minister Sergei Ivanov threatened to react if the US and Europe persisted in meddling in the domestic politics of states belonging to the former Soviet space. He denounced the West for not having 'abandoned stereotypes of the past, which [was] proven by the reaction of certain circles in Europe and the USA to the political crisis in Ukraine'.[125] He threatened to 'react ... to exports of revolution to the CIS'.[126] He stated that even prior to the presidential election in Ukraine there had been clear signals that the West would not recognise the ballot results if, according to Western political leaders, the wrong candidate won the elections.[127]

One of the most influential formulations of the Russians' increasing hostility towards the EU was published by the Russian news agency Regnum. Modest Kolerov, Regnum's president and a close Kremlin consultant, launched the discussion with an inflammatory polemic published on 18 March entitled 'The Front against Russia: "Sanitary Cordon" and "External Management"'. This article, which was later published in book form with an introduction by the Kremlin's 'political technologist' Pavlovsky, criticised Europe's plans to destroy Russia as a state. He wrote that it

[was] not the perimeters of Russia's borders or the squeezing of Russia out of its border areas that [was] currently at issue; [but] Russia's split along the Volga axis, which in practice [implied] the demand to introduce 'external management' by Brussels in Russia's European zone.[128]

Enlarged EU and the Orange Revolution   99

The significance of 'The Front against Russia' became evident when Kolerov was appointed as chief of the newly created Russian president's Directorate for Interregional and Cultural Ties with Foreign Countries and the CIS on 23 March 2005. Kolerov was a direct subordinate to Dmitry Medvedev, the head of the presidential administration.[129] His directorate had an important role to play in the contest with the EU. Pavlovsky asserted that the directorate would 'have to tackle those tasks in the post-Soviet area with which the Ministry of Foreign Affairs failed to cope: Russia should prove to its neighbours that it is a greater bearer of European values, than the EU itself'.[130] This statement revealed that some Russian policymakers were afraid of the EU's attraction as an upholder of values to certain states in the former Soviet space. This was the case when EU norms were seen as appealing to members of the Ukrainian political elite as well as citizens seeking to enhance integration with the EU, as demonstrated by the EU flags waved by many protestors during the Orange Revolution.[131]

Pavlovsky, the Kremlin's political adviser and a collaborator with Putin, was the most influential theorist of anti-EU rhetoric in Russia. In an article he published in April 2005 on Russia's policy within the CIS, he referred to the rising tension in EU–Russia relations stemming from their 'competition for space' in the former Soviet zone.[132] He denounced Kwasniewski's leading role in seeking to resolve the political crisis in Ukraine by stressing that his 'doctrine' that Ukraine was better off without Russia would be 'rejected in Russia officially by the majority of political forces'.[133] He condemned Kwasniewski's 'doctrine' for being 'as anti-Russian as it [was] anti-European'. Furthermore, he warned of the creation of a new dividing line within Europe, stating that Kwasniewski's dogma was based on the assumption that 'Europe will build a wall, a *new line of confrontation*, and countries will be asked to take sides.... [S]ome of the Baltic states have tried to play this game'.[134] A delegate of the International Affairs Committee of the State Duma and member of United Russia acknowledged the ability of the 'new' EU member states to influence EU foreign policy by declaring that the 'Balticisation of the EU' was ongoing.[135] This was an obvious allusion to Lithuanian President Adamkus' leading role as an envoy in the EU's diplomatic mission to Ukraine, which destroyed the Kremlin's ambitions for integration with Kiev.

Russia's accusations about the 'Balticisation of the EU' received additional corroboration during the Victory Day celebrations on 9 May 2005 commemorating the sixtieth anniversary of the Allied victory over Germany in the Second World War. This event was overshadowed by a severe clash between Russia and the EU over the Soviet occupation of the Baltic States. Two of the new EU member states, Lithuania and Estonia, rejected the Kremlin's invitation to the commemoration. They stressed that the end of the Second World War marked the beginning of the Soviet occupation of their countries.[136] The day before the celebration, Latvian President Vaira-Vike Freiberga, who was present at the commemoration ceremony, stated that she planned to voice her criticisms of the Soviet occupation of Latvia. She urged the Kremlin to admit that the Soviet occupation of the Baltic States had been illegal.[137]

The clash between Russia and the Baltic States turned into a confrontation between the EU and Russia. The European Commissioner for Enterprise and Industry Guenther Verheugen condemned Soviet rule in the Baltic States. He urged the Kremlin to admit the illegality of the Soviet Union's rule in these countries. He added that it was important for the EU that 'our relations are based on truth.... We should not hide the fact that the three Baltic [countries] were occupied against their will for a long time.'[138] Putin's presidential aide Sergey Yastrzhembsky dismissed Verheugen's comment as 'inappropriate and inopportune'.[139] He declared that 'deployment of Russian troops took place with the clearly expressed agreement of the existing authorities in the Baltic states'.[140] He accused the Baltic countries of having nursed 'historical phobia and prejudices'.[141]

This clash on Victory Day overshadowed the EU–Russia summit on 10 May, which achieved no significant results. Despite a joint statement boasting about the progress concerning the establishment of the Four Common Spaces, tension in other issue areas became evident after the summit.[142] The chairman of the Russian State Duma International Affairs Committee, Kosachev, referred to the tension at the summit. He criticised the meaninglessness of the summit by dismissing the significance of the agreements which had been signed during the meeting. He belittled them as 'memoranda of intent rather than specific agreements'.[143]

He acknowledged that the EU expected more predictability and consistency from Russia when it came to long-term goals, such as Russia's accession to the EU, for instance, which was a prospect he would welcome.[144] Kosachev claimed that Russia should be confident that its application for EU membership would be accepted.[145] It became evident that the reason for his longing for Russia's accession to the EU was his fear that Russia might lose its influence in the CIS if certain states in the former Soviet space joined the EU. He declared that 'otherwise former socialist countries or Soviet states where so-called botanical revolutions [in reference to revolutions in the post-Soviet space] have taken place will become EU members while Russia will be counting its lost chances'.[146] Kosachev's reference to Russia's 'lost chances' should not be overestimated. It has to be noted that Russia's prospect of EU membership was unlikely for many reasons. First, during the Putin era, Russia's foreign policy orientation was not characterised by the quest for approximation to the EU's standards. Both the RMTS and the Foreign Policy Concept had expressed Russia's preference for autonomy in its foreign policy, instead of association with the EU.[147] However, Kosachev's statement was crucial because it referred to the repercussions of competition between the EU and Russia over integration of the post-Soviet space. He expressed his fear that Russia might lose its grip over the former Soviet space when countries in which revolutions had taken place joined the EU.

A major report published by the European Parliament Committee of Foreign Affairs a fortnight after the EU–Russia summit demonstrated the EU's dissatisfaction with the relationship. In the report members of the Committee expressed their concern about the weakening of democracy, the human rights situation, freedom of speech, the conflict in Chechnya, the concentration of power in the Kremlin and Russia's increasingly assertive behaviour in the former Soviet

Enlarged EU and the Orange Revolution   101

states. It emphasised that this was the EU and Russia's 'common neighbourhood' and that it was in the EU's – and should also be in Russia's – interests to see the former Soviet states develop into peaceful democratic regimes. The report urged the EU institutions to formulate concrete objectives concerning EU–Russia relations.[148] The report also claimed that the attempts by political leaders of individual EU member states to forge special relations with Putin would harm the EU's ability to establish a common foreign policy towards Russia.[149] This was the second time that such a report had been published since the release of the Beelder report in November 2003, which admitted the EU's lack of a unitary stance in its policy towards Russia.[150]

The report's concerns regarding the attempts of individual leaders to forge special relationships was exemplified by divergent approaches from both the European Commissioner for EU External Relations and the ENP, Dr Benita Ferrero-Waldner, and Solana. Ferrero-Waldner praised the report as 'highly relevant' to the issues that had been discussed at the EU–Russia summit.[151] Ferrero-Waldner urged the EU to 'intensify its efforts to define and maintain a *common* EU line' in its relations with Russia.[152] But on the same day as her speech, Solana hailed achievements in EU–Russia relations underlining division in the EU regarding its policy towards Russia. While Ferrero-Waldner denounced Russia's drift into authoritarianism and the EU's lack of a coherent stance in its foreign policy towards Russia, an article by Solana in the Russian daily newspaper *Nezavisimaya Gazeta* paid tribute to EU–Russia cooperation. He stated that in areas where the partners cooperate they do so

> well and make a difference ... there is no better way to build trust between ourselves. This is not to say that it will be easy. The EU and Russia do not agree on everything and negotiations are often tough as both [partners] defended [their] respective interest.[153]

Solana highlighted that EU–Russia relations had improved massively. He declared that the relationship had 'indeed undergone a sea change, where old suspicions have been replaced by cooperation and trust'.[154] He added that the EU was concerned about human rights issues in Russia and about Chechnya, but declared diplomatically that a 'very frank and open discussion' was taking place, stressing that the EU and Russia had to find solutions 'on the basis of the shared values that underpin[ned] [their] strategic partnership'.[155]

The phrase 'open and frank dialogue' had become central in the political rhetoric of statements made by prominent European officials and policymakers about the relationship. According to Lars Grønbjerg, after 2004 it 'has been necessary for a Prime Minister from a certain country' or prominent European official to say the following after a meeting with Putin:

> 'I had a frank and open dialogue with Putin. I raised a number of human rights issues ...'. This was due to the fact that by then it had become evident that Putin did not move Russia in a democratic direction and it was no

102 *Enlarged EU and the Orange Revolution*

longer possible to keep the hope alive of a democratic and market oriented reformer. Therefore, the tone had changed in the European publics and the Prime Ministers [and/or EU officials] had to adjust.[156]

The legitimacy of Grønbjerg's statement became evident when the British Prime Minister, Tony Blair, who chaired the UK European Council Presidency, determined to maintain a cordial dialogue with Putin despite the increasing criticism from prominent members in both the European Parliament and the European Commission on Russia's policies. The joint press release from the EU–Russia summit on 4 October demonstrated that the representatives of the EU and Russia had discussed the implementation of the road maps aimed at establishing the Four Common Spaces, Russia's accession to the World Trade Organisation, energy policy, climate change and the future of EU–Russia relations after the expiry of the PCA.[157] The clearest confirmation of Blair's attempt to smooth relations with Putin was his praise of the EU's economic relations with Russia while sidelining the political aspects of the relationship.[158] At the summit press conference he emphasised the importance of economic issues in EU–Russia relations by saying that he and Putin would like to cooperate to take the relationship to a 'new ... more intense and strengthened level.... This is a relationship in economic terms that can only grow, ... prosper and strengthen.'[159]

Despite a BBC journalist's attempt to grill Blair on the EU justification for its cordial relations with Russia, Blair could not restrain himself from praising EU–Russia relations. He emphasised that Russia was the EU's strategic partner and had been its long-term supplier of energy. In order to support Blair's answer, Putin added that certain European countries obtained 90 per cent of their gas reserves from Russia and emphasised that none of these countries had been unhappy with their supply.[160] The journalist asked Blair how the EU could justify its continuing dialogue with Russia without being afraid of becoming too dependent on Russian energy resources to the extent that it was 'forced to reconcile itself to violations of democratic principles, human rights and freedom of speech in Russia'.[161] Blair simply dismissed the journalist's concern.

Conclusion

The EU intervention in the resolution of the Orange Revolution resulted in a crisis in EU–Russia relations. It was caused by both the EU's refusal to accept the results of the fraudulent election and its launch of a diplomatic mission to Kiev which led to repeated presidential elections resulting in victory for the pro-EU candidate.

The EU advanced its foreign policy in Ukraine through diplomacy in defiance of and to the detriment of the interests of the Russian political elite. Its diplomatic mission was planned strategically. Kwasniewski's role as mediator had been supported by the chairman of the Dutch European Council Presidency, Prime Minister Balkenende, because of his personal relations with the Ukrainian elite and his role as chairman of the Presidency of the Council of Europe.

Enlarged EU and the Orange Revolution   103

In resolving the political crisis in Ukraine, the EU was able to act coherently. This coherence is significant because previously the EU's foreign policy towards Russia when seeking to react to a conflict in a third-party state had been marked by internal division. This was the case during the second Chechen War when the EU did not manage to maintain a coherent and firm stance towards Russian human rights abuses in Chechnya. On the contrary, as demonstrated in Chapter 2, the EU's internal wavering stance regarding the conflict and the strategic importance of relations with Russia resulted in a gradual muting of EU condemnation of the situation in Chechnya.

The EU intervention in the political crisis resulted in the formation of a pro-Western government which jeopardised the Kremlin's foreign policy with Ukraine. From an economic point of view, Yushchenko's professed aspiration for Ukraine membership of the EU had worked to the detriment of Russia's plan to convince the Ukrainian leadership to become a member of the SES. From a political point of view, Russian policy makers regarded the Ukrainian revolution as a geopolitical catastrophe because it had shaken Russia's international order by having caused the diminution of Russia's influence in the post- Soviet space.

The Kremlin was outraged by the fact that the EU had intervened in a matter of Ukrainian domestic politics. At the same time, it was shocked by the fact that Poland and Lithuania, two 'new' EU member states, were spearheading the EU intervention in Ukraine. The most influential policy adviser in the Duma, Kosachev, condemned the role of new EU member states in determining EU foreign policy. According to Kosachev, the 'Balticisation process had turned the EU into an aggressive organisation'.[162] This was the clearest confirmation of the resulting crisis in EU–Russia relations after the Orange Revolution. This represented a reversal of the Kremlin's earlier perceptions of the EU reflected in the cordial atmosphere in EU–Russia relations five years prior to the Orange Revolution. During the Kosovo War – the most severe crisis in Russia's relations with the US and NATO since the end of the Cold War – Russian leaders perceived the EU as benign because of its limited capacity in external relations. At the time of the resolution of the revolution in Ukraine, the EU was at its most assertive because two of its new member states were steering EU foreign policy towards the former Soviet space. Afraid of losing its grip, the Kremlin began to perceive the EU as a hostile power, seeking to draw Ukraine into the EU's sphere of influence.

In retrospect, the crisis between the EU and Russia over Ukraine was just a pretext for a deeper, more complex confrontation, which contributed to Ukraine's drift into instability after November 2013. It is torn between Brussels and Moscow in terms of its future political orientation. The EU's lukewarm reception of Ukrainian aspirations for EU accession and the absence of a clear agenda to fulfil this objective was a major ingredient for the emerging Ukraine crisis nine years after the Orange Revolution. The current, ongoing crisis in Ukraine and its effects on EU–Russia relations are discussed in Chapter 7 which seeks to answer the question 'What lessons did the EU and Russia learn from their confrontation over the Orange Revolution?'

104 *Enlarged EU and the Orange Revolution*

The next chapter demonstrates that Ukraine's role as a transit country for Russian gas to Europe was crucial but resulted in increasing EU concerns regarding long-term security of the energy supply when Gazprom interrupted its delivery. In addition to increasing concerns about securing the EU's energy resources, EU–Russian confrontation over human rights, bilateral disputes between EU member states and Russia, as well as a deadlock concerning the renewal of the PCA, were continuing sources of confrontation in the 'strategic partnership'.

Notes

1 Babich (2004).
2 Yushchenko (2004).
3 Ibid.
4 Ibid.
5 Ibid.
6 Ibid.
7 BBC Summary of World Broadcasts. Source: Sislki Visti, Kiev. Ukrainian premier committed to ties with Russia, welfare state. 17 November 2004.
8 Yanukovich (2004).
9 *Ukrainskaya Pravda* (2004a).
10 *Ukrainskaya Gazeta* (nd); Petrov and Ryabov (2006), p. 152.
11 *Ukrainskaya Pravda* (2004b).
12 BBC Summary of World Broadcasts. Source: *Kommersant*. Russian paper sees Putin's Ukraine trip as attempt to sway presidential vote. 11 November 2004; Ragozin (2004).
13 Ragozin (2004).
14 Wilson (2005), p. 105.
15 BBC Summary of World Broadcasts. Source: UNIAN news agency, Kiev. Ukrainian Premier upbeat on CIS free trade zone. 25 February 2003.
16 Aptekar (2004), p. 1; United Nations Economic Commission for Europe (2004); BBC Summary of World Broadcasts. Source: Interfax. Russian, Ukrainian, Belarus, Kazakh leaders to create single economic zone. 23 February 2003.
17 Interfax (2004a).
18 Ibid.
19 Interfax (2004b).
20 Ibid.
21 BBC Summary of World Broadcasts. Source: Halytski Kontrakty, Kiev. Russian spin doctor says Moscow distrusts Russian opposition leader. 5 August 2004.
22 Isachenkov (1999).
23 BBC Summary of World Broadcasts. Source: UT1, Kiev. Ukrainian presidential candidates clash in TV debate. 15 November 2004. p. 11.
24 Ibid. p. 13
25 Romanova (2004).
26 BBC Summary World Broadcasts. Source: Interfax. Foreign minister denies politics prompted postponement of EU–Russia summit. 12 November 2004.
27 Wielaard (2004).
28 Nedbaeva (2004).
29 Ibid.
30 Wilson (2005), p. 6.
31 Ibid., p. 125.
32 Ibid., p. 128.

Enlarged EU and the Orange Revolution   105

33 International Election Observation Mission quoted in Pifer (2007), p. 29.
34 Agence France Presse (2004a).
35 MacAskill and Walsh (2004).
36 BBC Summary of World Broadcasts. Source: Antena 1 Radio. Lisbon. Commission chief says 'EU not happy' with Ukraine elections. 24 November 2004; Bridge (2004).
37 Bridge (2004).
38 BBC Summary of World Broadcasts. Source: Ekho Moskvy. Ukraine not major topic for EU–Russia summit – Putin aide. 24 November 2004.
39 Ibid.
40 Ibid.
41 Ibid.
42 BBC Summary of World Broadcasts: Source: ITAR-TASS. EU should concern itself with Cyprus, Kosovo, not Ukraine–Russian minister. 24 November 2004.
43 Ibid.
44 Agence France Presse (2004a).
45 Edwards (2004); Agence France Presse (2004b).
46 Gutterman (2004a).
47 Perrot (2004).
48 Avril (2004).
49 Ibid.
50 Ibid.
51 Pifer (2007), p. 30.
52 *Independent* (2004).
53 Ibid.
54 Gutterman (2004b).
55 Gutterman (2004c).
56 Melikova (2004).
57 Council of the European Union (2004).
58 Ibid.; Medvedev (2007), p. 5.
59 Council of the European Union (2004).
60 Ibid.
61 Quoted in Pifer (2007).
62 Wilson (2005), p. 192.
63 Baltic News Service (2004).
64 Gera (2004).
65 BBC Summary of World Broadcasts. Source: NTV Mir, Moscow. Update on Ukraine. Main players interviewed on Russian NTV special. 27 November 2004.
66 Ibid.
67 Wilson (2005), p. 138.
68 Dempsey (2004a).
69 BBC Summary of World Broadcasts. Source: Lithuanian Radio. Lithuanian leader arrives in Ukraine, explains his mission. 26 November 2004.
70 Pifer (2007), p. 31.
71 Wilson (2005), p. 139.
72 BBC Summary of World Broadcasts. Source: TVP1, Warsaw. Ukrainian president welcomes start of round-table talks. 26 November 2004.
73 *Guardian* (2004).
74 Strauss (2004).
75 Ibid.
76 Lavrov interview with *Handelsblatt* quoted in Averre (2005), p. 187.
77 Ibid.
78 BBC Summary of World Broadcasts. Source: Inter TV. Ukrainian president urges street protests to end. 26 November 2004.
79 Sushko and Prystayko (2006), pp. 139, 140.

106 *Enlarged EU and the Orange Revolution*

80 BBC Summary of World Broadcasts. Source: RTR Russia TV. Russian deputy speaker urges EU not to meddle in Ukrainian affairs. 25 November 2004.
81 Ibid.
82 Perrot (2004).
83 Dempsey (2004b).
84 Ibid.
85 Ibid.
86 BBC News (2004).
87 Wilson (2005), p. 153.
88 Tassinari (2005), p. 53.
89 Gardiner (2004).
90 Patten (2006), p. 167.
91 Ibid., p. 220.
92 Ibid.
93 Ibid.
94 Ibid.
95 Ibid.
96 Ibid., p. 159.
97 Ibid.
98 European Parliament (2005a).
99 Ibid.
100 Ibid.
101 Yushchenko (2005). See also Gaenzle (2008), p. 215.
102 Gaenzle (2008).
103 Ibid.
104 Ibid.
105 Ibid.
106 Ibid.
107 Ricard (2005).
108 Patten (2006), p. 158.
109 MacDonald and Croft (2015).
110 *The Times* (2005).
111 BBC Monitoring Central Asia Unit. Source: ITAR-TASS. EU says non-violence principle vital in search for solution in Kyrgyzstan. 22 March 2005.
112 Ibid.
113 BBC Monitoring Former Soviet Union. Source: ITAR-TASS news agency. Russian foreign minister criticises EU foreign policy chief over Kyrgyzstan. 23 March 2005.
114 Lavrov (2005).
115 BBC Monitoring Former Soviet Union. Source: ITAR-TASS. EU foreign policy chief heading for Moscow to discuss Kyrgyzstan. 23 March 2005.
116 Dempsey (2005).
117 Ibid.
118 Ibid.
119 Ibid.
120 Ibid.
121 Kosachev (2005).
122 Ibid.
123 Ibid.
124 Kondrashov (2005).
125 Ivanov quoted in Herd (2005), p. 19.
126 Ibid.
127 Ibid.
128 Kolerov (2005).
129 *Kommersant* (2005).

130 BBC Monitoring International Reports. Putin appoints a spin doctor to 'prevent velvet revolutions' in CIS. 23 March 2005.
131 Dannreuther (2006), p. 184.
132 Pavlovsky (2005).
133 Ibid.
134 Ibid. Added emphasis.
135 Regnum (2005).
136 Tsygankov (2006), p. 163; Raik (2007), p. 219.
137 Euractiv (2005).
138 Ibid.
139 Ibid.
140 Ibid.
141 Ibid.
142 Council of the European Union (2005a).
143 BBC Monitoring Former Soviet Union. Supplied by BBC Worldwide Monitoring. Source: Radio Russia. Russia should offer EU greater consistency – envoy. 11 May 2005.
144 Ibid.
145 Ibid.
146 Ibid.
147 European Council (1999); Ministry of Foreign Affairs of the Russian Federation (2000).
148 European Parliament (2005b).
149 Lobjakas (2005).
150 European Parliament (2004).
151 Russian Chamber of Commerce (2005).
152 Ibid. Emphasis added.
153 Solana (2005).
154 Ibid.
155 Ibid.
156 Email interview with Lars Grønbjerg. Interview conducted on 3 March 2011.
157 Council of the European Union (2005b).
158 *Moscow Times* (2005).
159 *Independent* (2005). Putin stresses Russia is 'equal' with EU states. 5 October 2005.
160 BBC World Wide Monitoring (2005).
161 Ibid.
162 Kondrashov (2005).

Bibliography

Agence France Presse. (2004a). Début du sommet Russie-UE à la Haye. 25 November 2004.

Agence France Presse. (2004b). Poutine félicite Ianoukovitch pour son élection à la présidence ukrainienne. 25 November 2004.

Aptekar, P. (2004). Odin s soshkoi, ostal'nye s lozhkoi. *Gazeta*. 16 September 2004.

Aslund, A. and McFaul, M. (2006). *Revolution in Orange. The origins of Ukraine's democratic breakthrough*. Washington DC: Carnegie Endowment Centre for International Peace.

Averre, D. (2005). Russia and the European Union: Convergence or divergence? *European Security*. 14(2): 175–202.

Avril, P. (2004). L'Europe dénonce la fraude mais reste impuissante. Alors qu'un constat de désaccord a clos le sommet UE-Russie, le scénario catastrophe d'une séparation est brandi par le clan au pouvoir pour faire barrage à l'opposition. *Le Figaro*. 26 November 2004.

108 *Enlarged EU and the Orange Revolution*

Babich, D. (2004). Lekarstvo ot Evropy. U Mosckvy est' rychagi vozdei'stviia na ES. *Vremya Novostei*. No. 75. 29 April 2004.

Baltic News Service. (2004). Lithuanian President leaves for Kiev on mediation mission (expands). 26 November 2004.

BBC Monitoring Central Asia Unit. Source: ITAR-TASS. EU says non-violence principle vital in search for solution in Kyrgyzstan. 22 March 2005.

BBC Monitoring Former Soviet Union. Source: ITAR-TASS. Russian Foreign Minister criticises EU foreign policy chief over Kyrgyzstan. 23 March 2005.

BBC Monitoring Former Soviet Union. Source: ITAR-TASS. EU foreign policy chief heading for Moscow to discuss Kyrgyzstan. 23 March 2005.

BBC Monitoring Former Soviet Union. Supplied by BBC Worldwide Monitoring. Source: Radio Russia. Russia should offer EU greater consistency- envoy. 11 May 2005.

BBC Monitoring International Reports. Putin appoints a spin doctor to 'prevent velvet revolutions' in CIS. 23 March 2005.

BBC News. (2004). Polish head rejects Putin attack. 24 December 2004. Retrieved 15 October 2011 from: www.news.bbc.co.uk/2/hi/europe/4122721.stm.

BBC Summary of World Broadcasts. Source: Interfax. Russian, Ukrainian, Belarus, Kazakh leaders to create single economic zone. 23 February 2003.

BBC Summary of World Broadcasts. Source: UNIAN news agency, Kiev. Ukrainian Premier upbeat on CIS free trade zone. 25 February 2003.

BBC Summary of World Broadcasts. Source: Halytski Kontrakty, Kiev. Russian spin doctor says Moscow distrusts Russian opposition leader. 5 August 2004.

BBC Summary of World Broadcasts. Source: Interfax. Russia–EU summit may be held in The Hague before the end of the year. 9 November 2004.

BBC Summary of World Broadcasts. Source: *Kommersant*. Russian paper sees Putin's Ukraine trip as attempt to sway presidential vote. 11 November 2004.

BBC Summary World Broadcasts. Source: Interfax. Foreign minister denies politics prompted postponement of EU–Russia summit. 12 November 2004.

BBC Summary of World Broadcasts. Source: UT1, Kiev. Ukrainian presidential candidates clash in TV debate. 15 November 2004.

BBC Summary of World Broadcasts. Source: Sislki Visti, Kiev. Ukrainian premier committed to ties with Russia, welfare state. 17 November 2004.

BBC Summary of World Broadcasts. Source: Antena 1 Radio. Lisbon Commission chief says 'EU not happy' with Ukraine elections. 24 November 2004.

BBC Summary of World Broadcasts. Source: Ekho Moskvy. Ukraine not major topic for EU–Russia summit – Putin aide. 24 November 2004.

BBC Summary of World Broadcasts: Source: ITAR-TASS. EU should concern itself with Cyprus, Kosovo, not Ukraine–Russian minister. 24 November 2004.

BBC Summary of World Broadcasts. Source: RTR Russia TV. Russian deputy speaker urges EU not to meddle in Ukrainian affairs. 25 November 2004.

BBC Summary of World Broadcasts. Source: Inter TV. Ukrainian president urges street protests to end. 26 November 2004.

BBC Summary of World Broadcasts. Source: Lithuanian Radio. Lithuanian leader arrives in Ukraine, explains his mission. 26 November 2004.

BBC Summary of World Broadcasts. Source: TVP1, Warsaw. Ukrainian president welcomes start of round-table talks. 26 November 2004.

BBC Summary of World Broadcasts. Source: NTV Mir, Moscow. Update on Ukraine. Main players interviewed on Russian NTV special. 27 November 2004.

BBC World Wide Monitoring. Source: NTV Mir, Moscow. Putin explains visa-free proposal at EU–Russia summit in London. 4 October 2005.

Enlarged EU and the Orange Revolution 109

Bridge, R. (2004). Ukraine dominates EU–Russia summit. Moscow News Russia. 1 December 2004.

Council of the European Union. (2004). The Hague. 14th EU–Russia summit. 25 November 2004. Retrieved 12 April 2011 from: www.consilium.europa.eu/uedocs/cms_Data/docs/pressdata/en/er/82799.pdf

Council of the European Union. (2005a). 15th EU–Russia summit. Road Maps. Road Map for the Common Economic Space. Building Blocks for sustained economic growth. Brussels, 11 May 2005. 8799/05. ADD 1 (Presse 110).

Council of the European Union. (2005b). 16th EU–Russia summit. London, 4 October 2005. 12946/05 (Presse 254).

Dannreuther, R. (2006). Developing the Alternative to Enlargement: The European Neighbourhood Policy. *European Foreign Affairs Review*. 11(2): pp. 183–201.

Dempsey, J. (2004a). Ukraine resentments sank EU's mediation. Poland and Germany avoid the vacuum. Standoff in Ukraine. Events take on a momentum of their own. *International Herald Tribune*. 30 November 2004.

Dempsey, J. (2004b). Moscow's 'hands off!' doesn't dissuade EU; Europeans will call Ukraine 'our border' too. *International Herald Tribune*. 4 December 2004.

Dempsey, J. (2005). Russia tries to force cuts in rights monitoring, fund block is feared as threat to Europe security organization. *International Herald Tribune*. 30 March 2005.

Edwards, R. (2004). Ukraine opposition in all-out strike call. *Evening Standard*. 25 November 2004.

EurActiv. (2005). Verheugen remarks cast shadow over EU–Russia summit. 9 May 2005. Retrieved 3 February 2011 from: www.euractiv.com/en/security/verheugen-remarks-cast-shadows-eu-russia-summit/article-139151

European Council. (1999). Russia's response to the Common Strategy of the European Union of 4 June 1999 on Russia. (1999/414/CFSP). Section 5. Securing the Russian interests in an expanded European Union.

European Parliament. (2004). Session Document. Report with a proposal for a European Parliament recommendation to the Council on EU–Russia relations. (2003/2230 INI). Committee on Foreign Affairs, Human Rights, Common Security and Defence Policy. Rapporteur: Bastiaan Beelder. Final A5–0053/2004. 2 February 2004.

European Parliament. (2005a). European Parliament resolution on the election results of Ukraine. 13 January 2005. Retrieved 17 March 2011 from: www.europarl.europa.eu/sides/getDoc.do?type=TA&reference=P6-TA-2005-0009&format=XML&language=EN

European Parliament. (2005b). European Parliament resolution on EU–Russia relations. (2004/2170) (INI). Brussels. Final edition. EU–Russia relations. 26 May 2005. Retrieved 28 February 2011 from: www.europarl.europa.eu/sides/getDoc.do?type=TA&reference=P6-TA-2005-0207&language=EN&ring=A6-2005-0135

Gaenzle, S. (2008). EU–Russia relations and the repercussions. In Schmidtke, O. and Yekelchyk, S. (eds). *Europe's Last Frontier? Belarus, Moldova and Ukraine between Russia and the European Union.* Basingstoke, UK: Palgrave Macmillan.

Gardiner, B. (2004). World leaders welcome new Ukraine vote. Associated Press. 3 December 2004.

Gera, V. (2004). Driven by bad memories, Poland gets involved in neighbor Ukraine standoff. Associated Press. 25 November 2004.

Guardian. (2004). Ukraine vote on hold after court ruling. 26 November 2004.

Gutterman, S. (2004a). Putin arrives in Netherlands for EU summit as Ukrainian election strains ties. Associated Press. 25 November 2004.

Gutterman, S. (2004b). EU, Russia fail to clinch partnership accord at summit overshadowed by Ukraine crisis, predict deal next May. Associated Press. 25 November 2004.

110 *Enlarged EU and the Orange Revolution*

Gutterman, S. (2004c). Putin and EU urge peaceful settlement in Ukraine, but East-West divide on results persist. Associated Press. 25 November 2004.

Herd, G.H. (2005). Russia and the 'Orange Revolution': Response, rhetoric and reality. *The Quarterly Journal.* 4(2): 15–28.

Independent. (2004).Ukraine's Supreme Court to hold inquiry into vote-rigging claims. 26 November 2004.

Independent. (2005). Putin stresses Russia is 'equal' with EU states. 5 October 2005.

Interfax. (2004a). Common Economic Space will become a strong regional structure – Kuchma. 15 September 2004.

Interfax. (2004b). CEC way to European living standards-Putin. 15 September 2004.

Isachenkov, V. (1999). Yeltsin meets with German EU leaders. Associated Press. 18 February 1999.

Kolerov, M. (2005). Front protiv Rossii: 'sanitaryi kordon' i 'vneshnee upravlenie.' Regnum. 18 March 2005. Retrieved 18 March 2011 from: www.regnum.ru/news/ 423582.html#ixzzlEAxQ6Xs4

Kommersant. (2005). Vladimir Putin naznachil barzhatnava kontrrevoliutsionera. 23 March 2005. Retrieved 27 April 2011 from: www.kommersant.ru/Doc/556859

Kondrashov, D. (2005). Front protiv Rossii: napravlenia agressii. Regnum. 28 March 2005. Retrieved 23 October 2011 from: www.regnum.ru/news7428347.html

Kosachev, K. (2005). From the Logic of 'Near Abroad' to the Community of Interests. *International Affairs* (Moscow). 51(3): 85–91.

Lavrov, S. (2005). Democracy, International Governance and the Future World Order. 9 February 2005. *Russia in Global Affairs* No. 1 Jan–March 2005. Retrieved 15 January 2011 from: http://eng.globalaffairs.ru/number/n_4422

Lobjakas, A. (2005). Russia: EU Parliamentarians criticise Moscow over democracy. 27 April 2005. Radio Free Liberty Europe. Retrieved 30 January 2011 from: www.rferl. org/content/article/1058662.html.

MacAskill, E. and Walsh, N.P. (2004). Ukraine crisis: EU anger at Putin's role in election: diplomacy turmoil highlights simmering tensions with Russia. *Guardian.* 25 November 2004.

MacDonald, A. and Croft, A. (2015). EU defies Russian 'bully' but disappoints ex-Soviets. Reuters. 22 May 2015.

Medvedev, S. (2007). The crisis in EU–Russia Relations: Between 'Sovereignty' and 'Europeanization.' *Political Theory and Political Analysis.* Working Paper. WP 14/2007/02. pp. 1–20.

Melikova, N. (2004). Putin vstretitsia so svoimi krutikami. V Gaage ego tiazhelye shesti-chasovye peregovory. *Nezavisimaya Gazeta.* 25 November 2004. Retrieved 12 April 2011 from: www.ng.ru/politics/2004-11-25/1_putin.html.

Ministry of Foreign Affairs of the Russian Federation. (2000). The Foreign Policy Concept of the Russian Federation. Approved by the President of the Russian Federation. V. Putin. 28 June 2000.

Moscow Times. (2005). Putin and Blair pledge to fight terrorism. 6 October 2005.

Nedbaeva, O. (2004). La crise ukrainienne s'oriente vers une nouvelle élection. Agence France Presse. 29 November 2004.

Patten, C. (2006). *Cousins and Strangers. America, Britain and Europe in a new century.* New York: Times Books.

Pavlovsky, G. (2005). Russia's policy within the post-Soviet space. 28 April 2005. Retrieved 30 February 2011 from: www.america-russia.net/eng/face/85193608?user_ session=480f37b22dc8b6a25f659dee5d4c25a.

Enlarged EU and the Orange Revolution   111

Perrot, P.L. (2004). Poutine a décidé de marquer à tout prix son territoire en Ukraine. Agence France Presse. 25 November 2004.

Petrov, N. and Ryabov, A. (2006). Russia's role in the Orange Revolution. In Aslund, A. and McFaul, M. (2006). *Revolution in Orange*. Washington DC: Carnegie Endowment for International Peace.

Pifer, S. (2007). Ukraine Looks West. European mediators and Ukraine's Orange Revolution. *Problems of Post-Communism.* 54(6): 28–42.

Ragozin, L. (2004). Ukraine's east-west showdown. 22 November 2004. Retrieved 18 January 2011 from: http://news.bbc.co.uk/2/hi/europe/4023043.stm

Raik, K. (2007). A Europe divided by Russia? The new Eastern Member States and the EU's policy towards the East. In Gower, J. and Timmins, G. *Russia and Europe in the Twenty-first Century. An uneasy partnership*. London: Anthem Press.

Regnum. (2005). Nakanue sammita Rossiia-ES v Moskve: 'krizis', 'Besperspektivnost' i 'baltizatsiia'. 10 May 2005. Retrieved 20 October 2011 from: www.newkaliningrad.ru/news/politics7k39068.html.

Ricard, P. (2005). Il n'existe pas de modèle sociale européen. Chaque pays a ses traditions. Guenther Verheugen- vice-président de la Commission européenne. *Le Monde*. 3 September 2005.

Romanova, L. (2004). The party meeting is not cancelled. *Gazeta*. 9 November 2004.

Russian Chamber of Commerce. (2005). Ferrero-Waldner, B. Speech. 25 May 2005. Retrieved 25 January 2011 from: www.ruscham.com/en/news/business_news/64/119.html

Solana, J. (2005). The EU and Russia: towards a strong and united Europe. Article by Javier Solana, EU High Representative for the CFSP on EU - Russia relations. 25 May 2005. Retrieved 15 February 2011 from: www.consilium.europa.eu/ueDocs/cms_Data/docs/pressData/en/articles/84926.pdf

Strauss, J. (2004). Moscow accuses EU of meddling in Ukraine. *Daily Telegraph*. 29 November 2004.

Sushko, O. and Prystayko, O. (2006). Western influence. In *Revolution in Orange. The origins of Ukraine's democratic breakthrough*. Washington DC: Carnegie Endowment Centre for International Peace.

Tassinari, F. (2005). A Riddle Inside an Enigma: Unwrapping the EU–Russia strategic partnership. *The International Spectator*. 40(1): 45–57.

The Times. (2005). From west to east rolling revolution gathers pace across the former USSR. 15 February 2005.

Tsygankov, A.P. (2006). New challenges for Putin's foreign policy. Orbis 50(1): 153–165.

Ukrainskaya Gazeta. (nd). O deyatel nosti Rossiiskogo kluba. Retrieved 1 September 2011 from: www.ukr.ru/club/docs/61349482.

Ukrainskaya Pravda. (2004a). Priktytiem dlya Pavlovskogo budet klub. 19 July 2004. Retrieved 1 September 2011 from: www.pravda.com.ua/ru/news/2004/7/19/10621.htm.

Ukrainskaya Pravda. (2004b). Rossiiskoe lobbi Yanukovicha-est' li ugolovnyi sled? 12 November 2004. Retrieved 1 September 2011 from: www.pravda.com.ua/ru/news/2004/11/12/13453.htm.

United Nations Economic Commission for Europe. (2004). Regional Trade Agreements in the ECE. SES presidents sign agreements on VAT. 16 September 2004. Retrieved 23 October 2011 from: http://ecetrade.typepad.com/rtas/recent_developments/

Wielaard, R. (2004). EU–Russia summit postponed due to lack of progress in difficult negotiations. Associated Press. 5 November 2004.

Wilson, A. (2005). *Ukraine's Orange Revolution*. Yale: Yale University Press.

112 *Enlarged EU and the Orange Revolution*

Yanukovich, V. (2004). Ukraine's European future. *International Herald Tribune*. 29 September 2004.

Yushchenko, V. (2004). Whither Ukraine. Plotting Europe's eastern border. *International Herald Tribune*. 10 September 2004.

Yushchenko, V. (2005). Ukraine's future is in the EU. Speech given on 23 February 2005 at the European Parliament. Retrieved on 23 October 2011 from: www.eu-un.europa.eu/articles/fr/article_4382_fr.htm

5 Towards confrontation: 2006–2008

From January 2006 until the eve of the Russian presidential election in March 2008, EU–Russia relations were marked by a series of disagreements. These quarrels ranged from the deadlock over the renewal of the EU–Russian PCA, to clashes over human rights and energy policy. When Gazprom's interruption of the supply of gas to Ukraine undermined delivery to several EU member states, EU leaders became increasingly concerned about Russia's reliability as a supplier of energy resources. Tensions over energy policy further intensified when the Kremlin rejected the EU's request to liberalise the Russian energy market and instead tightened state control over this sector. The resulting EU–Russian clash over energy policy was followed by a struggle over the adoption of a new PCA. These tensions in the relationship coincided with the increasing divergence between the values the EU sought to uphold in its relations with Moscow and Russia's political reality.

This chapter seeks to examine the reasons for these emerging sources of confrontation in EU–Russia relations.[1] It argues that the root causes for these tensions were the following three factors. First, the EU's internal fragmentation – in particular, frictions between 'old' and 'new' member states, the European Council Presidency, the European Parliament and the European Commission concerning EU–Russia relations – made it impossible for the EU to adopt a coherent policy towards Moscow. EU policy oscillated between extremes of accommodation and confrontation. The direction of this wavering was influenced by the EU's rotating European Council Presidencies. In 2006, the Finnish Council Presidency adopted an accommodating line towards Russia and prioritised the discussion of energy policy. In contrast, Germany's chairmanship of the European Council from January until June 2007 maintained a confrontational stance and made human rights a centrepiece of the Presidency.

Second, long-standing bilateral tensions between Russia and three of the EU's 'new' member states led to conflicts in EU–Russia relations. Clashes between Russia, and Poland, Lithuania and Estonia ranged from trade-disputes to the legacy of the Soviet occupation of the Baltic States. When these countries faced confrontations with Russia, the EU rallied to their support. As a consequence, Russian diplomats and political leaders attacked the EU.

114 *Towards confrontation: 2006–2008*

Third, confrontation between the EU and Russia between 2006 and 2008 was influenced by the increasing divergence between the values the EU attempted to promote in relations with Moscow and Russia's increasing authoritarianism. The latter was signalled by increasing manipulation of the political system by the Kremlin, the tightening of controls over state television and violent dispersals of demonstrations by opponents of the Putin regime in 2006 to 2007. Even though European politicians sought to promote EU values in its partnership with Russia, their aspirations were limited by Russia's principle of sovereignty in its foreign policy during Putin's second term as president. Brussels' lack of power in this regard became evident. EU leaders used summits with Russia as an opportunity to lecture the Russian political elite on human rights but without success, resulting in acrimonious clashes between European and Russian politicians at the EU–Russia summits in May and October 2007.

The clash over energy policy

Discord between the EU and Russia over energy policy was an example of the increasing confrontation in their relationship. It was caused by both the EU's attempt to urge Russia to liberalise its energy market and its growing fear about Russia's reliability as a supplier of energy after Gazprom interrupted its delivery to Ukraine, a major transit country for gas from Russia to Europe. As a result of this disruption, the gas supply to EU member states in Central and Eastern Europe was significantly affected by a decrease in the pressure in the pipelines. In 2006 EU member states such as Slovakia, Finland and the three Baltic States had to import 100 per cent of their gas from Russia. In comparison, France only imported 23 per cent of their gas requirements from Russia whereas Germany imported 40 per cent.[2] In January 2006, when Gazprom disrupted the supply to Ukraine, EU member states were importing about 40 per cent of their total requirements for natural gas, half of which came from Russia.[3]

The divergence in dependency on external resources encouraged EU member states to develop plans to safeguard the long-term security of their energy supplies. A Green Paper on a European strategy for sustainable, competitive and secure energy summarised the EU's concerns.[4] Stating that the EU had to ensure the 'diversity of energy type, country of origin and transit', the paper proposed options to tackle challenges in the European energy market such as competitiveness, solidarity among member states concerning energy policy, sustainable development, innovation and technology, as well as the establishment of a common external energy policy.[5]

The EU regarded Russia's liberalisation of its energy market as a means to safeguard the EU's energy supply. It sought to achieve this liberalisation by urging Russia to ratify the European Energy Charter Treaty (ECT), a framework for cooperation in energy trade, investment, efficiency and dispute settlement. It had been signed on 17 December 1994 and aimed at 'strengthening the rule of law' on energy related issues by ensuring mutual access to transport infrastructure and the protection of investment.[6] Its signatories had to obey the principles

Towards confrontation: 2006–2008 115

of encouraging free movement of investment in the energy sector, state sovereignty over natural energy resources and market access.[7]

Deliberations over Russia's ratification of the ECT became a symbol of EU–Russian divergence over energy policy. While the EU was seeking to make Russia liberalise its market, Russia increased state control over the energy sector. This was exemplified by the appointment of state officials, who had close relationships with Putin, as members of the board of Gazprom. The Russian Vice Premier Dmitry Medvedev, who was elected as president in March 2008, worked for the board of Gazprom from 2000 until 2006.[8] No less significant as evidence of Russia's increasing state control in the energy sector was the Kremlin's intervention in preparations by Mikhail Khodorkovsky, the founder of Russia's second largest oil company, Yukos, to build an independent export pipeline. As this plan threatened the Kremlin's monopoly on oil exports, agents of Federalnaya Sluzba Bezopasnosti (FSB), the federal security service, arrested Khodorkovsky in October 2003 on grounds of fraud and tax evasion.[9] Six years later, he was sentenced to nine years in prison, but was released in December 2013.[10]

The Russian government's reluctance to de-monopolise its gas sector enabled the Kremlin to use energy policy as a geopolitical weapon. The so-called 'coloured revolutions' in the former Soviet space were a factor which contributed to Russia's politicisation of energy policy. In March 2005, ten months before Gazprom interrupted its supply to Ukraine for the first time, there were the first indications that Russia was considering the manipulation of energy policy. Konstantin Kosachev, chairman of the International Affairs Committee of the State Duma, stated that the 'velvet changes of orientation', had created an 'unusually unanimous feeling within the Russian political class' about the need to respond to the revolutions in the former Soviet space. According to Kosachev, the politicians' options included 'tighten[ing] the gas noose' in countries in the former Soviet space where the coloured revolutions had originated.[11]

In January 2006, Kosachev's options were acted upon. Gazprom 'tightened the gas noose' on Ukraine, which resulted in a crisis for the EU. As a consequence of the interruption of supply by Gazprom, nine of the 25 EU member states were hit by shortages.[12] In four of the nine affected states, the supply of gas dropped by 30 per cent.[13] The French provider Gaz de France stated that supplies from Gazprom had decreased to 30 per cent.[14] In Poland, the supply decreased to almost 39 per cent.[15] Due to the absence of a common EU energy policy, gas reserves in EU member states affected by the shortages varied. Germany and France had relatively 'comfortable crisis cushions' of 75 and 45 days respectively, but Poland, in contrast, could only maintain the supply for about a fortnight.[16] The fact that supplies to countries in Eastern Europe were stopped during a very cold winter demonstrated the severe impact that the interruption of supply from Gazprom could have on the EU. Andris Piebalgs, EU Commissioner for Energy and Transport, stressed that the 'situation has shown how vulnerable the Union is to shortages of gas supply'.[17] He declared that the Ukrainian–Russian gas 'dispute [kept] us worried because 20 per cent of our gas supplies [went] through this route' and could thus undermine the EU's security of energy supply.[18]

The Russian–Ukrainian gas dispute prompted the European Commission to establish plans to launch a common EU external energy policy. The European Commission's paper entitled 'An External Policy to serve Europe's energy interests' warned that 'increasing dependence on imports from unstable regions and suppliers present a serious risk'.[19] In an indirect reference to the Russian–Ukrainian gas crisis it stated that 'some major producers and consumers have been using energy policy as a political lever'.[20] The paper criticised the EU's lack of a coherent and focused external EU energy policy, which meant that each EU member state was able to pursue its national energy interests by negotiating deals with third parties.[21] The establishment of a common external energy deal sought to prevent individual EU member states from concluding their own energy deals with Russia and thus create more coherence in the EU's external energy market. It was hoped this would prevent Gazprom from operating a divide and rule policy in price disputes with EU states in the future.

In a resolution, the European Parliament supported the Commission's proposal for a common external energy policy. It declared that 'protectionist support for national market leaders distorted the EU's energy [sector]'.[22] Given the recent disputes over gas prices between Russia and its neighbours, which 'ha[d] revealed the vulnerability of the supply and distribution of energy', the European Parliament urged the Commission and the Council to develop a mechanism for 'cases of conflict concerning the delivery and distribution of energy supply'.[23]

The push for a common EU energy policy provoked a war of words between the European Commission and Gazprom. On 21 April after a meeting with EU ambassadors, Gazprom's CEO Alexei Miller warned that limiting Gazprom's access to European markets 'will not lead to good results'.[24] He emphasised that the Russian gas monopoly was 'actively seeking' new markets in North America and China. Back then, Miller's thinly veiled threat caused concern in the European Commission. According to a European Commission spokesman, Miller's statement gave 'ground to our concerns on the growing foreign dependency of European energy supply and ... our supply routes'.[25] About a week after Miller announced Gazprom's intention to supply North America and China with gas rather than the EU, the European Commission President José Manuel Barroso sought to broker an ambitious agreement allowing European companies access to Russian gas fields and pipelines.[26] However, Russia's protectionism in energy policy constrained Barroso's ambitions. Since 2006, Miller's statement about exploring alternative markets such as China has become more concrete. In 2014 a Russian–Chinese gas deal was signed which opened up China as a market for Russian gas while meeting China's energy requirements.[27] As a result of the economic downturn in China in 2015, it remains to be seen whether this gas deal will be implemented.

The first EU–Russia summit in May 2006 following the Russian–Ukrainian gas dispute was overshadowed by the crisis caused by Gazprom's disruption of gas supplies. The EU High Representative for CFSP, Javier Solana, admitted that Russia had to 'ensure the reliability of supplies. We believe that it can be best achieved through transparency, openness to competitiveness and equal access to investment, markets and infrastructure.'[28] Apart from concerns over Russia's reliability as a supplier, a further source of confrontation in EU–Russian energy relations remained Russia's reluctance to ratify the ECT. The Commissioner for EU External Relations and the ENP, Dr Benita Ferrero-Waldner, pleaded with Russia to ratify the ECT, explaining that Russia's ratification would 'create a win-win energy relationship'.[29]

Putin refused to compromise on ratification of the ECT. At the press conference after the summit, he expressed his strong opposition to liberalisation of the Russian energy market. He declared that

> if our European partners [were] expecting us to let them into the holy of the holies of our economy, the energy sector, and we let them in ... we, for our part, [were] expecting reciprocal moves on the critical and most important directions for our economies.[30]

Deadlock at the Lahti summit

Due to the clash over both the security of energy supply and the liberalisation of the Russian energy market, the chairman of the Finnish European Council Presidency, Matti Vanhanen, sought to work towards safeguarding the EU's long-term provision of energy resources. Vanhanen attempted to maintain cordial relations with the Kremlin while continuing to encourage Russia to liberalise its gas market. He invited President Putin as a special guest to a meeting of EU heads of state and government in Lahti in Finland. The Finnish Presidency's stance towards Russia was controversial given that Vanhanen aimed to maintain cordial relations with Putin despite apparent lawlessness in Russian domestic affairs.

A tragic confirmation of the breakdown of the rule of law was the assassination of the Russian journalist Anna Politkovskaya on 7 October 2006. Politkovskaya, who worked for *Novaya Gazeta*, one of the last Russian newspapers critical of the Putin regime, became well known for her detailed reports on human rights violations in Chechnya and her account of Russia's increasing authoritarianism during Putin's second term as president.[31] A sign of authoritarianism was the Kremlin's violent dispersal in 2006 of demonstrations by those who opposed the Putin regime.[32]

The fact that the Lahti summit took place on 20 October, about a fortnight after Politkovskaya's assassination, made this encounter with Putin highly contentious. At the same time, this summit was unique in the regard that Putin attended a meeting at which all heads of state of governments of EU member states were present. Usually, at the biannual EU–Russia summits, only the head of state in charge of the rotating European Council Presidency met with Putin, Russian ministers and members of the European Commission as well as the High Representative for the EU CFSP.

118   *Towards confrontation: 2006–2008*

This summit in Lahti revealed internal fragmentation of the EU in its stance towards Russia. Unlike the Finnish European Council Presidency, the presidents of the European Parliament and the European Commission did not refrain from confronting Putin with questions concerning the curbing of democracy in Russia. Heads of state from some of the 'new' EU member states voiced their criticisms of Russia's drift into authoritarianism. As during the second Chechen War, internal division in the EU frustrated the establishment of a coherent policy towards Russia.

Heads of states of Poland, Hungary, Lithuania and Estonia adopted a confrontational stance towards Russia. The Estonian Prime Minister Andrus Ansip urged the EU to take a 'strong' position regarding human rights at the summit, stressing the need to 'find a good balance between values and economic interests'.[33] In an obvious reference to some common practices in EU–Russia relations, Ansip stated that it was 'totally wrong to pay attention only to interests'.[34] This confrontational line encouraged the Russian deputy foreign minister and envoy to the EU, Vladimir Chizhov, to raise Russia's perception of human rights violations in Europe. In an attempt to blame the EU for not respecting human rights, Chizhov warned that 'President Putin will be dissatisfied if European leaders in Finland want to read him a lecture about human rights, at a time when ethnic Russians in Estonia and Latvia have the status of non-citizens'.[35]

Division was evident between the European Commission and the Parliament on the one hand, and the European Council Presidency on the other. European Commission President Barroso sought to use the summit in Lahti as an opportunity for a 'frank discussion' with Putin about Politkovskaya's murder. He added that the investigation of this crime was a 'question of credibility for the Russian government'.[36] In contrast to Barroso, deliberations on Politkovskaya's assassination were not a priority on the summit agenda for Council Presidency chairman Vanhanen. He sought to use the summit as an opportunity to work towards the establishment of a more coherent stance on energy policy. He declared that Putin's presence in Lahti would 'result in a more united EU, creating a positive spirit of cooperation where many expressed a will to put an end to the internal controversy about energy policy'.[37] Vanhanen added that this summit would put 'positive pressure on European leaders to find a common position'.[38] Unlike Vanhanen, the European Parliament President Josep Borrell used the summit to raise EU concerns about human rights in Russia. He declared that the investigation of Politkovskaya's murder was a 'test for human rights and freedom of expression in Russia'.[39] Borrell acknowledged that Russia's deteriorating human rights record created tensions for the EU between the fulfilment of its strategic interests on the one hand, and its attempt to urge Russia to safeguard democracy and human rights on the other hand. Seeking to maintain the EU's aura as an actor whose foreign policy reflects the maintenance of democracy and human rights, he warned that 'Europe would lose its credibility if it began to trade human rights against energy'.[40] This statement reflected previous condemnation by human rights activists who accused the EU of maintaining a 'business as usual' approach with Russia, namely the prioritisation of energy policy over respect for human rights, while Russia's military operation in Chechnya was still ongoing.[41]

The tense tone of the meeting was exacerbated when Putin deflected Borrell's criticisms by accusing the EU of corruption. Challenged by Borrell, who asked questions about corruption in Russia, Putin countered by reminding Borrell, who is of Spanish origin, of recent cases of alleged corruption in Spain where mayors had been imprisoned.[42] In an attempt to strike back, Putin reminded the European heads of state and government of cases of corruption in other European countries by asking rhetorically whether the word 'mafia' was not Italian.[43] According to the scholar Thomas Ambrosio, Putin's rhetoric reflected the use of the *tu quoque* ('you also' in Latin) concept to defend Russia against criticism from democratic states as it drifted into authoritarianism during the Putin presidency. Ambrosio described the concept *tu quoque* as a

> legal defence in which the accused does not defend him/herself on the basis of fact or law, but rather points the finger at the actions of their accuser, claiming that they … have committed the same offence and therefore have no right to accuse another.[44]

Another major source of confrontation at the Lahti summit was Vanhanen's attempt to encourage Putin to ratify the ECT, which was reciprocated by the Kremlin's intransigence. The Kremlin emphasised three public justifications for its inflexibility. First, Putin was opposed to the commitments Russia had to make when ratifying the ECT without knowing what Russia would obtain in return.[45] That was the reason why he requested either clarification of the principles of the ECT or a re-draft of the document.[46] Second, the Kremlin was reluctant to ratify the ECT because of the Russian government's intention to increase state control in its energy market, a strategy which ran counter to the ECT provisions. Putin stressed that

> we intend to retain state control over the gas transport system and over Gazprom. We will not split Gazprom up. And the European Commission should not have any illusions. In the gas sector, they will have to deal with the state.[47]

Third, Russia's opposition towards the ECT was exacerbated by its reluctance to adjust the Russian price for gas to the world market price. The Russian deputy foreign minister and permanent envoy to the EU, Vladimir Chizhov, stated that the EU's demand to bring Russian prices for gas into line with world prices would need to be accomplished gradually in order not to harm the Russian economy.[48] No less critical towards the ECT than Chizhov was the Russian presidential aide Sergey Yastrzhembsky, who criticised 'certain provisions in the documents [as] discriminatory for Russia, [stressing that Russia] would not work towards its own detriment'.[49]

120 *Towards confrontation: 2006–2008*

The Finnish European Council Presidency's attempt to rescue EU–Russia relations at the Lahti summit failed. Vanhanen's assertion at the press conference that this summit had 'provided [the EU] with an opportunity to demonstrate to [Putin] that [it was] united' was a distorted reflection of reality.[50] Even prior to the Lahti summit, frictions in EU relations with Russia became evident. 'New' EU member states adopted a critical stance towards Moscow and urged the EU to address human rights at its summits with Russia. There was also disparity among EU institutions regarding the continuation of the EU relations with Russia. While the presidents of both the Parliament and the Commission expressed their criticism of human rights issues in Russia, Vanhanen attempted to engage Russia in a constructive discussion on energy policy. The EU's internal divisions in its relations with Russia remained a factor which undermined its capacity to determine a clear and assertive foreign policy towards Russia. This was still an issue for EU–Russia relations after the war in Georgia, which is the focus of Chapter 6. Internal friction in the EU was equally significant in hampering the development of a principled EU reaction to Russian aggression towards Ukraine from November 2013. The effect of this on EU reactions to the Ukraine crisis is examined in Chapter 7.

Deadlock over renewal of the PCA

The clash over energy policy and human rights, which characterised the Lahti summit, also overshadowed the EU's and Russia's negotiations concerning the update of the PCA. Such partnerships intend to provide a suitable framework for political dialogue, to strengthen the countries' democracies, develop their economies, including fostering their transition to a market economy, and encourage trade and investment.[51] The EU–Russian PCA set out the guiding principles for their relationship, such as trade liberalisation, the harmonisation of standards and political dialogue in return for the continuation of reforms. It had entered into force in 1997 and was valid until 1 December 2007 when it would be automatically renewed unless one of the contracting parties was not content with the agreement in its current form and sought to review it. Some EU figures used the expiry of the PCA as an opportunity to make its renewal conditional upon improvement of Russia's human rights record and liberalisation of its energy policy. This controversy within the EU was exacerbated by clashes between 'new' EU member states and Russia, further aggravating EU–Russia relations. Referring to these clashes, the Russian deputy foreign minister and ambassador to the EU, Chizhov, stated that 'the EU has never been easy to deal with for anyone. Things have gotten worse since the expansion, especially when it comes to Russia. Some of the new member countries have brought ghosts of the past into the EU.'[52]

The terms of the PCA became more contentious due to the normative divergence between the EU and Russia. The PCA contained moral obligations in terms of 'common values' as a basis for the partnership. According to article two, 'respect for democratic principles and human rights ... underpins the internal and external policies of the Parties and constitutes an essential element of partnership and of this agreement'.[53] According to Hiski Haukkala, the PCA's aim was to increase 'Russia's basic compatibility with European practices through the harmonisation of its norms and values along European models'.[54] Haukkala's claim concerning the PCA's normative dimension was validated when certain EU officials urged against renewal because of increasing evidence that Russia was not subscribing to the allegedly commonly accepted values set out in the agreement. A proponent of this approach was Graham Watson, leader of the European Parliament's Alliance of Liberals and Democrats in Europe, who made PCA renewal conditional upon Russia applying the rule of law. Watson called on the EU not to sign a renewed PCA with Russia until 'freedom, transparency and the rule of law [were] established and the legal certainty for investors, which follow[ed] from them'.[55] He added that the discussion concerning the PCA update was a 'unique opportunity for the [EU] to have a serious dialogue with Russia about human rights'.[56] Despite Watson's call to maintain a firm line towards Russia, the EU was unable to maintain a firm position in negotiating the basis for its future relations with Russia because of diverging views within the EU over renewal of the PCA.

The requirement that all EU member states had to agree and sign the PCA before the agreement could enter into force was an obstacle to updating it.[57] The unanimity requirement became an even more severe stumbling block for the EU following its eastern enlargement. This expansion had resulted in divergence in the representation of political interests between 'new' and 'old' member states and thus complicated the EU's decision making. Poland's Europe Minister Witold Sobkow lamented that in contrast to the 'new' member states, the 'larger, "old" member states were able to defend their interests'.[58] He declared that it was 'difficult to be understood in the EU. There [was] still this kind of division – EU 15 and EU 10'.[59] In an obvious reference to Poland's veto of the launch of negotiations on the PCA, he stated that 'if the countries in the EU 15 defend their national interests it is OK, but if we do, we are just "blocking"'.[60] The tensions within the EU concerning its ability to establish a coherent foreign policy since its expansion provoked a fierce debate. This was affirmed by Lithuania's Deputy Foreign Minister Zygimantas Pavilionis who stated that it 'was a litmus case to see if the EU was effective in defending each member's interest'.[61]

The Finnish European Council Presidency made strenuous efforts to prevent the Polish government from vetoing the launch of talks on the PCA due to a Polish–Russian dispute over meat exports to Russia. Four days before the EU–Russia summit where negotiations on the PCA were due to resume, Vanhanen, the chairman of the Presidency, stressed in his meeting with the Polish Premier Jaroslaw Kaczynski that several EU member states hoped that Poland would soften its stance 'in the name of solidarity' because they considered it 'very important for the negotiations with Russia [on the PCA] to start'.[62] In an attempt to solve the dispute as quickly as possible, he assured the Polish

122 *Towards confrontation: 2006–2008*

government of the EU's support on the matter of meat exports. Food inspectors from the European Commission were investigating the conditions in meat processing plants in Poland after Russia had accused Warsaw of having used false sanitary documents to import poor quality meat to Russia. As a result, Russia had imposed an import ban on Polish meat.[63] After the European Commission expressed its support, Andrey Krawcyz, the under-secretary of state and foreign policy adviser to Polish President Lech Kaczynski, announced that the EU–Russia summit would take place after all. He added that 'we hope it is a victory for us'.[64]

The summit was overshadowed by the Polish–Russian trade dispute. The Polish government reiterated that it would veto the negotiations on the PCA due to its dispute with Russia, which had been a source of conflict since 2005.[65] EU and Russian leaders focused solely on the impact of the Polish veto on EU–Russian relations and failed to address the human rights issue posed by the death by poisoning of Alexander Litvinenko, a former KGB agent, the day before the summit. Litvinenko had become an anti-Putin dissident and had begun investigating the death of Politkovskaya. On his deathbed, Litvinenko stated that Putin was responsible for his poisoning.[66] Vanhanen, who chaired the Finnish European Council Presidency, was unsure whether or not to raise the Litvinenko case at the EU–Russia summit and stated that 'we do [not] actually know very much about it'.[67] A similar statement was given by the EU official who was asked on behalf of the Danish European Council Presidency to draft a statement regarding the hostage crisis in Beslan in 2004. The official acknowledged the difficulty of this task, given that the Presidency was not fully aware of the developments and circumstances of the Beslan tragedy.[68] Both Vanhanen's reference to the Litvinenko case and the statement on the Beslan tragedy from the Danish European Council Presidency demonstrate the impact of EU–Russian relations in that the EU's official response in such cases can be hampered by a lack of or delay in the receipt of sufficient information from the Russian authorities. Language barriers could be responsible for the lack of information but is also likely that Russia's interest in maintaining its autonomy in domestic politics is also a factor.

At the summit press conference, the European Commission and the European Council Presidency were divided over the Polish–Russian dispute. Following Putin's criticism of the fact that the Polish government was linking this 'entirely technical issue, [the Polish–Russian quarrel over meat imports] with the overall status of Russian–EU relations', Vanhanen also dismissed the Polish–Russian dispute as an 'absolutely technical, not political' one.[69] Barroso, on the other hand, opposed Vanhanen's stance. He denounced Russia's ban on Polish meat imports as 'disproportionate'.[70] At the summit, he had urged Putin to lift the ban because the European Commission's investigations of Polish meat producing factories had provided evidence that Russia's concerns about the lack of quality of the meat were unfounded.[71]

Putin regarded the EU's internal divisions as the root cause of the problems over the PCA's renewal. He declared that the EU 'had not yet developed its position' on the PCA and added that

Russia was prepared to launch these talks. Delay [would] not affect in a negative way the entire set of relations between the EU and Russia. We extend the document on an annual basis, so there will be no legal gap in our relations. We will be patient, wait for an agreed position by the EU and finally we will hope we can all contribute to achieving this.[72]

Asserting that the Commission played a significant role in EU foreign policy, Putin stressed that 'when there [is] a common position in the EU, then [the EU and Russia] ... talk in a single voice'.[73] He stated, 'certainly where the European Commission has not yet received a mandate of course it is more difficult for us – we have to resolve the issue with each ... EU member'.[74] Putin's statement implied that he perceived the European Commission to be significant in steering the direction of EU foreign policy towards Russia. The EU's lack of a common stance was further exacerbated by the Russian political elite's conduct of negotiations with individual EU member states in some issue areas such as energy policy.

When journalists at the press conference were much more confrontational than EU leaders and grilled Putin on Litvinenko's poisoning and Politkovskaya's assassination, Putin applied the *tu quoque* rhetoric again and accused Europe of hypocrisy. He stated that 'we should not forget that such crimes do not only happen in Russia. In other European countries there are well-known political murders that have not yet been resolved. This is our common problem.'[75] Given that the summit took place about a month after Politkovskaya's assassination, Putin's allusion to political murders in other European countries was controversial. In a deliberate attempt to shift the focus to problems which, according to Putin, pose threats to Europe's internal security, he continued:

let's look at what is happening with the mafia in several EU countries which, not in an isolated incident but systematically, destroys representatives of law-enforcement agencies, judges, prosecutors, investigators, journalists and political figures. It takes decades to catch these mafiosi in European countries.[76]

The German European Council Presidency

Unlike the Finnish European Council Presidency, its German successor made human rights a centrepiece of its agenda. On 17 January 2007, in a speech given by the German chancellor Angela Merkel at the beginning of the Presidency, she stressed that Berlin could not ignore issues like the 'freedom of the press [and] civil liberties' in EU–Russia relations.[77] The fact that Merkel's stance towards Russia was more critical exacerbated EU–Russian confrontation during the German Presidency.

Merkel's attitude towards Russia was exemplified by the fact that she made PCA renewal conditional upon the inclusion of an article which would bind Russia to warn the EU about potential interruptions in energy supply.[78] When she proposed this idea to Putin, he was unwilling to agree to this commitment.[79]

124 *Towards confrontation: 2006–2008*

Putin launched a counter attack.[80] He accused the EU of promoting policies which would create dividing lines and thus failed to respect Russian interests. He stated that 'bloc mentalities [should not] prevail in European politics, nor should ... new dividing lines appear on our continent or unilateral projects to be implemented to the detriment of the interests and security of our neighbours'.[81]

Putin asserted that the update and renewal of the PCA was undermined by internal problems in the EU in adopting a unified position on renewal. He stated that 'we understand all the difficulties of our partners in developing one position'.[82] Putin's warning that 'any pause in the dialogue is always going to be counterproductive' was a reversal of his stance on the PCA negotiations following the Lahti summit, when at the press conference, he denied that a delay in the talks would have negative repercussions for Russia's relations with the EU.[83] Opposed to both associate membership and accession to the EU, for Putin the PCA seemed to be the only way to develop EU–Russia relations. He emphasised that in the 'foreseeable future, Russia had no intention of either joining the EU or establishing any form of institutional association with it'.[84] Putin's repeated disavowment of integration with the EU had been emphasised in the RMTS which stated that 'Russia should retain its freedom to determine and implement its domestic and foreign policies, its status and advantages of a Euro-Asian state, ... independence of its position and activities at international organizations'.[85] The fact that Putin reiterated this line at this point in the PCA negotiations indicated his intention to safeguard Russia's autonomy in its external relations.

The Russian government's intention to maintain its autonomy became a source of conflict in its relations with the EU. Referring to Putin's statement that Russia neither intended to become closely integrated with the EU nor to join it, Peter Mandelson, European Commissioner for Trade, argued that this 'picture which [the EU] would call Russian isolationism [could] only lead Russia in the wrong direction'.[86] Russia's shift in the 'wrong direction' was exacerbated by the considerable discrepancy between the EU's and Russia's understanding of values. According to Mandelson, 'some in Russia' were not convinced that the rule of law was decisive for Russia's long-term political and economic development. He stated that it was the EU's obligation to explain to Russian politicians their 'commitment to a relationship based on mutual interdependence, guaranteed for both sides by predictable rules'.[87]

Mandelson pleaded for the development of a unitary policy towards Russia. He emphasised that the EU needed 'a clear, single Russia policy based on our common interest, not multiple Russia policies based on mistrusts of the past'.[88] Mandelson condemned the EU's lack of a common policy towards Russia as 'frankly alarming' because

> no other country reveals our differences as does Russia. This was a failure of Europe as a whole, not any Member State in particular. But it does our interests no good. And by feeding misunderstanding about the nature and condition of the EU, our divisions lead to disappointment and disillusion in Russia, which does not serve Russia's interests either.[89]

Such an assessment of the state of EU–Russia relations would have been unthinkable in 1999 when Russia and the EU were united in their mutual interest to work together to resolve the Kosovo War. The EU's internal fragmentation, Russia's drift into increasing authoritarianism and the partners' divergence about the significance of values in their relationship contributed to a crisis. According to Mandelson, the relationship incorporated a 'level of misunderstanding or even mistrust we have not seen since the end of the Cold War'.[90] Mandelson's perception of EU–Russia relations was in strong contrast to the relationship in 1999 when mistrust informed Russia's relations with the US and NATO, which were facing the most severe crisis since the end of the Cold War, while EU–Russia relations were blooming.[91]

The repercussions of the lack of a unified EU foreign policy with Moscow increased tensions between Russia, the EU and some of its 'new' member states. An Estonian-Russian stand-off was caused by the relocation of the Monument to the Liberators of Tallinn. For Estonians, the monument symbolised Soviet repression, whereas for Estonian Russians it represented the heroism of the struggle against Hitler.[92] To prevent further escalation, the Estonian Prime Minister Anders Ansip moved the monument, a bronze statue of a soldier. This resulted in violent protests between Estonian nationalists and pro-Soviet demonstrators.[93] The crisis between Estonia and Russia became evident when Russian diplomats did not participate in Ansip's ceremony to mark the moving of the statue on Victory Day.[94] The severity of the crisis was reflected in the Russian Foreign Ministry's warning of 'most serious consequences for relations between Estonia and Russia'.[95] Meanwhile the Estonian embassy in Moscow was blocked by the state-sponsored Russian youth movement *Nashi* [Ours] for a week.[96] As a sign of provocation they placed speakers in front of the embassy which played military music from the Stalin era.[97] When the situation deteriorated, Estonia's Foreign Minister Urmas Paet requested support from the EU. He issued a dramatic declaration which stated that 'the EU was under attack, as Russia attacked Estonia'.[98] Urging the EU to be as 'vigorous as possible', he called on the EU to postpone the negotiations on the PCA with Russia.[99]

The stand-off escalated when the EU rallied behind Estonia. Solana, the High Representative of the EU CFSP, and the European Commission called on the Russian authorities to 'honour relations with Estonia'.[100] Frank-Walter Steinmeier, the German Minister for Foreign Affairs acting on behalf of the European Council Presidency, mediated a compromise to end the crisis.[101] The fact that the German European Council Presidency played a significant role in resolving the crisis in Russian–Estonian relations demonstrated that a crisis in one of the EU's 'new' member states with Russia had become a matter of EU policy instead of remaining an issue of domestic politics for this member state.

EU support of Estonia demonstrated that the accession of former Soviet satellite states had transformed EU foreign policy towards Russia. This was the second time in EU–Russia relations since 1999 that bilateral conflicts between EU member states and Russia occurred. Concerns were raised in Russian policy-making circles that EU support to member states in bilateral disputes with Russia

126   *Towards confrontation: 2006–2008*

might damage public opinion of Russia in the EU. Russian presidential aide Sergey Yastrzhembsky raised his concerns about Tallinn's attempt to ally with the EU, stressing that the Kremlin was

> trying to ensure that the EU hears us and understands the in-depth reasons for our concern at the Estonian authorities' actions, which fit in the trend to glorify Nazism. Above all, they are gradually pushing European countries towards a global revision of WWII results.... We do not want the so-called EU neophytes, people who oftentimes have an exaggerated ego and deeply rooted historic complexes, to instigate a U-turn in Europe's public opinion.[102]

Yet another layer of tension

The quarrels over energy policy and the deadlock over PCA extension between January 2006 and May 2007 coincided with clashes over human rights. The EU–Russia summit in Samara on 18 May 2007 highlighted a range of confrontations in the relationship.

A 'Dissenters March' staged by the opposition Other Russia coalition coincided with and overshadowed the summit in Samara. The fact that Other Russia had chosen to demonstrate in Samara testified to the enduring importance of the EU's normative objections to the Russian opposition. Having failed to ban the march with the use of strong arms, the Russian authorities placed protestors under house arrest, sent them to jail and detained journalists who were intending to interview some participants in the protest.[103] Chancellor Angela Merkel, who held the German European Council Presidency, condemned the Russian authorities' use of violence against the protestors.[104] Seeking to ensure this issue would not undermine the EU–Russia summit, the mayor of Samara, Viktor Tarkhov, gave the 'dissenters' permission to stage the protest on 18 May.[105]

The Samara summit was dominated by bilateral disputes between new member states and Russia. Frictions between Russia and Estonia, Poland and Lithuania obstructed progress on the ambitious agenda of the summit, which included collaboration on energy policy, cooperation in the common neighbourhood and PCA renewal.[106] The EU and Russia's failure to adopt a new PCA was triggered by their inability to resolve the Polish–Russian dispute over meat imports.[107] The attempt to renew the agreement was further undermined when Lithuania also vetoed PCA negotiations because Transneft, the Russian oil pipeline operator, decided to shut a pipeline delivering Russian oil to the Baltic States.[108]

Before the summit, Barroso had expressed solidarity with these three new member states. He explained the EU position on Russia's clashes with Poland, Lithuania and Estonia and stressed that 'a difficulty for a member state [was] a difficulty for all of us' because the EU was 'based on the principle of solidarity'.[109] He declared that a 'Polish problem is a European problem; a Lithuanian problem is a European problem as well'.[110] As a consequence of these continuing bilateral disputes with Russia, a new PCA was not negotiated. However,

Towards confrontation: 2006–2008 127

since the PCA was about to expire on 1 December 2007 and Russia had not been willing to lift the import ban on Polish meat (in fact it only declared the ban void on 19 December 2007), the agreement was extended for a year.[111]

EU solidarity with its new member states provoked obvious frustration in the Kremlin. Speaking on the day of the summit, Putin mockingly expressed satisfaction that after a year during which the Polish government would not talk to Russia, 'it is good that now chancellor Merkel is speaking on behalf of Poland'.[112] According to Russia's Deputy Foreign Minister and permanent representative to the EU, Chizhov, EU solidarity was likely to result in further conflicts in its relations with Russia. Referring to the EU's mediation efforts in the Estonian-Russian clash over the bronze soldier in Tallinn, Chizhov stated that

> we have seen that intra-EU solidarity is more important than elementary objectivity. This [cannot] help but put one on guard. After all, if later, on other issues, this kind of solidarity is going to dominate, then, knowing the characteristics of the policy of some of the EU's new member-nations, Russia and the European Union may run into problems.[113]

The following EU–Russia summit in Mafra on 26 October faced deadlock. Two days prior to the summit, the Commissioner for EU External Relations and the ENP, Dr Benita Ferrero-Waldner, echoed the German European Council Presidency's outspokenly critical stance towards Russian human rights abuses. She declared that 'concerns about human rights issues, such as the limitations on press freedom, attacks on journalists, pressure on NGOs and the situation in the North Caucasus' should be raised at the summit.[114] She emphasised that it would be an important opportunity to 'assess the state of our relationship. While several issues [would] not be solved ... we [would] lay the ground for future work at this moment of transition in Moscow', which was a reference to the parliamentary and presidential elections taking place in Russia in March 2008. According to Ferrero-Waldner, the elections would be an 'important test [for the] implementation of democratic principles and human rights commitments'.[115]

In addition to concerns about human rights and democratisation, EU dependence on Russia as its major supplier of energy remained a factor in the instability of the relationship. The EU's concerns intensified to the extent that it developed plans to diversify its energy supply by bypassing Russia as a supplier. The Nabucco pipeline, seeking to bring Caspian gas to Europe through Turkey and the Balkans, was one of the EU's new plans to diversify the source of its energy and its access to it.[116] Even though the quantities of gas this pipeline would be able to transport would not be significant, it demonstrated to the Kremlin that Europe aimed to avoid overdependence. Russia's ambassador to the EU, Chizhov, rebutted EU concerns about Russia's reliability as an energy supplier for Europe, stating that 'we do [not] mix energy and economic problems with political ones'.[117]

The plans for the establishment of the Nabucco pipeline were profoundly flawed. The European Commission had difficulties concluding agreements with

128 *Towards confrontation: 2006–2008*

countries which would deliver the gas. This was a major issue affecting the feasibility of the Nabucco pipeline.[118] According to the European Commissioner for Energy Policy, Piebalgs, it was initially expected that the Nabucco pipeline would carry gas from Azerbaijan, Iran, Iraq and Egypt, but later on the possibility of obtaining gas from Kazakhstan and Turkmenistan was taken into consideration.[119] Seeking to resolve the issue of suppliers for the Nabucco pipeline, in April 2008, the Commissioner for EU External Relations and the ENP negotiated a gas deal with Turkmenistan, to supply a fraction of gas for the Nabucco pipeline.[120] In 2008, Turkmenistan possessed 1.6 per cent of global gas reserves and thus had the second highest reserves after Russia.[121]

Conclusion

This chapter examined the underlying causes for the clash in EU–Russia relations from January 2006 until the end of Putin's second term as president. It argued that the EU's internal fragmentation, the increasing gap between the values the EU sought to promote in its relations with Moscow and Russia's political reality, as well as bilateral disputes between Russia and Poland, Lithuania and Estonia contributed to the confrontation.

The EU's internal fragmentation was demonstrated by the opposing positions on Russia taken by the European Commission and the Finnish European Council Presidency. At the Lahti summit, European Commission President Barroso, Commissioner for EU External Relations Ferrero-Waldner and Mandelson, the European Commissioner for Trade Policy, were outspoken in their criticism of Russia's drift into authoritarianism, human rights abuses and the Kremlin's politicisation of energy policy. In contrast, the chairman of the European Council Presidency, Finnish Prime Minister Vanhanen, prioritised the discussion of energy policy.

This confrontation in EU–Russia relations was exacerbated by the increasing normative divergence between the partners. Whereas the EU sought to establish 'common values' which would form the basis of the partnership, the Russian political elite aspired to remain autonomous. This drive to autonomy was reflected in the Kremlin's energy and foreign policies. Regarding the Kremlin's external relations, Putin declared that Russia was neither willing to establish associate membership with the EU nor to become a member state. As a result, the EU was not in a position to encourage Russia to implement political and economic reforms as the price of a future in an integrated Europe. The strategic partnership between the EU and Russia rested on shaky ground as a result of the failure to agree a shared set of values as a basis for EU–Russia relations.

The Kremlin was no less intransigent when it came to any measures which might jeopardise its autonomy in the energy market. Putin emphasised that Russia would not de-monopolise its gas market and instead increased state control in the energy sector. As the EU had sought to encourage the liberalisation of Russia's gas market in an attempt to secure the EU's energy supply by making Russia ratify the ECT, a severe clash over energy policy unfolded after

Towards confrontation: 2006–2008   129

Gazprom's interruption of supply to Ukraine in January 2006. This disruption increased EU concerns about safeguarding its energy supply and resulted in the plan to build the Nabucco pipeline. The EU's attempt to circumvent Russia as a supplier was another indication of the shift from cooperation to confrontation in EU–Russia relations.

Previously, cooperation in energy policy had been perceived as one of the hallmarks of the 'strategic partnership' between the EU and Russia. In 2000, European policy makers muted their condemnation of Russian human rights abuses in Chechnya in view of the prospect of cordial relations with Russia's newly elected president and the lure of the EU–Russian Energy Dialogue, the first contract for energy cooperation with Russia in anticipation of the EU's biggest enlargement in its history. As a consequence, the EU sacrificed its role as a promoter of fundamental values in its relations with Russia.

There were two reasons for the problems in resolving EU–Russian clashes over energy policy and human rights. First, the EU and Russia's understanding of both human rights issues and their approach to energy policy was fundamentally different. The partners did not manage to overcome their differences regarding these two issues. Second, the partners did not have time to discuss ways to minimise their differences because diplomatic relations were overshadowed by the Georgian war, the impact of which is discussed in Chapter 6.

Notes

1 For other scholarly accounts on the confrontation in EU–Russia relations see: Averre (2007); Lukyanov (2008); Light (2008).
2 Lucas (2008), p. 213.
3 Neft Trader Weekly (2006).
4 Email interview with an expert in the Directorate General Energy in the European Commission. Interview conducted on 4 May 2011.
5 European Commission (2006).
6 International Energy Charter (nd); Oil and Gas Weekly. Russia and CIS. Russian officials diss energy charter treaty. 25 October 2006.
7 Antonova, Zubkov, and Sergeyev (2006).
8 Medvedev (nd).
9 Sakwa (2014), p. xv.
10 Lucas (2008), p. 65; Sakwa (2014), p. xv.
11 Kosachev (2005).
12 Agence France Presse (2006).
13 Ingram (2006).
14 Bilefsky and Dougherty (2006); Agence France Presse (2006).
15 Agence France Presse (2006).
16 Euronews (2006).
17 Borowiec and Sands (2006).
18 BBC News (2006a).
19 European Council (2006); Email interview with an expert in the Directorate General Energy in the European Commission. Interview conducted on 4 May 2011.
20 Email interview with an expert in the Directorate General Energy in the European Commission. Interview conducted on 4 May 2011.
21 Ibid.

130 *Towards confrontation: 2006–2008*

22 European Parliament (2006).
23 Ibid.
24 Milner (2006).
25 Ibid.
26 Watt (2006a).
27 Paton and Guo (2014).
28 BBC Monitoring Former Soviet Union – Political. Supplied by BBC Worldwide Monitoring. Europe pins high hopes on energy cooperation with Russia – EU official. 24 May 2006.
29 Page (2006).
30 BBC Monitoring Former Soviet Union – Political. Russian TV hails Sochi summit as success despite few disagreements. 26 May 2006.
31 Ackerman, Filkenstein and Glucksmann (2007), p. 53.
32 Horvath (2013), p. 182.
33 Bilefsky (2006b).
34 Ibid.
35 Dubnov (2006).
36 BBC News (2006b).
37 European Report (2006a).
38 Finnish European Council Presidency (2006a).
39 Brand (2006).
40 Ibid.
41 The shift from EU condemnation of the Chechen War to pragmatic relations with Russia was examined in Chapter 2.
42 Parker (2006).
43 Europolitique (2006); Watt (2006b).
44 Ambrosio (2008).
45 BBC Monitoring Former Soviet Union – Political. Supplied by BBC Worldwide Monitoring. Putin reassures EU leaders on energy security, migration. 25 May 2006.
46 Nikolayevna and Kashin (2006).
47 Fredholm quoted in Lucas (2008), p. 212.
48 Bilefsky (2006a).
49 Petrova (2006).
50 European Report (2006b).
51 European Commission (nd).
52 BBC Monitoring Europe – Political. Supplied by BBC Worldwide Monitoring. Finnish Prime Minister tries to mediate in dispute between Russia and Poland. 20 November 2006.
53 European Commission (1997).
54 Haukkala (2010), p. 87. For a detailed analysis of the negotiations of the first PCA see pp. 68–91.
55 European Report (2006b).
56 EUX.TV (2007a).
57 Haukkala (2010), p. 73.
58 Rettman (2006).
59 Ibid.
60 Ibid.
61 Dempsey (2006a).
62 BBC Monitoring Europe – Political. Supplied by BBC Worldwide Monitoring. Finnish Prime Minister tries to mediate in dispute between Russia and Poland. 20 November 2006.
63 Ibid.
64 Dempsey (2006a).
65 Bilefsky and Dempsey (2006); EurActiv (2007).

Towards confrontation: 2006–2008 131

66 Grierson (2015). See also BBC News (2016).
67 Dempsey (2006b).
68 The Beslan tragedy was discussed in Chapter 3 of this monograph.
69 Medetsky (2006).
70 Finnish European Council Presidency (2006b).
71 Ferrero-Waldner (2006).
72 Finnish European Council Presidency (2006b).
73 Ibid.
74 The Kremlin (2006).
75 Ibid.
76 Ibid.
77 Radio Free Europe (2007).
78 Ibid.
79 Kreimeier (2007).
80 Ibid.
81 Putin (2007), emphasis added. See also: BBC Monitoring Former Soviet Union – Political. Supplied by BBC Worldwide Monitoring. Source: President of the Russian Federation website, Moscow, in English. Russia wants stable, prosperous and united Europe. 25 March 2007.
82 Putin (2007), emphasis added.
83 Ibid.
84 Ibid. See also: BBC Monitoring Former Soviet Union – Political. Supplied by BBC Worldwide Monitoring. Source: President of the Russian Federation website, Moscow, in English. Russia wants stable, prosperous and united Europe. 25 March 2007.
85 The Delegation of the European Union to Russia (1999).
86 Mandelson (2007).
87 European Commission (2007).
88 Mandelson (2007).
89 European Commission (2007).
90 European Commission (2007).
91 For a detailed analysis of the emerging EU–Russian partnership during the Kosovo War, see Chapter 1.
92 Roth (2009), p. 13; Lucas (2008), p. 199.
93 Light (2008), p. 10.
94 Ibid.
95 Russian Federation Ministry of Foreign Affairs quoted in Roth (2009), p. 13.
96 Ibid; Korchmarek (2007).
97 Lucas (2008), p. 200.
98 Ibid.
99 Ibid.
100 Roth (2009), p. 14.
101 Ibid.
102 BBC Monitoring Former Soviet Union – Political. Supplied by BBC Worldwide Monitoring. Putin aide details 'friction' in EU–Russia relations. 17 May 2007.
103 BBC Monitoring Former Soviet Union – Political. Supplied by BBC Worldwide Monitoring. Russian authorities using intimidation to thwart EU summit march-paper. 16 May 2007.
104 Agence France Presse (2007a).
105 BBC Monitoring Former Soviet Union – Political. Supplied by BBC Worldwide Monitoring. Russian authorities using intimidation to thwart EU summit march-paper. 16 May 2007.
106 European External Action Service (2007). Emphasis added.
107 Council of the European Union (2007).

132 *Towards confrontation: 2006–2008*

108 Interfax (2007).
109 EUX.TV. Fruitless EU–Russia summit in Samara. Retrieved 21 January 2011 from: www.youtube.com/watch?v=F7g9hYqTC_A.
110 Ibid.
111 BBC Monitoring Europe – Political. Supplied by BBC Worldwide Monitoring. German chancellor stresses EU interest in partnership with Russia. 18 May 2007; EurActiv (2007).
112 Agence France Presse (2007b).
113 BBC Monitoring Former Soviet Union – Political. Supplied by BBC Worldwide Monitoring. Russia's EU envoy hopes summit will advance political, economic dialogue. 17 May 2007.
114 Ferrero-Waldner (2007).
115 Ibid.
116 The Nabucco pipeline would compete with Gazprom's South Stream pipeline, which would deliver Russian gas to Europe through the Balkans. In this sense, it would use the same route as the Nabucco pipeline. See: Lucas (2008), p. 230.
117 Vogel (2008).
118 Email interview with Lars Grønbjerg, former seconded national expert working at the Unit for Relations with Russia at the DG RELEX of the European Commission. Conducted on 6 October 2012.
119 O'Byrne (2007).
120 Giuli (2008), p. 6.
121 Giuli (2008), p. 2.

Bibliography

Ackerman, G., Filkenstein, S. and Glucksmann, A. (2007). *Hommage à Anna Politkovskaïa.* Paris: Buchet/Chastel.

Agence France Presse. (2006). Gaz russe: l'UE subit déjà les effets de l'arrêt des livraisons à l'Ukraine. 3 January 2006.

Agence France Presse. (2007a). German. Merkel und Putin liefern sich Schlagabtausch zu Menschenrechten. 18 May 2007.

Agence France Presse. (2007b). German. Eiszeit an der Wolga. 18 May 2007.

Ambrosio, T. (2008). Tu quoque: How the Kremlin redirects external criticism through rhetorical attacks. Retrieved 7 October 2012 from: www.wiscnetwork.org/ljubljana2008/papers/WISC_2008-69.pdf.

Antonova, G., Zubkov, K. and Sergeyev, M. (2006). Informal EU summit will discuss energy security and innovation policy. WPS Russian Media Monitoring Agency. 20 October 2006.

Averre, D. (2007). Sovereign Democracy and Russia's relations with the European Union. *Demokratizatsiya.* 15(2): 173–190.

BBC Monitoring Europe – Political. Supplied by BBC Worldwide Monitoring. Finnish Prime Minister tries to mediate in dispute between Russia and Poland. 20 November 2006.

BBC Monitoring Europe – Political. Supplied by BBC Worldwide Monitoring. German chancellor stresses EU interest in partnership with Russia. 18 May 2007.

BBC Monitoring Former Soviet Union – Political. Supplied by BBC Worldwide Monitoring. Europe pins high hopes on energy cooperation with Russia – EU official. 24 May 2006.

BBC Monitoring Former Soviet Union – Political. Supplied by BBC Worldwide Monitoring. Putin reassures EU leaders on energy security, migration. 25 May 2006.

Towards confrontation: 2006–2008   133

BBC Monitoring Former Soviet Union – Political. Russian TV hails Sochi summit as success despite few disagreements. 26 May 2006.

BBC Monitoring Former Soviet Union – Political. Supplied by BBC Worldwide Monitoring. Source: President of the Russian Federation website, Moscow, in English. Russia wants stable, prosperous and united Europe. 25 March 2007.

BBC Monitoring Former Soviet Union – Political. Supplied by BBC Worldwide Monitoring. Russian authorities using intimidation to thwart EU summit march-paper. 16 May 2007.

BBC Monitoring Former Soviet Union – Political. Supplied by BBC Worldwide Monitoring. Russia's EU envoy hopes summit will advance political, economic dialogue. 17 May 2007.

BBC Monitoring Former Soviet Union – Political. Supplied by BBC Worldwide Monitoring. Putin aide details 'friction' in EU–Russia relations. 17 May 2007.

BBC News. (2006a). Ukraine gas row hits EU supplies. 1 January 2006. Retrieved 31 January 2011 from: http://news.bbc.co.uk/2/hi/europe/4573572.stm

BBC News. (2006b). EU Relations. On Sunday 15 October 2006 Huw Edwards interviewed José Manuel Barroso. Retrieved 18 March 2011 from: http://news.bbc.co.uk/2/hi/programmes/sunday_am/6052808.stm

BBC News. (2016). Alexander Litvinenko: Profile of murdered Russian spy. 21 January 2016. Retrieved 22 January 2016 from: www.bbc.com/news/uk-19647226

Bilefsky, D. (2006a). Russia won't yield to the EU on energy; European demands for pact on supplies face stiff resistance. *International Herald Tribune.* 19 October 2006.

Bilefsky, D. (2006b). Putin rejects EU demands that Russia ratify energy charter. *International Herald Tribune.* 21 October 2006.

Bilefsky, D. and Dempsey, J. (2006). Meat ban threatens Russia's WTO entry. EU trade chief warns that some EU states could move to block Moscow's accession. *International Herald Tribune.* 25 November 2006.

Bilefsky, D. and Dougherty, C. (2006). As supplies drop, EU officials appeal to Moscow. *International Herald Tribune.* 3 January 2006.

Borowiec, A. and Sands, D.R. (2006). Gas price dispute worries Europeans; Russian clout as supplier of energy raises reliability fears. 4 January 2006.

Brand, C. (2006). European leaders push Russia on energy. Associated Press Online. 20 October 2006.

Council of the European Union. (2007). EU–Russia summit in Samara. Press conference. 18 May 2007.

Dempsey, J. (2006a). Russia targets more EU exports. All animal products from bloc to be banned, Moscow vows. *International Herald Tribune.* 23 November 2006.

Dempsey, J. (2006b). Before dying, ex-spy accused Putin; UK experts find toxic radioactive isotope in victim's body. *International Herald Tribune.* 25 November 2006.

Dubnov, A. (2006). Uyhin s Evropoi. *Vremya Novostei.* 23 October 2006.

EurActiv. (2007). Russia lifts embargo on Polish meat. 21 December 2007.

Euronews. (2006). Russia–Ukraine gas crisis felt throughout EU. 2 January 2006.

European Commission (nd). Summaries of EU legislation. Partnership and Cooperation Agreements (PCAs): Russia, Eastern Europe, the Southern Caucasus and Central Asia. Retrieved from: http://europa.eu/legislation_summaries/external_relations/relations_with_third_countries/eastern_europe_and_central_asia/r17002_en.htm.

European Commission. (1997). Agreement on partnership and cooperation establishing a partnership between the European Communities and their member states, of one part, and the Russian Federation, of the other part. Retrieved July 2012 from: www.trade.ec.europa.eu/doclib/dosc/2003/november/tradoc_114138.pdf.

134 *Towards confrontation: 2006–2008*

European Commission. (2006). Green Paper on a European Strategy for sustainable, competitive and secure energy. 8 March 2006. COM 0105 final. Retrieved 3 February 2011 from: http://eurlex.europa.eu/smartapi/cgi/sga_doc?smartapi!celexplus!prod!DocNumb er&lg=en&type_doc=COMfinal&an_doc=2006&nu_doc=105

European Commission. (2007). Peter Mandelson. EU Trade Commissioner. The EU and Russia: our joint political challenge. Conference in Bologna: 'The future relationship between Russia and the European Union: Which kind of opportunity for the Italian economy?' Bologna, Italy, 20 April 2007. Press release. Speech/07/242. Retrieved 21 January 2011 from: http://europa.eu/rapid/pressReleasesAction.do?reference= SPEECH/07/242

European Council. (2006). An external policy to serve Europe's energy interests. Paper from Commission/SG/HR for the European Council. S160/06. 15 June 2006. Retrieved 8 June 2011 from: www.consilium.europa.eu/uedocs/cms_data/docs/pressdata/en/reports/ 90082.pdf

European External Action Service. (2007). EU–Russia summit. Samara, 17–18 May 2007. Press release. Retrieved 3 February 2011 from: http://eeas.europa.eu/russia/ sum05_07/index_en.htm

European Parliament (2006). 23 March 2006. European Parliament Resolution on the Security of Energy Supply in the European Union. Retrieved 3 February 2011 from: www.europarl.europa.eu/sides/getDoc.do?objRefId=112190&language=EN

European Report. (2006a). Interview/Finnish PM: Vanhanen highlights EU support for new EU–Russia deal. TV Broadcast. 24 October 2006.

European Report. (2006b). Lahti European Union summit: presidency and MEPs divided on summit results. TV Broadcast. 27 October 2006.

Europolitique. (2006). Sommet de Lahti: le diner avec Poutine plus franc que prévue n'a rien réglé. 24 October 2006.

EUX.TV. (2007a). EU–Russia Relations. Towards a new partnership and cooperation agreement. March 2007. Programme produced for the European Parliament. Retrieved 21 January 2001 from: www.youtube.com/watch?v=kugarffHB7c&feature=channel

EUX.TV. (2007b). Fruitless EU–Russia summit in Samara. TV Broadcast. 28 May 2007. Retrieved 21 January 2001 from: www.youtube.com/watch?v=F7g9hYqTC_A.

Ferrero-Waldner, B. (2006). Statement on EU–Russia summit. European Parliament Plenary. 29 November 2006. Speech 06/758. Retrieved 3 February 2011 from: http:// europa.eu/rapid/pressReleasesAction.do?reference=SPEECH/06/758&format=HTML &aged=0&language=en&guiLanguage=en.

Ferrero-Waldner, B. (2007). EU–Russia: Preparations for the summit. 24 October 2007. Speech 7/653. Retrieved 03 February 2011 from: http://europa.eu/rapid/pressReleases-Action.do?reference=SPEECH/07/653&format=HTML&aged=0&language=en&gui Language=en

Finnish European Council Presidency. (2006a). official website. The presidency meets the press. In Helsinki: Prime Minister Matti Vanhanen. In Brussels: journalists from different countries. 18 October 2006. Retrieved 30 March 2011 from: www.eu2006.fi/ MEDIA-SERVICES/EN-GB/presidency-meets-press/index.htm.

Finnish European Council Presidency. (2006b). EU–Russia summit press conference. 24 November 2006. Retrieved 7 April 2011 from: www.eu2006.fi/MEDIA_SERVICES/ WEBCASTS/EN_GB/ARCHIVE_NOVEMBER/INDEX.HTM

Giuli, M. (2008). Nabucco Pipeline and the Turkmenistan Conundrum. *Caucasian Review of International Affairs*. 2(3): 1–9.

Towards confrontation: 2006–2008 135

Grierson, J. (2015). Alexander Litvinenko lawyer points finger at Putin as enquiry ends. 31 July 2015. Retrieved 13 November 2015 from: www.theguardian.com/world/2015/jul/31/alexander-litvinenko-inquiry-ends-lawyer-blames-vladimir-putin

Haukkala, H. (2010). *The EU–Russia Strategic Partnership. The limits of post-sovereignty in international relations.* Routledge.

Horvath, R. (2013). *Putin's Preventive Counter-revolution. Post-Soviet authoritarianism and the spectre of velvet revolution.* London and New York: Routledge.

Ingram, J. (2006). Ukraine crisis hits gas supply to Europe. *The Advertiser.* 3 January 2006.

Interfax. (2007). Central Europe. Lithuania supports Polish veto of EU–Russia negotiations – Lithuanian PM. 23 April 2007.

International Energy Charter. (nd). About the charter. Website. Retrieved 28 March 2011 from: www.encharter.org/index.php?id=7

Korchmarek, N. (2007). Nashi vzialis'za Tallinskuiu ulitsu. *Izvestia.* 7 June 2007.

Kosachev, K. (2005). From the Logic of 'Near Abroad' to the Community of Interests. *International Affairs* (Moscow). 51(3): 85–91.

Kreimeier, N. (2007). Merkel ruegt Putin fuer Energiekonflikt; Kanzlerin verlangt Regeln fuer Krisenkommunikation. *Financial Times* (Germany). 22 January 2007.

Light, M. (2008). Keynote Article: Russia and the EU: Strategic partners or strategic rivals. *Journal of Common Market Studies.* 46: 7–27.

Lucas, E. (2008). *The New Cold War. How the Kremlin menaces both Russia and the West.* London: Bloomsbury.

Lukyanov, F. (2008). Russia–EU: The partnership that went astray. *Europe–Asia Studies.* 60(6): 1107–1119.

Mandelson, P. (2007). Russia, its future and the World Trade Organisation. 27 March 2007. Moscow. Joint Event. Association of European Business (AEB) and the Russian Confederation of Business Industries (RSPP). Reference: Speech/07/192. Retrieved 21 January 2011 from: http://europa.eu/rapid/pressReleasesAction.do?reference=SPEECH/07/192&format=HTML&aged=1&language=EN&guiLanguage=en

Medetsky, A. (2006). Overflight feed cancelled but meat ban stays. *Moscow Times.* 27 November 2006.

Medvedev, D. (nd). CV of Dmitry Medvedev. Head of the Board of Trustees of Skolkovo Foundation, Russian Prime Minister. Retrieved from: www.sk.ru-RU/Model/Team/Popechsovet/Medvedev.aspx?sc_Lang=en.

Milner, M. (2006). Gazprom threatens Europe's gas supply. *Guardian.* 21 April 2006.

Neft Trader Weekly. (2006). European Union officials discuss Russia–Ukraine gas row. 6 January 2006.

Nikolayevna, A., and Kashin, B. (2006). Putin ne uslyshal ES. *Vedomosti.* 23 October 2006.

O'Byrne, D. (2007). Piebalgs backs Gazprom-ENI gas pipeline; says new link is no threat to Nabucco project. Platts Oilgram News. 27 June 2007.

Oil and Gas Weekly. (2006). Russia and CIS. Russian Officials diss energy charter treaty. 25 October 2006.

Page, J. (2006). Summit set for angry clash over energy. *The Times.* 25 May 2006.

Parker, G. (2006). Putin swats EU criticism aside as energy talks loom. *Financial Times.* 22 October 2006.

Paton, J. and Guo, A. (2014). Russia, China add to $400 Billion gas deal with accord. *Bloomberg.* Retrieved 21 January 2014 from:: www.bloomberg.com/news/articles/2014-11-10/russia-china-add-to-400-billion-gas-deal-with-accord

136 *Towards confrontation: 2006–2008*

Petrova, N. (2006). Otvet Evropeiskomu khory. *Gazeta*. 23 October 2006.

Putin, V. (2007). Russia is Europe's natural ally. *The Sunday Times*. 25 March 2007. Emphasis added. Retrieved 25 April 2011 from: www.timesonline.co.uk/tol/comment/columnists/guest_contributors/article1563806.ece

Radio Free Europe. (2007). German chancellor calls for reliable relations with Russia. 18 January 2007. Retrieved 28 January 2011 from: www.rferl.org/content/article/1143793.html

Rettman, A. (2006). Meat exports hang over Polish veto on EU–Russia treaty. EUobserver.com. 13 November 2006.

Roth, M. (2009). Bilateral disputes between EU member states and Russia. Centre for European Policy Studies (CEPS). Brussels. Working Document No. 319/August 2009. pp. 1–32. Retrieved 17 April 2016 from: http://aei.pitt.edu/11434/1/1900.pdf

Sakwa, R. (2014). *Putin and the Oligarch. The Khodorkovsky–Yukos affair*. London and New York: I.B.Tauris.

The Delegation of the European Union to Russia. (1999). The Russian Federation's Middle Term Strategy towards the EU (2000–2010). Retrieved 18 November 2009 from: www.delrus.ec.europa.eu/en/p_245.htm

The Kremlin. (2006). Joint Press Conference with the Prime Minister of Finland Matti Vanhanen, President of the European Commission Jose Manuel Barroso, Secretary-General of the EU Council and the EU High Representative for the Common Foreign and Security Policy Javier Solana, Prime Minister of Norway Jens Stoltenberg and Prime Minister of Iceland Geir Haarde following the Russia–EU meeting. President of Russia. Official Web Portal. 24 November 2006. Retrieved 6 May 2015 from: www.archive.kremlin.ru/eng/speeches/2006/11/24/2355_type92914type82915_114506.shtml.

Vogel, T. (2008). The EU seeks alternative fuel routed to Europe bypassing Russian-controlled gas pipelines. *European Voice*. 14–20 February 2008.

Watt, N. (2006a). Europe: Putin revives energy row with US but promises to help fight terrorism: Russian leader rejects blackmail accusations: President denies gas cut off to intimidate Europe. *Guardian*. 26 May 2006.

Watt, N. (2006b). Putin blames Georgia for Caucasus unrest. Tbilisi accused of moving towards bloodshed. Russian leader angry over criticism at summit with EU. *Guardian*. 21 October 2006.

6 The repercussions of EU diplomacy in Georgia

According to Moscow, its military invasion of Georgia in August 2008 was necessary to defend its citizens when military was mobilised in Abkhazia and South Ossetia, Georgia's breakaway regions. In contrast, the EU regarded Russia's intervention in Georgia as both illegitimate and disproportionate. As a result of these clashing views, it comes as no surprise that the Russian–Georgian War had negative repercussions for the development of EU–Russian diplomatic relations.

This chapter contends that even though the Russian–Georgian War had negative ramifications for EU–Russia relations, it did not culminate in an EU–Russian political crisis like that following the EU's intervention in the Orange Revolution in Ukraine. The different outcomes of the EU's diplomatic intervention in Kiev in 2004 and the European Council's involvement in the conflict in Tbilisi seem to be paradoxical at first sight. The main difference between the role the EU played in the resolution of the Ukrainian revolution and in the conflict between Moscow and Tbilisi was that in the latter case, the EU was mainly acting as a mediator between the conflicting parties. During the revolution in Ukraine, in contrast, the EU systematically and carefully planned the composition of a diplomatic mission to Kiev. The mere fact that the EU had interfered in Kiev and then managed to jeopardise the Kremlin's strategic interests with Ukraine resulted in Russian policy makers' hostility towards the EU's involvement in Ukrainian domestic politics. Hence, in Ukraine in 2004, the EU was a game changer in the Kremlin's foreign policy objectives with Kiev, which resulted in a political crisis between Brussels and Moscow.

Despite the absence of an EU–Russian political crisis over EU involvement in the resolution of the Russian–Georgian War, the war resulted in three negative repercussions for relations between Brussels and Moscow. First, the renewal of the EU–Russian PCA was postponed once again after previous attempts to renew this agreement since 2006 were overshadowed by clashes over both human rights and the security of energy supply. Second, after the Georgian war, the EU developed an integrative framework for enhancing political and economic integration with six former Soviet satellite states within the framework of the Eastern Partnership Initiative (EaP). The launch of this integrative project intensified EU–Russian rivalry over the post-Soviet space, which had begun to take

138 *Effects of EU diplomacy in Georgia*

its toll on the 'strategic partnership' after EU involvement in the resolution of the Orange Revolution. The Kremlin perceived the EU's integrative efforts in the post-Soviet space as jeopardising the Kremlin's sphere of influence over the region. Third, the European Council review of EU–Russia relations reflected the EU's disenchantment with its relations with Moscow in the aftermath of the Russian–Georgian War.

The road to Russian–Georgian confrontation

Even though the origins of the Russian–Georgian War remain contested, two factors are likely to have increased tensions.[1] According to Ronald D. Asmus, Deputy Assistant to the US Secretary of State, the acceptance of Kosovo's declaration of independence and the NATO summit in Bucharest 'had increased the pressure by taking steps that amounted to a creeping annexation of the two separatist [Georgian] enclaves', Abkhazia and South Ossetia.[2] Russia warned that a decision which recognised Kosovo's status 'would set a precedent which could encourage separatism in other parts of the world, including post-Soviet Eurasia'.[3] Asmus stated that Georgia was the 'perfect target for Russia's retaliation' following their acceptance of Kosovo's declaration of independence, because both the US and the EU regarded Moscow's warnings about the consequences of recognition for the Georgian breakaway regions as 'bluffs'. As a result, neither the US nor the EU hesitated to respect Kosovo's new status. Their assumption had been proven wrong and there was no contingency plan for the West's support of Georgia in place.[4] Five days after the declarations of independence of Abkhazia and South Ossetia, the Georgian president, Sakaashvili, stated that there were no similarities between Kosovo's status and that of Georgia's breakaway regions because the latter sought to gain independence from Moscow rather than from Tbilisi.[5] On March 6, less than three weeks after Kosovo's declaration of independence, Russia declared an embargo on the supply of arms to Abkhazia and South Ossetia dating from 1996 void, and provided Russian separatists in these Georgian secessionist regions with arms.[6] About a fortnight later, Putin confirmed this support in a letter to the leaders of the separatists in South Ossetia and Abkhazia.[7]

The NATO summit in Bucharest from April 2 to 4 was another factor accelerating the Russian–Georgian War.[8] The debate about eventual incorporation of Georgia and Ukraine into the NATO Membership Action Plan (MAP) was intended to prepare the way for the accession of potential future members to the alliance. In the end, these countries did not become part of MAP as a result of disagreements within NATO. Instead, it was merely decided that Ukraine and Georgia would become NATO members in the future.[9] According to Professor Richard Sakwa, France and Germany feared that granting Ukraine and Georgia MAP status would be perceived as a provocation by Russia.[10] Putin expressed his opposition to NATO enlargement when he warned the US Secretary of State, Condoleeza Rice, and the Secretary of Defense, Robert Gates, that Georgia's accession to NATO was a 'red line' because he considered the 'appearance of a military bloc' on Russia's frontiers as a 'direct threat to its security'.[11]

Effects of EU diplomacy in Georgia   139

The eventual outbreak of the Russian–Georgian War was a further setback in EU–Russian diplomatic relations. The last EU–Russia summit under President Putin's presidency in Mafra in October 2007 (before Medvedev became president in March 2008) was marked by tensions over human rights and limits on freedom of the press in Russia as well as EU concerns about security of energy supply.[12] The first summit under President Medvedev was perceived by both parties as a 'fresh start' in their relationship. After a period of confrontation between 2002 and 2007, the summit in Khanty Mansiisk on 27 June had a 'friendly atmosphere'.[13] According to a joint statement concerning the PCA updates, a renewed agreement 'will build on the international commitments which bind the EU and Russia. It will contain the appropriate institutional provisions to ensure the efficient functioning of the ... relationship'.[14] It remained unclear what an 'efficient functioning of the relationship' entailed in practice. The anticipated date for the negotiation of the agreement was 4 July.[15] The purpose was to come to an agreement which 'will provide a comprehensive framework of EU–Russia relations for the foreseeable future and help to develop the potential of our relationship'.[16]

At the summit, EU officials were determined to work towards the improvement of EU–Russia relations. This motivation reflected the need to escape the deadlock caused by clashes over human rights, energy policy and bilateral disputes between EU member states and Russia, which had prevented an earlier update of the EU–Russian PCA.[17] European Commission President Barroso considered the new PCA as 'provid[ing] a good opportunity to develop the potential of our strategic partnership'.[18] Dr Benita Ferrero-Waldner, Commissioner for EU External Relations and the ENP, reiterated Barroso's view while alluding to the promotion of EU values. This summit, she stated, 'will lay the foundations for a *constructive relationship with the new administration, defending our values* and promoting our growing mutual interest'.[19]

Ferrero-Waldner's and Barroso's ambitious plans regarding the development of relations were jeopardised by the breakout of the Russian–Georgian War in August 2008. The war resulted in the European Council's decision to postpone the PCA negotiations. Increasing friction over the post-Soviet space, in addition to the postponement of the PCA update, marked a gloomy period in EU–Russian diplomatic relations. Tensions between Russia and Georgia had been simmering since 2001 when the Kremlin blamed the Georgian government for having supported terrorists in Chechnya.[20] A year later, the Russian Defence Minister Sergei Ivanov emphasised that Georgia required Russia's support in the combat of terrorism: 'Georgia will never resolve this problem without Russia's participation, armed forces and special-operation troops'.[21] Several days after Ivanov's statement, the Pankisi Gorge, a valley in North East Georgia separating Chechnya from Russia, was bombed by what were supposedly Russian aircrafts. Georgia responded with the deployment of troops to the Pankisi Gorge. As a consequence, President Putin declared that

Today, no one can deny ... that Georgian territory has been chosen as a haven by those who were complicit in planning the terrorist attacks in the

140 *Effects of EU diplomacy in Georgia*

US a year ago [11 September 2001] and those who blew up houses in the Russian Federation [September 1999, in reference to several bombing attacks in different cities in Russia before Russian troops invaded Dagestan]. I ask the General Staff to submit proposals on the feasibility of delivering strikes on terrorists bases in the course of hot pursuit.[22]

As well as the Kremlin's assumption of a link between Georgia and a terrorism network, the Beslan hostage crisis on 4 September 2004 fanned Russia's more confrontational stance against Georgia. The FSB claimed that staff from a Georgian TV team was at the school where the hostages were held so quickly after the crisis that the Georgian government must have known about the tragedy. Russian media reported that one of the terrorists behind the attack was Georgian.[23]

The Georgian government, on the other hand, was equally suspicious of Russia. It felt provoked by Putin agreeing to Russia's exclusion from the Conventional Forces in Europe Treaty, which had been negotiated in the last years of the Cold War to significantly reduce military equipment. It was signed in November 1990 by the 16 NATO member states and the Warsaw Pact states.[24] Russia's refusal to sign the treaty was interpreted as an indication of Moscow's intention to initiate a military strike against Georgia.[25]

On 7 August 2008, the tensions between Russia and Georgia reached the point of no return. The exact details of the development of the hostilities remain contested.[26] From the Russian perspective, the Russian government reacted to an attack on South Ossetia by Georgia. This explanation was challenged by the West because Russia's argument that it intervened to protect Russian citizens was not considered credible. The argument that they were protecting Russian citizens was based on the grounds that 'Russian passports have been distributed to locals in the separatist regions, effectively creating Russia[n] ... citizens where there had been none'.[27] The distribution of passports was termed 'creeping annexation' by Houman Sadri and Nathan Burns.[28] Hence, it was vaguely claimed in the West that Russia intervened in Georgia 'for other strategic purposes'.[29]

The EU reaction to the crisis

France, as holder of the European Council Presidency, began to play a leading role in negotiating a ceasefire. This was the second time since the EU's carefully planned intervention in the revolution in Ukraine that the EU was involved in resolving a crisis in the post-Soviet space. However, the repercussions of French diplomacy did not result in a political crisis between Russia and the EU, unlike the case of the Orange Revolution.

The need for EU intervention became evident when the Georgian Foreign Ministry's initial attempts to negotiate a conflict resolution with Russia broke down very quickly. Despite President Medvedev's and Sakaashvili's discussion at the CIS summit about the details of 'changes in peace talks ... to de-escalate' the situation, the Georgian proposal on the format of the peacekeeping forces and conflict

Effects of EU diplomacy in Georgia 141

resolution, hand-delivered to Moscow after the president's discussion, failed. This proposal, which was not intended for public debate, was leaked in a Russian newspaper. According to the then acting Georgian Foreign Minister, Eka Tkeshelashvili, this 'meant that Russians were already killing' the proposal.[30] The Russian response to the proposal was a rejection of all of its elements, including the return of refugees. In the meantime Russian troops entered the country, which put the Georgian government under pressure to explain to its population why the presence of troops was necessary. Tbilisi gave Russia an ultimatum to withdraw the troops within four weeks and then to begin negotiations, a decision which was supported by the UK, France, Germany and the US. The Georgian government was asked by Georgia's Group of Friends to prepare a proposal for a change in the format of the negotiations.[31] According to Tkeshelashvili,

> we were told that at this time, Germany would put the political capital behind [the proposal] as well ... and with that the chances of implementation and potential success for the new negotiating process would have been higher. The idea was that because of the special relationship of Germany with Russia, Germany playing the leading role would have contributed to ... meaningful changes of the format of negotiations.[32]

Therefore, the German Foreign Minister Frank-Walter Steinmeier sought to resolve the dispute between Georgia and Abkhazia prior to the outbreak of the war.[33]

Initial steps towards conflict resolution in Georgia were taken by Steinmeier about three weeks before Russia invaded Georgia. His objective was to mediate between Georgia and Russia over Abkhazia. He flew to Moscow to discuss the development of the conflict in Georgia with his Russian counterpart Sergei Lavrov. According to Lavrov, who had previously criticised the German draft proposal as 'unrealistic' with regard to the return of refugees to Georgia, such a proposal was 'extremely helpful for looking for compromises and a way out of the crisis'.[34] Lavrov considered Steinmeier's proposal to be a 'step in the right direction' but stated that it was 'unrealistic' to seek to sign a peace agreement to avoid violence while signing another agreement concerning the 'return of refugees'.[35] According to Tkeshelashvili, who met with Steinmeier prior to his departure for Moscow,

> his plan was crashed [because] Russians said that the idea was to have negotiations in Berlin on 5 August. They said that they had vacation time and [thus] cannot come to negotiations. That was the signal that they were not getting behind an idea of a comfortable resolution in terms of a diplomatic way of solving the escalated situation. That meant that nothing was happening in a meaningful way in terms of negotiations.[36]

Moscow's strategic objectives regarding Abkhazia caused Russian–Georgian confrontation, as Tbilisi perceived Russia's advances towards Georgia's breakaway regions as gradual steps towards annexation. After having met with

142 *Effects of EU diplomacy in Georgia*

Abkhazia's president Sergei Bagapsh, Steinmeier acknowledged that 'both sides' positions are still very far from each other and we need to create the conditions for a dialogue'.[37] As a consequence, ten days after Steinmeier's efforts to create a peace plan were not reciprocated, the existing tensions between Russia and Georgia culminated in the Russian invasion of Georgia on 7 August.

No less challenged than Steinmeier in the attempt to find a breakthrough in negotiations was the French European Council Presidency. Several factors impeded the Presidency's reaction to the Russian–Georgian War. President Sarkozy had brought forward two demands to which the Russian government should adhere: a ceasefire by the time of his arrival in Tbilisi and Russian troops refraining from advancing to the Georgian capital.[38]

Finnish Foreign Minister Alexander Stubb, in his role as chairman of the OSCE presidency, and the French Minister for Foreign Affairs, Bernard Kouchner, got involved in the negotiations as well. They acted as 'high-level envoys of the EU, whose Special Representative for the South Caucasus Peter Semneby was already in Tbilisi'.[39] After a dinner with Georgia's President Saakashvili, Stubb and Kouchner agreed on a draft for a ceasefire with the Georgian Foreign Minister Eka Tkeshelashvili.[40] After obtaining Sakaashvili's signature to the draft, Stubb and Kouchner intended to submit the draft plan for a ceasefire to the Russian government. Mrs Tkeshelashvili acknowledged that this draft 'was not the perfect text, but [Kouchner and Stubb] had the mandate to talk on that text when in Moscow'.[41] According to the Chief of Cabinet and political adviser to the EU's Special Representative for the South Caucasus and the crisis in Georgia, the

> French European Council Presidency decided to take the lead and coordinate international efforts, which then led to the signing of the six point agreement on 12 August. This was a natural continuation of and based on the efforts of Kouchner and Stubb.[42]

Sarkozy intended to negotiate with his Russian counterpart Medvedev in Moscow on a peace deal, but Prime Minister Vladimir Putin was present as well. Tkeshelashvili argued that Putin's presence

> was the right decision for him to make because we all know that Lavrov is not the decision maker but he is a bit of a technician when it comes to the diplomatic way of delivering on something that has been decided.[43]

When the Kremlin's influential adviser Gleb Pavlovsky stated that the Kremlin had objections to a ceasefire and instead intended to invade Georgia and 'maybe [go] further than Tbilisi', the likelihood of negotiating a peace deal seemed close to zero.[44]

The initial attempts of Kouchner, Stubb and Saakashvili to draft a peace deal were undermined by both the EU's initial difficulties in coordinating a peace plan, and by Putin's stance towards Saakashvili. First, when negotiations with

Effects of EU diplomacy in Georgia 143

Sarkozy and Medvedev began, Kouchner realised that the proposal for a peace plan which he had agreed with Stubb had not been taken into account by the French government. Sarkozy's security adviser considered it to be a diplomatic fauxpas to present Medvedev with a proposal which had been discussed with Saakashvili rather than directly with Medvedev.[45] A second factor undermining the negotiation of a peace plan was Prime Minister Putin's unaccommodating stance towards Saakashvili. Putin vulgarly expressed his intention to overthrow the Georgian president: 'I want to hang Saakashvili by the balls'.[46] Presumably, one of the reasons for Putin's attitude towards Saakashvili was the Georgian president's intention to turn Georgia into an energy hub which would gain autonomy from Moscow by receiving resources from Azerbaijan instead.[47]

President Sarkozy sought to overcome the deadlock in peace negotiations by drafting a new proposal for a peace agreement which extended Kouchner's and Stubb's initial plan by two points.[48] The concluded ceasefire agreement contained the following six objectives: (1) it should refrain from the use of force; (2) hostilities should be stopped; (3) free access to humanitarian aid should be granted; (4) Georgian military forces should be withdrawn; (5) Russian military forces should go back to the positions which they held prior to the conflict and implement additional measures of security; (6) international mediations should begin on the establishment of peace and security in Abkhazia and South Ossetia.[49] These points were agreed on 12 August 2008 between President Sarkozy and his Russian counterpart before they were sent to the Georgian president two days later. This peace plan resulted in the ceasefire between Russia and Georgia. An additional document from 8 September led to the creation of a mediation forum for peace-building in Georgia which involved the EU, OSCE, the UN and the US, as well as Georgia and Russia.[50]

Even though the agreement of the peace plan was a success given the obstacles to the negotiation process, the plan contained three internal contradictions. First, it did not give deadlines by which each of its six points had to be implemented.[51] Second, when the peace plan was translated into Russian, it was not checked against the original French text which resulted in discrepancies between Russia and France regarding the adopted agreement.[52] When Sarkozy and Medvedev presented the peace deal during a press conference, the Russian president omitted the safeguarding of Georgia's independence and sovereignty, which were crucial criteria for Sarkozy.[53] Medvedev did not answer a question from a journalist about the reason why Georgia's territorial integrity was not included in the ceasefire agreement. Sarkozy, however, alluded to the limitations of the peace plan in his response:

> we can try to resolve all the issues now and end up achieving no result at all, or we can try to restore peace and attempt through dialogue to find a long-term solution and that is what we have tried to do.[54]

Third, while Medvedev and Sarkozy were giving a press conference, President Saakashvili realised that he had signed a draft of the peace plan containing

144 *Effects of EU diplomacy in Georgia*

a clause on the protection of Georgia's territorial integrity, which had been excluded in the final ceasefire agreement.[55] This omission was a concern for the Georgian government, but according to Sarkozy, this issue could not be discussed anymore. The final point in the agreement, the 'international debate on the future status of South Ossetia and Abkhazia', was very vaguely worded and thus remained a major bone of contention for the Georgian government.[56] About three weeks after adoption of the peace plan on 6 September, French Foreign Minister Kouchner acknowledged its limitations. He stated that 'of the six points, only two or let's say two and a half, perhaps three, have been implemented'.[57] The Russian government's non-compliance with the agreement was acknowledged by the Polish and Lithuanian presidents about three months after its adoption. They stated that Russian troops had not yet been withdrawn to 'pre-conflict positions'.[58]

The limitations of the peace plan were also reflected in a letter clarifying the agreement issued by Sarkozy in the context of the French European Council Presidency. According to Tkeshelashvili this

> letter clarified some of the aspects ... but still the text was so flawed itself that it needed some further clarification. At least you had one set of interpretations that could have been used for a formal interpretation of the treaty.[59]

Despite the peace agreement, relations between Russia and Georgia remained tense. On 26 August, Russia recognised both South Ossetia and Abkhazia as independent republics, which triggered Georgia's freezing of diplomatic relations with Russia.[60]

An emergency meeting of European foreign ministers seeking to find a common stance in the EU response towards the continuing conflict in Georgia reflected divergence in the EU position on its relations with Russia. French Foreign Minister Kouchner, who chaired this meeting, expressed the need for the presence of 'monitors ... controllers ... and facilitators' in Georgia.[61] Kouchner's proposition was not supported by his Polish counterpart Radislaw Sikorski, who stated that the presence of 'international forces would be more credible' than the deployment of European monitors. His view was reinforced by the Finnish Foreign Minister Alexander Stubb, possibly because Finland was chairholder of the OSCE presidency at the time.[62] Steinmeier, the German foreign minister, took a different stance from both Kouchner and Sikorski. According to Steinmeier, an urgent solution was required to the issue of the composition of a peacekeeping mission in Georgia and he thought it should be carried out by the EU. He stated that 'we should not have a long discussion on how to respond to the escalation of the last days. The EU must decide which role it plays in the future'.[63] The fact that it was launched two months after the ceasefire agreement made it 'so far the fastest deployment in the history of the EU'.[64] The European Union Monitoring Mission (EUMM) was a 'temporary mission ... established by the Council on ... 15 September 2008 as an autonomous civilian monitoring mission, under the [European Security and Defence Policy]'.[65]

Effects of EU diplomacy in Georgia 145

It aimed to achieve stability in Georgia in line with the ceasefire agreement. About 300 'unarmed European monitors' were deployed. They managed to enter the breakaway region South Ossetia, which was condemned by Russia.[66] According to the EUMM's Deputy Head of Mission, the EUMM's staff 'are eyes and ear, the delegation is the wallet and the EU Special Representative to the Caucasus is the brain'.[67] However both the fact that the EUMM's border guards were not allowed to enter Georgia's secessionist regions and their pure observer status raises some doubts about the efficacy of the mission.[68] The potential limitations of the EUMM were acknowledged by its Deputy Head of Mission, who stated that 'we are patrolling, we are reporting, but we cannot act'.[69]

The EU's stance regarding the future development of relations with Russia was wavering. EU foreign ministers were also divided on the development of future diplomatic relations with Russia. The Estonian Foreign Minister, Urmas Paet, drew conclusions from Russia's war in Georgia for the development of EU–Russia relations. He asserted 'I am sure what happened in Georgia will change the level of relations between the EU and Russia.... I would say it is impossible that everything continues as if nothing had happened'.[70] In a similar vein, the Finnish Foreign Minister Alexander Stubb explained that 'I am sure we will have a very tough discussion about EU–Russia relations in the future'.[71] Unlike Stubb and Paet, their German counterpart adopted a much more conciliatory stance. According to Steinmeier, 'channels to Moscow and Tbilisi [should be kept] open', instead of making 'strong statements and one-sided condemnations'.[72]

In a speech delivered at the French Institute for International Relations between 6 and 8 October 2008, in front of heads of states of EU members and the Russian president, Sarkozy acknowledged that Medvedev and he could 'not hide' the fact that 'Russia and the EU had been through a very challenging period'.[73] Sarkozy concluded from this that 'Russia and the EU should not separate themselves from each other, provoking fears of divisions in Europe, even reviving fears of a "new Cold War" [which] would be a historic error'.[74] Sarkozy alluded to one of the major issues in EU–Russia relations, namely emerging tensions over the shared neighbourhood when he stated that 'Russia's near abroad is ... as well that of the EU. It is in fact our "common neighbourhood". It should be a field of cooperation, not a terrain of rivalries.'[75] The aspirations of some of the countries of the post-Soviet space such as Ukraine to achieve closer ties with the EU resulted in serious confrontation between the EU and Russia which is examined in Chapter 7.

Sarkozy's words concerning EU observation of its relations with Russia carried weight. A month after his speech, an extraordinary session of the European Council discussed the prospects for EU relations with Russia. The pressure on Russia had increased before this summit. A group of EU member states sought to pursue a more hard-line policy towards Russia after its military invasion of Georgia. Poland, the Baltic States and the UK were in favour of implementing sanctions against Russia, but some EU member states sought to continue a conciliatory position.[76] Before the summit, President Medvedev

146 *Effects of EU diplomacy in Georgia*

stressed that 'we are not partisans of sanctions [but] if necessary we can adopt them'.[77] President Sarkozy sought to ease tensions over the imposition of sanctions. He expressed his opposition towards restrictive measures when he stated 'let us not launch a Cold War ... demonstrate strength ... sanctions, counter-sanctions; this does not serve anybody'.[78] Sarkozy's hesitance regarding the implementation of restrictive measures against Russia reflected his attempt to avoid burning bridges with Moscow.

The conclusion of this extraordinary Council session demonstrated the EU's wavering stance towards Russia.[79] This conclusion denounced Russia's 'unilateral decision' regarding the recognition of Abkhazia and Ossetia as 'unacceptable', urged all parties to implement the six point plan negotiated by President Sarkozy, and stated that 'with the crisis in Georgia, relations between the EU and Russia have reached a crossroads'.[80] The reference to 'crossroads' suggests that the EU had to choose the direction of its future policy towards Russia, but does not give any indication of how it should proceed in its relations with Russia. The statement that there

> is no desirable alternative to a strong relationship, based on cooperation, trust and dialogue, respect for the rule of law and [the EU's] call on Russia to join with us in making this fundamental choice in favour of mutual interest, understanding and cooperation

reveals the EU's wish for future cooperation and progress in the relationship.[81] The seriousness of the repercussions of the Russian–Georgian War was reflected in an indirect warning in the Council conclusion:

> We are convinced that it is in Russia's interest not to isolate itself from Europe. We expect Russia to behave in a responsible manner, honouring all its commitments. The Union will remain vigilant; the European Council requests the Council, with the Commission, to conduct a careful, in-depth examination of the ... various aspects of EU–Russia relations; this evaluation must begin now and continue in the run-up to the forthcoming summit.[82]

The Kremlin's response to the extraordinary European Council summit oscillated between optimism and indifference regarding the development of EU–Russia relations in the aftermath of the Georgian war. A day after the Council, Prime Minister Putin expressed his appreciation of the EU summit. He stated 'Thank God, common sense has prevailed'.[83] He added that it was good that Russia did not see 'any extreme conclusions or propositions and that is very good.... There has been a lot of emotion during the summit's preparation. There have been very tough proposals, I would even say extremist.'[84] President Medvedev regretted that the EU 'had not entirely understood' the Russian government's motives for its invasion of Georgia, but he declared that this 'was sad, but not fatal, because everything changes in the world'.[85] After the summit

Medvedev stated 'despite certain divisions among the EU states ... a reasonable, realistic point of view prevailed because some of the states were calling for some mythical sanctions'.[86]

The review of EU–Russia relations, which was published on 5 November, nine days prior to the next summit, was informed by developments in the Georgian crisis. According to the review, the Russian–Georgia War

> cast a serious shadow over the EU Russia partnership: the violation of Georgia's territorial integrity with the use of force, and Russia's unilateral recognition of Abkhazia and South Ossetia remain unacceptable, while the principles of foreign policy recently articulated including the resurgence of spheres of influence, is a cause for concern.[87]

The statement continued in a constructive tone, which was the basis for the European Commission's stance towards Russia for several consecutive years.[88] It stated that

> the EU can approach its relations with Russia with a certain confidence. Economically Russia needs the EU. The EU is an important market for the export of its raw materials, notably energy.... The recent financial crisis has underlined how acutely Russia needs to modernise and diversify its economy. The EU is the natural partner for this process and is the main source of its foreign investments, Russia desires engagement with the EU for its own purposes, for example to achieve visa abolition.[89]

According to Lars Grønbjerg, the 'confidence' which was referred to in the review, 'was very much alive in the Commission in the following years, i.e. in connection with the two annual summits'.[90]

The fact that this was the second time that such a review had been published indicated the increasing and deepening strain on the former 'strategic partnership'. The goal of the review was to reconsider EU–Russia relations, in particular by 'making a sober assessment of where the EU's *own* interests now lie. The scope for pursuing and widening these interests has been established in the recently-agreed mandate to open negotiations on a successor agreement to the [PCA].'[91] The emphasis on representing the EU's interests in contrast to those of Russia was reflected in the use of italics in this statement. The need for this had already been reflected in a review of EU–Russia relations published by the European Commission four years earlier.[92] The backdrop to the 2004 review was concern in the European Parliament, the Commission and among several EU officials about the lack of unity in the EU position on relations with Russia following Berlusconi's advocacy of Putin, in direct contradiction to the EU stance on Chechnya, during Italy's European Council Presidency.[93] The European Commission instigated the 2004 review with the intention of creating a 'more coherent and effective approach to relations with Russia reflecting the views of the EU 25'[94] because of the EU's failure to 'send clear, unambiguous messages

148 *Effects of EU diplomacy in Georgia*

to Russia'.[95] The publication of a new review four years later reflected the lack of the progress with addressing the issues outlined in the 2004 review.

The 2008 review reflected the negative repercussions of the Russian–Georgian War on EU–Russia relations. First, it mentioned the Council's decision of 1 September to postpone meetings concerning PCA renewal. However, the negotiations were resumed on 10 November.[96] This did not come as a surprise considering that the European Council conclusions of 1 September stated that there was no desirable alternative to a strong relationship based on cooperation, trust and dialogue.[97] Second, it addressed the need to establish a 'genuine energy partnership based on the principles of the Energy Charter Treaty and notably transparency, reciprocity and non-discrimination', positions on Kosovo and the shared neighbourhood as well as human rights as the main issues of concern in EU–Russia relations.[98] Third, the review referred to EU–Russian cooperation over the shared neighbourhood. It stated that Russia was a 'key geopolitical actor, whose constructive involvement in international affairs is a necessary precondition for an effective international community'.[99] The expression 'constructive involvement' clearly alluded to the EU's expectations on Russia to cooperate both with the EU and other partners instead of implementing a unilateral foreign policy in the former Soviet space. The document also mentioned

> the will and the capacity of the *EU to act as one*, combining both Community instruments as well as those of CFSP/ESDP [European Security and Defence Policy] [as] key requirements for successfully engaging Russia in conflict resolution in their common neighbourhood.[100]

This was a reference to the EU's internal division in its relations with Russia, which was demonstrated in its inability to adopt a unified and constructive position on the implementation of sanctions following Russia's recognition of South Ossetia and Abkhazia as independent regions. Internal divisions had also characterised EU–Russia relations during the second Chechen War, as discussed in Chapter 2. Further evidence of friction within the EU on its stance towards Russia on the imposition of restrictive measures are examined in Chapter 7, which assesses the strategic partners' confrontation over Ukraine since 2013.

The relevance of the review was emphasised when its core messages were reiterated prior to the EU–Russia summit in February 2008. President Barroso's comments reflected the concern expressed in the review regarding the representation of EU interests. According to Barroso, the newly agreed PCA would be the 'best possibility for the EU to *advance its interests while defending its values*'.[101] The importance of Barroso's statement and the review was highlighted by the Commissioner for External Relations and the Neighbourhood Policy, Dr Ferrero-Waldner, who stated that the review had received overwhelming backing from EU member states:

> Our team will approach the forthcoming negotiations with Russia with a clear-eyed sense of where the EU sees its own advantage. At the same time,

Effects of EU diplomacy in Georgia 149

the EU stands firm on the positions we have adopted since the Georgia crisis: the Geneva process [the process of 'ending hostilities on the ground' after the ceasefire agreement] must advance, and the principle of territorial integrity must be upheld.[102]

About two weeks after the summit, fundamental problems in EU–Russia relations were reflected in a report on the implementation of the European Energy Strategy which referred to the discrepancy over values, mistrust, and the worsening of the relationship since the outbreak of the Russian–Georgian War. The report stated that 'our relations with Russia have deteriorated over the conflict with Georgia. The EU expects Russia to honour its commitments in a way that will restore the necessary confidence.'[103] Second, it mentioned that 'our partnership should be based on respect for common values, notably human rights, democracy, and rule of law, and market economic principles'.[104] Despite the ambition to uphold common values in the relationship, previous developments in EU–Russia relations, such as confrontations over human rights violations in Chechnya, demonstrated that Russia was not willing to listen to lectures given by Brussels. At the same time, division in the EU into two camps – proponents of cordial relations with Russia and those opposed to them – contributed to the limited effectiveness of criticism of Russian human rights violations in Chechnya. Third, according to the report, the relationship should also be based on common interests and objectives.[105] Fourth, the report referred to energy policy, stating that greater diversification of energy sources, of 'transit routes ... of respect for the rule of law and investment in source countries' was important.[106] The issues about common interests and energy policy were also reflected in the 2004 review of EU–Russia relations, which was examined in Chapter 3.

According to a Chief of Cabinet and political adviser to the EU Special Representative to the South Caucasus and the crisis in Georgia, President Sarkozy's efforts in Tbilisi

were well perceived and even welcomed in Moscow. Given the fact that other international actors already present on the ground through their respective field missions, had been strongly criticised by Moscow ... the EU, through the French Presidency could act as a new and 'more' fresh player.[107]

This positive reading of Sarkozy's negotiations of a peace agreement was presumably also influenced by the fact that his efforts were not regarded by Russian policy makers as EU diplomacy. Instead, 'the majority of the press reports and remarks by Russian officials at that time were mentioning ... Sarkozy solely as the "French President", without recalling that he was acting as President of the EU'.[108] This perception was presumably also due to the absence of Javier Solana, High Representative of the EU CFSP, during Sarkozy's negotiations in Moscow and Tbilisi. Solana discussed the crisis with both the Georgian president and the Foreign Minister.[109]

150   *Effects of EU diplomacy in Georgia*

The initial steps taken by the EU in seeking to resolve the emerging tensions between Russia and Georgia were less well coordinated and streamlined in comparison to EU diplomacy after the Orange Revolution. Both the composition and timing – at the point in time when negotiations between the Kuchma regime and the opposition were losing momentum – of the EU diplomatic mission to Kiev were well considered. The Polish and Lithuanian presidents spearheading the EU diplomatic mission had crucial local contacts in the Kuchma administration, which facilitated the negotiations. However, the price for the EU's successful resolution of the revolution was the first major political crisis in EU–Russia relations since 1999. The Kremlin reacted with hostility to the EU intervention, criticising EU influence in the post-Soviet space as a 'Balticisation process, which had turned the EU into an aggressive organisation'.[110] This perception demonstrated two aspects of EU–Russia relations. On the one hand, the tense relationship between 'new' EU member states and Russia can instigate major confrontation between Brussels and Moscow. On the other hand, the Kremlin's condemnation reflected the capacity of the EU thwart Moscow's plans for future relations with Ukraine.

In contrast to EU diplomacy in Ukraine in 2004, the EU's initial response to emerging tensions in the Southern Caucasus in 2008 was less well coordinated. The chairman of the OSCE presidency, together with the German and the French foreign ministers, made initial attempts to prevent conflict emerging between Russia and Georgia. The lack of success of their efforts reflected their lack of coordination and isolation, as well as opposition from the leading political groups in Abkhazia. When President Sarkozy took the lead in negotiations as chairman of the French European Council Presidency, the Kremlin took a less hostile view. Sarkozy's diplomacy was perceived by Russia as the effort of a head of state rather than a key official mediating on behalf of the EU. Sarkozy was operating in a less confrontational context compared with the situation in Ukraine in 2004, where the Kremlin had invested its efforts in bringing about a regime change which would have advanced Russia's geopolitical ambitions, including the launch of the SES. EU interference however thwarted achievement of these objectives.[111] In contrast, at the time of the Russian–Georgian War in 2008, there was less at stake for Russia in terms of the likelihood of Georgia being drawn towards the EU. However, the increasing tensions between the EU and Russia regarding Georgia and five other post-Soviet states was perceived by the Kremlin as a danger to its geopolitical control over those countries.

The aftermath of the Georgian War: the EU's efforts to increase integration with its Eastern neighbours

The Russian–Georgian War accelerated EU plans to enhance integration with Azerbaijan, Armenia, Belarus, Georgia, Ukraine and Moldova within the framework of the EaP. EU support for some future EaP member states, including Georgia, began in 1997 with the delivery of humanitarian aid, before 'rehabilitation programmes in the two conflict zones' became part of EU policy towards

Effects of EU diplomacy in Georgia 151

Georgia.[112] Despite this political engagement, the European Commission acknowledged that the conflicts over Abkhazia and South Ossetia were major 'impediments to development in Georgia'.[113] In 2002, the European Council had also expressed the intention of enhancing integration with Ukraine, Moldova and Belarus.[114] Six years later, the European Council proposed the development of the EaP to the European Commission.[115] The Extraordinary European Council Summit of 1 September 2008, which was dominated by the Georgian crisis, 'asked for this [draft of the EaP] to be accelerated, responding to the need for a clearer signal of EU commitment following the conflict in Georgia and its broader repercussions'.[116]

The overall objective of the EaP was to contribute to 'stability, better governance, economic development', and to provide 'additional, tangible support for their democratic and market-oriented reforms [as well as] the consolidation of their ... territorial integrity'.[117] These objectives should be fulfilled both with the strong involvement of EU member states as well as with the commitment by EaP members'.[118] Simultaneously, closer economic integration with the EU could be achieved through free trade areas and visa liberalisation within the framework of Association Agreements (AA). However, accession to the EU was not the EaP's ultimate objective.[119] In 2010, the EU began negotiations with Georgia regarding the development of its AA.

The absence of EU membership prospects for EaP members resulted in several challenges for EU foreign policy. On the one hand, it created a division between those member states within the EaP framework (insiders) and member states outside the framework. This reality contradicted the European Commission's initial statement that the ENP, the overall policy framework to which the EaP belonged, would not create dividing lines in Europe.[120] On the other hand, the launch of the EaP inflamed EU–Russian tensions. EU involvement in the Ukraine crisis in 2004 highlighted the Kremlin's strong opposition to EU interference in the post-Soviet space. Needless to say, EU efforts to increase integration with its six eastern neighbours resulted in increasing friction concerning the 'shared neighbourhood'. According to Erwan Lannon and Peter van Elsuwege, EU condemnation of Russia's war in Georgia and the launch of integration efforts with former Soviet satellite states to the east of the EU could well be perceived as 'an initiative directed against Russia'.[121] At the same time, the EaP had repercussions for its members' bilateral relations with Russia.[122] Despite the EU repeatedly emphasising that the EaP did not come at the expense of relations with Russia, this newly established policy was perceived with ambiguity. According to the former president of Moldova Vladimir Voronin, the EaP was an 'encirclement of Russia' and an attempt to found 'another CIS under EU control'.[123]

The negative repercussions of the EaP for the 'strategic partnership' were reflected at the EU–Russia summit a fortnight after its launch. President Medvedev expressed his opposition to EU integration with its Eastern partners. He declared that 'we do not want the [EaP] to turn into a partnership against Russia'.[124] He added that 'any partnership was better than a conflict, but it is

152 *Effects of EU diplomacy in Georgia*

confusing for us that some states attempt to use the structure [of the EaP] as a partnership against Russia'.[125] There had already been signs of EU–Russian rivalry over the post-Soviet space eight years prior to the launch of the EaP in the RMTS of 2000 which emphasised the Russian government's opposition to any involvement by external actors in the post-Soviet space. According to this strategy

> Russia, as a world power situated on two continents, should retain its freedom to determine and implement its domestic and foreign policies, its status and advantages of a Eurasian state and the largest country of the Commonwealth of Independent States.[126]

This strategy directly referred to Russia's strong opposition to integrative projects between third-party states and countries in the former Soviet space. According to the strategy, 'Russia will counteract any attempt at hampering economic integration in the CIS. In particular, it opposes "special relations" of the EU with individual countries of the CIS to the detriment of Russia's interests'.[127] The RMTS included a warning that Russia would counteract 'special relations with individual countries in the CIS to the detriment of Russia's interests' which gave a foretaste of the Kremlin's reaction to the EU's AA with Ukraine. The culmination of EU and Russian rivalry over integration with the Ukraine is discussed in Chapter 7.

An article published in August 2008 before the launch of the EaP by Fyodor Lukyanov, Deputy Chairman of the Council of Foreign and Defence policy, reflects the emerging EU–Russian competition over the post-Soviet space. Lukyanov refers to negative characteristics of EU foreign policy towards Russia. He stated that 'none of [the descriptions] fully correspond to reality, yet each defines certain features of the EU [and] different stages in Russia's perception of Europe in the last 15 years'.[128] He perceived the EU as an

> expansionist empire of a new type that is slowly yet steadily driving Russia out of its traditional sphere of influence, seeking to create a buffer zone on Russia's border and impose its own views, norms and rules on the Russians.[129]

This negative perception of the EU's increasing influence in the former Soviet space is comparable to Russian policy makers' perceptions of the EU's interference in the Orange Revolution. He stated that 'Moscow began to speak of the European Union as an "empire of a new type", as an unfriendly force that seeks to extend its influences into Russia's zone of interests'.[130] At the same time, Lukyanov referred to the 'enormous attraction of the EU model, which has created a great demand for countries to join or associate themselves with it'.[131] His statement acknowledged that EU values were appealing to several countries in the post-Soviet space, which undermined the Kremlin's ability to maintain its grip over this region.

Effects of EU diplomacy in Georgia 153

'Business as usual' in the aftermath of the Russian–Georgian War

About a year and a half after the launch of the review of EU–Russia relations, a new framework called the Partnership for Modernisation (PfM) was suddenly launched. The partnership was controversial due both to the context in which it emerged and the discrepancy between EU and Russian views of the notion of modernisation. The aim of the PfM was three-fold: to 'modernize Russia; to adapt the whole complex of Russian–European relations in accordance with the experience of the existing dialogue instrument of "sectoral" Russia–EU cooperation'; and to establish guidelines for EU–Russian cooperation aimed at addressing common challenges.[132]

The overall purpose of the PfM was difficult to discern. It did not address the negative issues raised in the review of EU–Russia relations in an attempt to ameliorate the relationship. According to a former official who worked for the Russia unit in the Directorate General for EU External Relations at the European Commission, the review of EU–Russia relations published in November 2008, was 'the basis for the PfM'.[133] European Council President Herman van Rompuy envisaged that the PfM would 'promote reform (ensure a functioning legal system as well as working towards the reduction of corruption, and give renewed momentum to our relationship)'.[134] Van Rompuy's reference to 'renewed momentum' alluded to difficulties in making the relationship between the partners more constructive.

The PfM's relationship to the institutionalised framework for EU–Russian relations was not clear. It was meant to 'update the relations between Moscow and Brussels' while a renewed PCA was in the making.[135] This suggests that the PfM provided interim guidelines for the continuation of EU–Russia relations prior to adoption of an updated PCA. The PfM 'built on the current achievements of the Four Common Spaces [economy; freedom, security and justice; external security; research, education and culture]' while neither replacing the road maps, nor becoming a 'reason for creation of new structural additions'.[136] It was intended to 'equip the partners with a more liberal and yet specific, down-to-earth programme'.[137] This description is very vague and does not provide the slightest indication of how the partnership would operate in practice. This vagueness is due to the absence of definitions of the notions 'liberal' and 'down-to-earth' in this particular context. Because of the way in which it relates to earlier frameworks for cooperation between the EU and Russia, a former official in the European Commission Directorate General for External Relations characterised the PfM as a 'new heading or frame [rather] than a new departure for our cooperation'.[138] He considered that the PfM was not a reset for EU–Russia relations, but rather 'business as usual under a new heading. The parties … [neither came] up with a new concrete idea [nor] with new institutions'.[139]

Due to difficulties in clearly determining the added value that the PfM brought to the existing frameworks for the conduct of EU–Russia relations, Paul Flenley questioned whether the PfM would 'suffer from the same problems as the earlier attempts at partnership'.[140] Seeking to address this question, Flenley pointed out that the PCA attempted to 'promote norms' in EU–Russia relations,

154 *Effects of EU diplomacy in Georgia*

but referred to the practical limitations of this approach. The EU's enlargement policy facilitates the export of its norms and values to new member states because they have to comply with the EU's acquis communautaire. Flenley pointed out that because EU membership was 'not on offer or even desired' by Russia, the extension of EU norms in the course of its relations with Russia was problematic.[141] Flenley emphasised the challenges faced by the EU in attempting to export its values to Russia by arguing that within the PCA, there was already an asymmetry of interests and priorities. For the EU, the key concerns were the promotion of democracy, human rights and the opening of markets. However, Russia was 'more concerned with the restoration of state power'.[142] Flenley suggested that due to its emphasis on technical rather than normative cooperation, the PfM addressed the main shortcomings of the PCA.

Differences in the definition of modernisation between the EU and Russia challenged the PfM. For Russia, modernisation entailed a focus on 'economic and technological aspects ... as well as respect to its culture and traditions'.[143] For the EU, in contrast, 'respect for democracy, human rights and the rule of law' were the hallmarks of modernisation.[144] According to Romanova and Pavlova, these diverging understandings of modernisation 'obstructed the EU's message to Russia', making the achievement of 'convergence' between the partners 'difficult'.[145] Two years prior to the launch of the PfM, the Kremlin defined its understanding of modernisation in the Russian Foreign Policy Concept in the following way:

> transformation of its economy along innovation lines, enhancement of living standards ... ensuring competitiveness of the country in a globalizing world [as well as] strengthening of the foundations of the constitutional system, rule of law and democratic institutions, realization of human rights and freedoms.[146]

In November 2011 Vladimir Chizhov, the Russian ambassador to the EU, linked the concept of modernisation directly to EU–Russia relations. In an 'ever-deepening and widening globalization', he said:

> no country ... can succeed in social, economic, scientific and technological developments alone.... Under these circumstances, the optimal alternative is to move forward jointly through mutually reinforcing diversity. And in the case of the Russian Federation and the European Union there is every reason and opportunity to achieve this.[147]

It has to be acknowledged that Chizhov's vision of pooling the EU and Russia's resources towards further development is very sensible, but 'reinforcing diversity' proved tremendously difficult to do. His proposal to 'move forward jointly' was rendered impossible by the dynamics of the EU–Russian relationship at the Vilnius summit in November 2013. The development by the EU and Russia of competing rather than mutually agreed integrative strategies with countries in the post-Soviet space became the major source of confrontation in contemporary EU–Russia relations.

Effects of EU diplomacy in Georgia   155

Convergence was not only challenging because of the different perceptions of the notion of modernisation held by the EU and Russia, but also because in addition to the overarching PfM, the 24 member states of the EU also concluded their own partnerships with Russia. According to Romanova and Pavlova, in the process of establishing PfMs with the 24 EU members, Russia 'sought to fine-tune its definition of modernization with whatever European partner had to add, hence keeping the interpretation of modernization tied to its social context'.[148] As a consequence, it was difficult to develop a single strategy for the modernisation of EU–Russia relations.

Officials working in the Russia unit in the Directorate General for EU External Relations in the European Commission were preparing the documents for President Barroso prior to the EU–Russia summit in Stockholm where the PfM was launched. Barroso's intention was to present President Medvedev and the press at the summit with 'something new and interesting. He was apparently bored with the long list of trivial and sour subjects which he knew all too well.'[149] An official involved in preparing the documents for the summit recalled that 'under this pressure I stole [the idea for the PfM] from [German foreign minister] Steinmeier. In the unit we had discussed the German–Russian PfM during the year, so it did not come quite out of the blue'.[150] There is no reference to the PfM by the Committee of Permanent Representatives in any European Council internal documents prior to the Stockholm summit which suggests that the idea of launching the PfM at the summit was spontaneous.[151]

The PfM failed to improve EU–Russia relations in the wake of acrimonious clashes over human rights and energy policy, despite the shift from a normative to a more pragmatic approach. The EU's intention to uphold its values in relations with Russia had been rejected by the Kremlin both in the RMTS and in its refusal of ENP membership. Vladimir Solovyov, an influential Russian journalist, condemned the focus on values in EU–Russia relations, stating that the PfM 'should direct attention to practical questions rather than to benefits of European values'.[152] According to Tom Casier, the PfM's focus on trade, investment and innovation made it a 'predominantly technical document [in which] normative aspects are limited to references to an independent judiciary, the fight against corruption and dialogues with civil society'.[153] Casier rightly stated that in 2000, the EU began to adopt a

> more pragmatic approach of 'constructive engagement' with Russia, where a partnership was seen as a requirement rather than a choice on the basis of shared values or norms. The role of the latter was gradually sidelined, while the credo of constructive engagement continued to resonate.[154]

This became evident when the EU prioritised economic and political considerations over humanitarian concerns by launching the first crucial energy cooperation with Russia, despite Russia's continuing human rights violations in Chechnya.[155]

Conclusion

This chapter sought to demonstrate that Russia's invasion of Georgia and its recognition of Abkhazia and South Ossetia as independent regions strained EU–Russia relations, but did not result in a political crisis, as had been the case when the EU intervened for the first time in the affairs of a post-Soviet state in the Ukraine in 2004. The EU's initially hesitant and uncoordinated attempts to seek to ease tensions between Russia and Georgia before the escalation of conflict failed. It was only with President Sarkozy's key role as mediator on behalf of the European Council Presidency that negotiations concerning a ceasefire gained momentum.

Despite Sarkozy's leading role in the adoption of the peace plan, Russian policymakers and diplomats did not perceive him as a mediator on behalf of the EU and thus did not feel threatened or concerned that the EU would intervene once again to encourage another country in the post-Soviet space to move towards closer integration with the EU. As a consequence, a political crisis in EU–Russia relations did not emerge after the Russian–Georgian War.

However, this war had several negative repercussions for EU–Russia relations. It resulted in the Council's decision to freeze negotiations regarding the update of the PCA by two months. At the same time, Russia's aggression towards Georgia resulted in divergence within the EU regarding the implementation of sanctions against Russia. The EU's stance diverged between a group of European heads of state who were convinced that the war with Georgia prevented continuing relations with Moscow on the basis of 'business as usual'. Several heads of government of EU member states were in favour of introducing sanctions in retaliation for Russia's aggression towards Tbilisi. Another group, in contrast, sought to maintain a cordial stance with Russia. The latter approach was also reiterated in the European Council conclusions of 1 September, which referred to the fact that relations with Russia were too crucial for the EU to simply discontinue them. Due to internal division in the EU and President Sarkozy's wish to continue engagement with Russia, restrictive measures were not implemented. However, the fact that this discussion took place highlighted the extent of the strain in the relationship.

Russia's aggression towards Georgia pushed the EU to seek to increase security in its eastern neighbourhood through the launch of the EaP. The creation of this integrative framework intensified EU–Russian rivalry over the post-Soviet space. Kremlin hostility towards the EU's involvement in the Ukrainian revolution in 2004 resulted in the country's turn towards the EU until a conflict over Ukraine's future political orientation re-emerged with utmost intensity in 2013, when Ukraine intended to sign its AA with the EU. The pressure exerted by the Kremlin on the Ukrainian government culminated in turmoil and resulted in the most severe confrontation in the diplomatic history of EU–Russia relations. Both the unfolding and repercussions of these events for relations between Ukraine, the EU and Russia are the focus of Chapter 7.

Notes

1 A comparison of the two articles reveals discrepancies between the Russian and Georgian accounts of the outbreak of the war: Medvedev (2008); Saakashvili (2008).
2 Asmus (2010), p. 24.
3 Antonenko (2007), p. 92.
4 Asmus (2010), p. 105.
5 Ibid., p. 106.
6 Ibid., p. 146.
7 Ibid.
8 Ibid., p. 48.
9 Ibid., p. 89.
10 Sakwa (2015), p. 4.
11 Asmus (2010), pp. 127, 137.
12 Ferrero-Waldner (2007).
13 Slovenian Presidency of the European Union (2008).
14 Ibid.; Slovenian European Council Presidency (2008).
15 Slovenian European Council Presidency (2008).
16 Van Elsuwege (2014), p. 447.
17 See Chapter 5 of this book.
18 European Commission (2008a).
19 Ibid. Added emphasis.
20 Quoted in Filippov (2009), p. 1833.
21 Quoted in Filippov (2009).
22 Putin speech quoted in Filippov (2009), p. 1834.
23 Ibid., p. 1835.
24 OSCE (1990).
25 Putin speech quoted in Filippov (2009), p. 1837.
26 Malek (2009) gives a short overview of the development of the Russian–Georgian conflict between March and August 2008.
27 Sadri and Burns (2010), p. 138.
28 Ibid.
29 Allison (2008), pp. 1145, 1146. See Allison's article for a detailed explanation of diverging views of Russia's military intervention in Georgia.
30 Interview with the former Foreign Minister and current President of the Georgian Institute for Strategic Studies Eka Tkeshelashvili. Interview conducted by phone on 13 July 2015.
31 Ibid.
32 Ibid.
33 Larsen (2009).
34 Deutsche Welle (2008a)
35 Ibid.
36 Interview with the former Foreign Minister and current President of the Georgian Institute for Strategic Studies Eka Tkeshelashvili. Interview conducted by phone on 13 July 2015.
37 Deutsche Welle (2008a).
38 Asmus (2010), p. 194.
39 Interview with Chief of Cabinet/Political adviser to the EU Special Representative for the South Caucasus and the crisis in Georgia. Interview conducted via email on 30 July 2015.
40 Asmus (2010), p. 195.
41 Interview with the former Foreign Minister and current President of the Georgian Institute for Strategic Studies. Eka Tkeshelashvili. Interview conducted by phone on 13 July 2015.

158 *Effects of EU diplomacy in Georgia*

42 Interview with Chief of Cabinet/Political adviser to the EU Special Representative for the South Caucasus and the crisis in Georgia. Interview conducted via email on 30 July 2015.
43 Interview with the former Foreign Minister and current President of the Georgian Institute for Strategic Studies. Eka Tkeshelashvili. Interview conducted by phone on 13 July 2015.
44 Asmus (2010), p. 198
45 Ibid., p. 199.
46 Ibid.
47 Ibid., p. 57.
48 Ibid.
49 Government of Georgia (2008).
50 Whitman and Wolff (2010), p. 93.
51 Asmus (2010), p. 202.
52 Ibid. p. 201.
53 Ibid.
54 Ibid.
55 Ibid., p. 204.
56 Ibid., p. 206.
57 Kouchner quoted in Asmus (2010), p. 212
58 President of the Republic of Lithuania (2011).
59 Interview with the former Foreign Minister and current President of the Georgian Institute for Strategic Studies Eka Tkeshelashvili. Interview conducted by phone on 13 July 2015.
60 Whitman and Wolff (2010).
61 Deutsche Welle (2008b).
62 Ibid.
63 Ibid.
64 EU Monitoring Mission Georgia (2015a).
65 Parmentier (2009). p. 56.
66 Ibid., p. 57.
67 EU Monitoring Mission Georgia (2015b).
68 Interview with the former Foreign Minister and current President of the Georgian Institute for Strategic Studies. Eka Tkeshelashvili. Interview conducted by phone on 13 July 2015.
69 EU Monitoring Mission Georgia (2015b).
70 Deutsche Welle (2008c).
71 Ibid.
72 Ibid.
73 Sarkozy (2008). Speech given at the World Policy Conference organised by IFRI, Paris.
74 Ibid.
75 Ibid., p. 7.
76 Blitz (2008).
77 *Le Monde* (2008a).
78 *Le Monde* (2008b).
79 Council of the European Union (2008a). Brussels, 6 October 2008 (07.10). (OR.fr) 12549/2/08 REV 2. CONCL 3. Extraordinary European Council, Brussels. 1 September 2008.
80 Ibid.; The change in the revised version was very minor and concerned the following sentence: 'To this end (the establishment of an observer mission), the European Council requests the President of the Council and the SG/HR to undertake all the necessary contacts and discussions.' In the revised version, the word 'discussion' was exchanged to 'work'. See Council of the European Union (2008b).

Effects of EU diplomacy in Georgia 159

81 Ibid.
82 Ibid.
83 *Le Monde* (2008c).
84 Ibid.
85 Ibid.
86 Blitz (2008).
87 European Commission (2008b).
88 Email interview with former seconded national expert working at the Unit for Relations with Russia and the Northern Dimension Policy at the DG RELEX of the European Commission. Interview conducted on 30 June 2015.
89 European Commission (2008b).
90 Email interview with Lars Grønbjerg, former seconded national expert working at the Unit for Relations with Russia and the Northern Dimension Policy at the DG RELEX of the European Commission. Interview conducted on 30 June 2015.
91 European Commission (2008b).
92 A detailed analysis of the review on EU–Russia relations in 2004 can be found in Chapter 3 of this book.
93 See Chapter 2 of this book.
94 European Commission (2004).
95 Ibid.
96 European Commission (2008c).
97 Council of the European Union (2008a).
98 European Commission (2008d).
99 Whitman and Wolff (2010), p. 97.
100 Ibid. Added emphasis.
101 European Commission (2008c). Added emphasis.
102 Ibid; Turunen (2011).
103 European Union (2008), p. 10.
104 Ibid.
105 Ibid.
106 Ibid., p. 5.
107 Interview with Chief of Cabinet/Political adviser to the EU Special Representative for the South Caucasus and the crisis in Georgia. Interview conducted via email on 30 July 2015.
108 Ibid.
109 The Delegation of the European Union to Georgia (1999).
110 Kondrashov (2005).
111 See Chapter 4 of this book.
112 Whitman and Wolff (2010), p. 89.
113 Whitman and Wolff (2010), p. 90.
114 Lannon and Van Elsuwege (2012), p. 285.
115 Council of the European Union (2008c).
116 European Commission (2008d), p. 2.
117 Ibid.
118 Ibid.; European Commission (2008d), p. 3.
119 Tumanov, Gasparishvili and Romanova (2012), p. 132.
120 This issue is discussed in Haukkala (2010).
121 Lannon and Van Elsuwege (2012), p. 312.
122 European Commission (2008d), p. 2.
123 Tumanov, Gasparishvili and Romanova (2012), p. 132.
124 Deutsche Welle (2009).
125 Tumanov, Gasparishvili and Romanova (2012), p. 133.
126 The Delegation of the European Union to Russia (1999).
127 Ibid.

160 *Effects of EU diplomacy in Georgia*

128 Lukyanov (2008), p. 1107.
129 Ibid.
130 Lukyanov (2008), p. 1115.
131 Lukyanov (2008), p. 1114.
132 EU–Russia Partnership for Modernisation (nd).
133 Interview with former official working in the Russia unit of the Directorate General for EU External Relations at the European Commission. Interview conducted via email on 28 August 2015.
134 Flenley (2015), p. 12.
135 Romanova and Pavlova (2014), p. 500.
136 EU–Russia Partnership for Modernisation (nd).
137 Ibid.; David and Romanova (2015), p. 2.
138 Interview with former official working in the Russia unit of the Directorate General for EU External Relations at the European Commission. Interview conducted via email on 28 August 2015.
139 Ibid.
140 Flenley (2015), p. 13.
141 Ibid.
142 Ibid.
143 Romanova and Pavlova (2014), p. 499.
144 Ibid.
145 Ibid.
146 Romanova and Pavlova (2014), p. 504.
147 David and Romanova (2015), p. 4.
148 Romanova and Pavlova (2014), p. 506.
149 Interview with former official working in the Russia unit of the Directorate General for EU External Relations at the European Commission. Interview conducted via email on 28 August 2015.
150 Ibid.
151 Ibid.
152 Solovyov (2010).
153 Casier (2013), p. 1380.
154 Ibid.
155 The reasons for the shift in the EU's policy towards Russia were assessed in Chapter 2.

Bibliography

Allison, R. (2008). Russia Resurgent? Moscow's campaign to 'coerce Georgia to peace.' *International Affairs*. 84(6): 1145–1171.

Antonenko, O. (2007). Russia and the Deadlock over Kosovo. *Survival: Global Politics and Strategy* 49(3): 9–106.

Asmus, R.D. (2010). *A Little War That Shook the World*. Basingstoke, UK: Palgrave Macmillan.

Blitz, J. (2008). NATO urged to bolster Baltic defence. *Financial Times*. 2 September 2008.

Casier, T. (2013). The EU–Russia Strategic Partnership: Challenging the normative argument. *Europe–Asia Studies*, 65(7): 1377–1395.

Council of the European Union. (2008a). Revised presidency conclusions. Extraordinary European Council, Brussels. 1 September 2008 (OR.fr) 12549/2/08 REV 2. CONCL 3. Brussels, 6 October 2008.

Council of the European Union. (2008b). Presidency conclusions. (OR.fr). 12594/08. CONCL 3. Extraordinary European Council, Brussels. 1 September 2008.

Effects of EU diplomacy in Georgia 161

Council of the European Union. (2008c). Brussels European Council 19/20 June 2008. Presidency conclusions. 17 July 2008. 11018/1/08 REV 1 CONCL 2.

David, M. and Romanova, T. (2015). Modernisation in EU–Russia Relations: Past, present, and future. *European Politics and Society* 16(1): 1–10.

Deutsche Welle. (2008a). Russia calls German peace plan for Caucasus 'helpful'. 18 July 2008. Retrieved 16 June 2015 from: www.dw.de/russie-calls-german-peace-plan-for-caucasus-helpful/1-3494076.

Deutsche Welle. (2008b). EU mulls sending peacekeepers to monitor Georgia ceasefire. 13 August 2008. Retrieved 28 September 2014 from: www.dw.de/eu-mulls-sending-peacekeepers-to-monitor-georgia-ceasefire/a-3560775.

Deutsche Welle. (2008c). Analysis: EU under pressure to be tough with Russia. 13 August 2008. Retrieved 28 September 2014 from www.dw.de/analysis-eu-under-pressure-to-be-tough-with-russia/a-3562329.

Deutsche Welle. (2009). EU–Russia summit reveals differences rather than agreement. 22 May 2009. Retrieved 9 July 2015 from: www.dw.com/en/eu-russia-summit-reveals-differences-rather-than-agreement/a-4271011.

EU Monitoring Mission Georgia. (2015a). Presentation to College of Europe study trip by the EUMM at its Headquarters in Tbilisi. March 2015.

EU Monitoring Mission Georgia. (2015b). Speech by the EUMM's Deputy Head of Delegation. to College of Europe study trip at the EUMM Headquarters in Tbilisi. March 2015.

EU–Russia Partnership for Modernisation. (nd). On the Russia–EU Initiative 'Partnership for Modernisation' (background information). Retrieved 7 September 2015 from: http://formodernization.economy.gov.ru/en/info/

European Commission. (2004). Communication from the Commission to the Council and the European Parliament on relations with Russia. COM (2004). 106 final. 9 February 2004.

European Commission. (2008a). EU–Russia summit on 26–27 June in Khanty Mansiisk to launch negotiations of the new framework agreement. Press Release. Brussels 25 June 2008. IP/08/1008. Retrieved from: www.ec.europa.eu/external_relations/russia/intro/index.htm.

European Commission. (2008b). Review of EU–Russia relations. Memo/08/678. Brussels, 5 November 2008. Retrieved 30 October 2014 from: http://europa.eu7rapid/press-release_MEMO-08-678_en.htm?locale=en

European Commission. (2008c). EU–Russia summit in Nice on 14 November. Brussels, 13 November 2008. IP/08/1701. http://europa.eu/rapid/press-release_IP-08-1701_en.htm

European Commission. (2008d). Communication from the Commission to the European Parliament and the Council. Eastern Partnership. SEC (2008) 2974. Brussels, 3.12.2008. COM (2008) 823 final.

European Union. (2008). Report on the Implementation of the European Energy Security Strategy – Providing Security in a Changing World. Brussels, 11 December 2008. Global Strategy. S407/08.

Ferrero-Waldner, B. (2007). EU–Russia: Preparations for the summit. 24 October 2007. Speech 7/653. Retrieved 03 February 2011 from: http://europa.eu/rapid/pressReleasesAction.do?reference=SPEECH/07/653&format=HTML&aged=0&language=en&gui Language=en

Filippov, M. (2009). Diversionary Role of the Georgia-Russia conflict: International constraints and domestic appeal. *Europe–Asia Studies* 61(10): 1825–1847.

Flenley, P. (2015). The Partnership for Modernization: Contradictions of the Russian modernisation agenda. *European Politics and Society* 16(1): 11–36.

162   Effects of EU diplomacy in Georgia

Government of Georgia. (2008). Letter from Nicolas Sarkozy. 14 August 2008. Russian Aggression of Georgia. Six Point Peace Plan. Le Président de la République. Protocole d'accord. State Ministry for Reconciliation and Civic Equalities. Retrieved 7 September 2015 from: http://new.smr.gov.ge/Uploads/9bbbc7.pdf

Haukkala, H. (2010). Explaining Russian reactions to the European Neighbourhood Policy. In Whitman, R. and Wolff, S. (eds). *The European Neighbourhood Policy in Perspective: Context, implementation and impact.* New York: Palgrave. Macmillan.

Kondrashov, K. (2005). Front protiv Rossii: napravlenia agressii. Regnum. 28 March 2005. Retrieved 23 October 2011 from: www.regnum.ru/news7428347.

Lannon, E. and van Elsuwege, P. (2012). *The European Neighbourhood Policy's Challenges.* Brussels: P.I.E. Peter Lang.

Larsen, H. (2009). The Russo-Georgian War and Beyond: Towards a European Great Power Concert. Danish Institute for International Studies (DIIS) working paper 2009: 32.

Le Monde. (2008a). Moscou multiplie les menaces avant le sommet européen sur la Géorgie. 1 September 2008.

Le Monde. (2008b). L'UE reporte ses négociations avec la Russie. 1 September 2008.

Le Monde. (2008c). Russie et Géorgie affichent leur satisfaction des Européens. 2 September 2008.

Lukyanov, F. (2008). Russia–EU: The partnership that went astray. *Europe–Asia Studies* 60(6): 1107–1119.

Medvedev, D. (2008). Why I had to recognize Georgia's breakaway regions. *Financial Times.* 26 August 2008.

Malek, M. (2009). Georgia and Russia: The 'unknown' prelude to the 'Five Day War'. *Caucasian Review of International Affairs.* 3(2): 227–232.

Miller, R.R. (2008). Lithuania's Lonely Gambit. Centre for European Policy Analysis. 15 May 2008. Retrieved 20 November 2015 from: www.cepa.org/content/lithuanias-lonely-gambit

OSCE. (1990). Treaty on Conventional Armed Forces in Europe. 19 November 1990. Retrieved 16 December 2014 from: www.osce.org/library/14087.

Parmentier, F. (2009). Normative Power, EU Preferences and Russia. Lessons from the Russian–Georgian War. *European Political Economy Review* 9: 49–61.

President of the Republic of Lithuania. (2011). Lithuanian and Polish Presidents issue joint declaration on Russian troops withdrawal from Georgia. 3 November 2011. Retrieved 10 November 2015 from: www.archyvas.lrp.lt/en/news.full/9789.

Romanova, T. and Pavlova, E. (2014). What Modernisation? The case of Russian partnerships for modernisation with the European Union and its member states. *Journal of Contemporary European Studies* 22(4): 499–517.

Sadri, H.A. and Burns, Nathan, L. (2010). The Georgia Crisis: A new Cold War on the Horizon? *Caucasian Review of International Affairs* 4(2): 126–144.

Saakashvili, M. (2008). Moscow's plan is to redraw the map of Europe. *Financial Times.* 27 August 2008.

Sakwa, R. (2008). Putin's Leadership: Character and consequences. *Europe–Asia Studies* 60(6): 879–897

Sakwa, R. (2015). *Frontline Ukraine. Crisis in the borderlands.* London: I.B. Tauris.

Sarkozy, N. (2008). L'Union européenne et la Russie dans la gouvernance mondiale. Politique Etrangère. Politique Etrangère 2008/4 Hiver, 723–732.

Slovenian Presidency of the European Union. (2008). EU–Russia Summit: The Start of a New Age. 27 June 2008. Retrieved 3 February 2011 from: www.eu2008.si/en/News_and_Documents/Press_Releases/June?2706KPV_EU_Rusija.html

Effects of EU diplomacy in Georgia 163

Slovenian European Council Presidency. (2008). Joint statement of the EU–Russia summit on the launch of negotiations for a new EU–Russia agreement. Retrieved 3 February 2011 from: www.eu2008.si/includes/Downloads/misc/JS_Negotiation_EU-RF_Agreement.pdf

Solovyov, V. (2010). Zakonnost, vpered! *Kommersant.* 11 February 2010. Retrieved 16 October 2015 from: www.kommersant.ru/doc/1319877

The Delegation of the European Union to Russia. (1999). The Russian Federation's Middle Term Strategy towards the EU (2000–2010). Retrieved 18 November 2009 from: www.delrus.ec.europa.eu/en/p_245.htm

Tumanov, S., Gasparishvili, A. and Romanova, E. (2012). *Eastern Partnership: A new opportunity for the neighbours*, edited by Elena Korosteleva, 122–143. London and New York: Routledge.

Turunen, A. (2011). Conflicts in Georgia – Challenges and Prospects for Settlement. A joint seminar organized by the Ministry for Foreign Affairs of Finland and the Aleksanteri Institute in Helsinki, 6 May 2011 Presentation by Ambassador Antti Turunen. Retrieved 19 June 2015 from:www.helsinki.fi/aleksanteri/english/projects/files/Challenges%20and %20prospects%20for%20the%20Geneva%20process-final.pdf

Van Elsuwege, P. (2014). The Legal Framework of EU–Russia Relations: Quo Vadis? In Govaere, I., Lannon, E., Van Elsuwege, P. and Adams, S. Nijhoff (eds). *The European Union in the World. Essays in honour of Marc Maresceau.* pp. 441–460.

Whitman, R.G. and Wolff, S. (2010). The EU as a Conflict Manager? The case of Georgia and its implications. *International Affairs* 86(1): 87–107.

7 The point of no return? EU–Russia relations after the Euro-Maidan

Following the EU's strategically planned intervention to resolve the political crisis in Ukraine in 2004, several Russian policy makers perceived the EU as an 'aggressive organisation' which was seeking to undermine Russia's influence in the post-Soviet space.[1] Both the Kremlin and key Russian officials accused Brussels of having sought to draw Ukraine into the EU sphere of influence. Almost a decade after the EU's intervention, Russian policy makers mocked the EU for its limited capacities in reacting to the Ukraine crisis in 2013.

The Kremlin belittled the imposition by the EU of restrictive measures against Russia. It referred to the potentially negative economic repercussions of sanctions for the EU itself. Key Russian policymakers declared that the EU demonstrated its failure in international politics. Russia's perception of the EU as a weak actor in international relations would have been unthinkable after the EU's diplomatic intervention in the Orange Revolution.

The purpose of this chapter is to explain this paradoxical shift in Russian perceptions of the EU. Unlike in 2004, EU diplomacy during the Ukraine crisis in 2013 had several limitations. First, the agreement which had been negotiated by the EU did not contribute to the resolution of the crisis. Second, another major shortcoming of the EU's diplomacy in the 2013 crisis was its inability to develop a common strategy to constrain Putin's authoritarian foreign policy towards Kiev.

This chapter argues that the shift in Russian perceptions of the EU from an aggressive proactive organisation interfering in Kiev in 2004 to a reactive bystander in the continuing crisis in Ukraine was affected by three factors. First, the EU was internally divided in its response to the gradually escalating crisis in Ukraine. Second, the sanctions the EU imposed were not an effective means of resolving this crisis. Third, the EU was unable to find appropriate ways of counterbalancing Russia's uncompromising foreign policy.

Déjà vue on Maidan: the EU–Russian clash over Ukraine

The launch in May 2009 of the EaP, a Polish and Swedish initiative for closer integration with six of the EU's 'Eastern' partners including Ukraine, increased the EU's influence in the post-Soviet space.[2] According to European Commission

President José Manuel Barroso, the EaP aims to support the partner countries' political and economic reforms, it assists the prospective members' modernisation process and moves these countries closer to the EU while respecting the degree of integration chosen by each country.[3] This choice was not in the Kremlin's interest. The EaP came at the price of alienating Russia. In 2004, prior and during the Orange Revolution Putin expressed his strong opposition to the prospect of closer EU–Ukrainian integration in the framework of the AA and the related Deep and Comprehensive Free Trade Agreement (DCFTA). After the triumph of the Orange Revolution, which resulted in Ukraine's turn towards the EU, according to a memorandum from the European Commission, the AA was the most 'ambitious agreement the EU has ever offered' to achieve fuller integration.[4]

The EU's objectives for closer integration with Ukraine impacted negatively on triangular relations between Ukraine, Russia and the EU. On the one hand, the signing of the proposed AA institutionalised Ukraine's political orientation towards Brussels. On the other hand, the struggle over the direction of Ukraine's foreign policy triggered a renewed conflict in EU–Russia relations a decade after the Orange Revolution triggered the first political crisis between the partners since 1999. Russian policy makers reacted immediately to the EU's strengthened efforts to enforce political and economic ties with Kiev and put the Ukrainian President Victor Yanukovich under pressure not so sign the EU–Ukrainian AA. Yanukovich succumbed to Russian pressure and abstained from signing the AA with the EU at the Vilnius summit on 28 to 29 November 2013.[5]

The first signs of President Putin's opposition to the EU–Ukrainian AA emerged three weeks before the Vilnius summit. Putin urged Yanukovich to 'freeze' the EU–Ukraine AA and to commence trilateral negotiations on the agreement's potential adoption between the EU, Russia and Ukraine instead.[6] Putin's suggestion would have provided the framework for joint negotiations regarding Ukraine's future political orientation. Due to the EU and Russia's clashing perspectives on the development of relations with Ukraine, the negotiations would have been both difficult and lengthy but would have provided an opportunity to prevent the escalation and violence which shook Ukraine.

Several Russian politicians joined Putin's chorus of criticism. Sergei Glazyev, Putin's adviser on regional economic integration, denounced the EaP as the EU's imposition of its own rules of integration on its Eastern partners.[7] The severity of the emerging clash between the EU and Russia became apparent when prominent Russian politicians accused the EU of meddling in Ukraine. Three days before the Vilnius summit, Glazyev declared that the West had been using 'its agents' in Ukraine to sign the AA. In an indirect condemnation of the EU's diplomacy during the Orange Revolution, Glazyev stated that 'during this revolution as well as during the latest pro-EU demonstrations in Kiev, protestors had been paid by the EU'.[8] He called on Ukraine to resist EU 'blackmail' and join the Eurasian Union, an integrative economic project between Russia, Armenia, Belarus, Ukraine and Kazakhstan, if it wanted to avoid becoming a 'colony' of Brussels.[9]

166 *Point of no return: after Euro-Maidan*

More outspoken than Glazyev against the EaP was Leonid Slutsky, the First Deputy Chairman of the State Duma Committee on International Affairs. He harshly denounced the EaP 'as a tactic of overt amputation of post-Soviet countries from the Eurasian project, their "polarisation" in the western direction as semi-colonies'.[10] This was an explicit allusion to the Kremlin's plan to create the Eurasian Union. Thus, he denounced the EU's unilateral tendency to entice the six EaP members to closer integration with Brussels to the detriment of the Kremlin's anticipated integration in the Eurasian Union. Several days later, the AA with Ukraine was also criticised for its negative economic repercussions. The chairman of the Council on Foreign and Defense Policy Fyodor Lukyanov, denounced the signing of the agreement as 'not just unprofitable for Ukraine today, but [for being] very risky.... [S]erious economic losses related with the change in the model of trade with Russia and a highly probable socio-economic crisis in this case will come literally tomorrow.'[11]

The intensification of the EU–Russian conflict over Ukraine was reflected in Barroso and van Rompuy's condemnation of Russia's position towards Ukraine. In a joint statement published on 25 November Barroso and van Rompuy demonstrated the EU's strong opposition to Russia's involvement in Ukrainian politics by advancing four points. First, they stated that people in Ukraine have indicated a preference for integration with the EU rather than allying themselves with Russia. According to Barroso and van Rompuy, 'Ukrainian citizens have shown again these last days that they fully understand and embrace the historic nature of the European association. We therefore strongly disapprove of the Russian position and actions in this respect'.[12] Second, van Rompuy and Barroso declared that they were 'aware of the external pressure that Ukraine is experiencing, [but stated that they] believe ... short-term considerations should not override the long-term benefits that this [EU–Ukrainian] partnership would bring'.[13] Third, the presidents of these two EU institutions stated that Ukraine should be able to choose freely its future political orientation:

> the European Union will not force Ukraine, or any other partner to choose between the European Union or any other regional entity. It is up to Ukraine to freely decide what kind of engagement they seek with the European Union.[14]

Fourth, they emphasised that neither the AA nor the DCFTA would be detrimental to EU–Russia relations. On the contrary, they stated that the agreements

> do not come at the expense of relations between our Eastern partners and their other neighbours, such as Russia. The EaP is considered as a win-win where we all stand to gain. The European Union continues to stand ready to clarify to the Russian Federation the mutual beneficial impact of increased trade and exchanges with our neighbours, whilst fully respecting the sovereignty and independence of our Eastern Partners and the bilateral nature of AAs and DCFTAs.[15]

Point of no return: after Euro-Maidan 167

Barroso and van Rompuy's statement was harshly rejected by President Putin. At a news conference after a meeting with the Italian Prime Minister Enrico Letta, Putin called on the EU to avoid criticism concerning Russia: 'I would like to ask our friends in Brussels, my personal good friends, to refrain from strong criticism'.[16] A day later, Putin ensured that his words were widely spread: the Kremlin's spokesman Dmitry Peskov rejected the accusations by the EU officials that Russia has used political blackmail to prevent Ukraine from signing the AA. Peskov declared that 'it is out of place to talk about any pressure'.[17]

Despite the Kremlin's rejection of any pressure issued against Ukraine, the Vilnius summit provided evidence of Russian manipulation of Yanukovich to refrain from signing the AA. President Yanukovich responded to the pressure at the summit's plenary session, where he made a plea to the EU to include Russia in the preparations for the EU–Ukrainian free trade agreement. He called on the EU to develop a

> coordinated plan of actions aimed at the elimination of contradictions and settlement of problems in trade and economic cooperation with Russia and other members of the Customs Union related to the establishment of a free trade area between Ukraine and the EU.[18]

Yanukovich reflected Putin's wish to proceed with the EU–Ukrainian integration efforts by including Russia. He declared that he would be 'grateful for your support in the issue of initiating respective cooperation in the format Ukraine–EU–Russia'.[19] Due to this direct reference to Putin's request to conduct tripartite negotiations on the EU–Ukrainian agreement, it became obvious that Ukraine's foreign policy decisions were not free from the Kremlin's orbit. Despite Yanukovich's announcement that he would not sign this agreement, he sought to avoid burning bridges with the EU. He 'reaffirm[ed] the intentions of Ukraine to sign the [AA] in the nearest future'.[20] The clearest empirical evidence for the fact that the Kremlin had exerted pressure on Yanukovich was a Russian–Ukrainian gas deal signed on 17 December. The price for Russian gas deliveries to Ukraine was lowered by a third. Both this decrease and Russia's offer of a loan of $15 billion to Ukraine were the country's reward for having abstained from signing the AA with the EU.[21]

Barroso, the European Commission president, sought to convince Yanukovich to reconsider his decision to abstain from signing the AA. At the press conference after the Vilnius summit, Barroso emphasised that 'the offer to sign these agreements remains on the table provided the government of Ukraine delivers on its commitments'.[22] He stated that this agreement would enable Ukraine to save about €500 million a year in import duties and would increase the Gross Domestic Product by more than 6 per cent in the longer-term. He expressed his solidarity with the Ukrainian people, who were protesting against Yanukovich's decision: 'we know how much Ukrainian people feel European, how much they aspire to be recognized as members of a democratic community of nations of Europe'. [23] In an obvious reference to President Putin's pressure on Yanukovich, Barroso stressed that 'we will always accept Ukraine's sovereign decisions'.[24]

168   *Point of no return: after Euro-Maidan*

At this press conference, Barroso and van Rompuy sought to rescue EU–Russia relations while emphasising that the AA would not harm Russia. Barroso explained that 'this partnership was never an imposition or rather a supposition. And all stand to gain.... Let me be clear. This is a process *for* something. It is not a process *against* someone.'[25] Van Rompuy referred to the benefits Russia could gain from the EU–Ukrainian AA. He declared that stronger relations with the EU did not come at the expense of relations between eastern neighbours and their other neighbours, such as Russia. 'Our strong conviction is that these kinds of agreements are also benefitting Russia because the better the economies in the neighbourhood of Russia are performing, the better it is for Russia'.[26] He added that 'we, [the EU] are on the side of the Ukrainian people.... We are helping Ukraine to become as other EU member states.'[27] This is precisely the underlying problem because assisting Ukraine to become as the EU member states was at odds with the Kremlin's interests.

Despite this attempt to rescue EU–Russia relations, van Rompuy could not ignore the extent of emerging tensions in the 'strategic partnership'. He denounced Russia's meddling in EU–Ukraine relations by stating that

> on numerous occasions, [we] reiterated that action taken by Russia vis-à-vis the eastern partners are incompatible with how international relations should function on our continent in the 21st century. The Union will continue insisting that any Russian actions [which] influence Eastern European partner countries' sovereign choices could be in breach of the [OSCE's] Helsinki principles which commit to respect each other's ... right to freely define ... relations with other states in accordance with international law.[28]

Ten days later, the European Commission made an attempt to soften the developing confrontation with Russia. Prior to the visit of Catherine Ashton, EU High Representative, to Kiev in December 2013, the European Commission's spokesperson, Pia Ahrenkilde Hansen, announced that the EU was not intending to interfere in Ukraine. She declared that it was not

> our role to be specific about actions taken on the ground. It is our role to support the freedom of the people of Ukraine to express their European aspirations.... In the past days we have been very clear in our condemnation of violence in that respect. This is our role in addition to engaging with a closer association, if that is the will of the sovereign people of Ukraine.[29]

This declaration carried some weight when bearing in mind that the EU's effective and carefully planned intervention in the resolution of the Orange Revolution in 2004 resulted in the first political crisis in EU–Russia relations since 1999 (see Chapter 4). Back then, the Kremlin accused the EU of deliberately attempting to steer Ukraine's policy away from Russia with the aim of enhancing its sphere of influence in the post-Soviet space.

The European Commission's announcement that it would refrain from interference in the Ukraine crisis was both appreciated and belittled by Fyodor Lukyanov, the chairman of the Council for Foreign and Defence Policies. Lukyanov stated that 'as compared with the activities during the Orange Revolution, their impact on the current events in the country is much more moderate. This is far from being the top priority for the EU now'.[30] In 2004, Lukyanov expressed his strong opposition to President Yushchenko's election, which had been brought about by the EU's diplomacy in Kiev. Lukyanov lamented that the 'end of the Kuchma regime was Russia's biggest foreign policy defeat since the collapse of the Soviet Union'.[31] When Lukyanov described the EU's role in the crisis in 2013 as moderate, the conflict was still at an early stage and not yet marked by severe violence. Although the early stage of the crisis and the limited protest could be regarded as a justification of the EU's rather passive stance, for Lukyanov, this was an imminent weakness. He downplayed the EU's capacities in foreign policy by criticising Ashton's role: '[a]s for Catherine Ashton's speech at the opposition rally staged against [President Yanukovich in December 2013], she is a minor EU official, [w]ho hardly takes any important decisions'.[32] According to Professor Richard Sakwa, Ashton was constrained in her ability to make an impact by the Kremlin's ruthless policy towards Kiev. Sakwa argued that the development of the Ukraine crisis showed that Ashton was 'unable to articulate an independent policy that could temper the militant rhetoric emanating from Moscow, Washington and Kiev. The EU has been marginalised – in a conflict that its actions have provoked and that is taking place in its "neighbourhood"'.[33]

A sign of growing tensions over the EU–Russian 'shared neighbourhood' was the diverging expectations concerning the summit agenda. The Russian presidential press service stated that visa-free travel, energy cooperation and talks on the renewal of the PCA would be discussed.[34] According to the Russian presidential aide Yury Ushakov, there was a 'great need for a frank, substantial conversation, including on the joint vision of EU–Russia relations'.[35] Ushakov considered integration efforts concerning the former Soviet space as a crucial point on the summit agenda. He stated that the EU and Russia 'should frankly and substantively discuss the massive, long-term task, the matching of two integration processes, the European and Eurasian ones'.[36] Ushakov was critical of EU–Russia relations. He stated that 'we are convinced that our cooperation is far from being fully used, there are significant reserves'.[37]

In a similar vein to Ushakov, van Rompuy indirectly referred to some problems the EU and Russia encountered. Prior to the summit, he stated that 'we have also had however a number of differences which need to be discussed and clarified. At this moment we need to focus on our common neighborhood, regional integration processes, trade questions and international commitments'.[38] These fundamental problems in EU–Russia relations probably prompted the EU to shorten the summit with Russia from a meeting lasting two days to an encounter of three hours.[39] This was interpreted as a sign of strained EU–Russia relations. According to an EU diplomat, the only time relations had been as tense as this was during the Russian–Georgian War in 2008.[40]

170   *Point of no return: after Euro-Maidan*

This view was reflected in the summit press release. Van Rompuy asserted that 'there can be different interpretations and misunderstandings on the association agreements and that is why we both agreed to pursue bilateral consultations at expert's level on the … AA and the economic consequences on both sides'.[41] European Commission President Barroso alluded to the strains inherent in the relationship when he stated that the EU and Russia

> have much to gain by strengthening our cooperation as strategic partners – but for this to be successful, we need mutual understanding and strategic trust. This is what we will try to consolidate at our next summit, by an open discussion on our common interests as well as on our differences and the best ways to overcome them.[42]

A day after the summit, Lukyanov compared Russia's strengths to the EU's inability to respond to the Ukraine crisis. According to Lukyanov, in 2013 when 'the [EU] tried to draw Ukraine into its sphere of influence … Russia withstood Western pressures with limited effort, relying exclusively on the power of persuasion and a moderate financial injection'.[43] He belittled the EU's impact in Ukraine by saying that the EU 'did not invest serious money or intellectual and political efforts in [resolution of the Ukraine crisis], assuming it would work anyway'.[44] Contrasting the EU's response to the crisis in 2013 to its prominent role in the resolution of the Ukraine conflict in 2004 enabled him to emphasise the EU's decreasing influence in resolving the Ukraine crisis: '[i]f Russia had been as passive or of as limited capability as it was at the start of the last decade, the EU might perhaps have succeeded in tethering Kiev, Yerevan, and others to itself even without any promises'.[45] He warned that 'Moscow has regained its qualities as a serious player and is recklessly making up for lost time. Rivalry has erupted with new force'.[46] Lukyanov's reference to EU–Russian rivalry would have been unthinkable in 1999, when the EU did not yet possess leverage in its external relations. However, the EU's growing influence in the post-Soviet space which emerged in the EU–Russian dilemma over Kaliningrad, the geopolitical consequences of EU eastern enlargement for EU–Russia relations and the EU's intervention in the Orange Revolution became sources of confrontation in the former strategic partnership, which culminated in the ongoing crisis in Ukraine.

Restrictive measures as a foreign policy tool

Three weeks later, when the situation in Ukraine reached its most violent phase and many protestors lost their lives on Euro-Maidan, the EU was forced to react. After EU High Representative Ashton agreed on a mediation mission consisting of the foreign ministers of Germany, France and Poland, EU-led negotiations between Yanukovich and the opposition began in Kiev. But the EU's involvement in the crisis resulted in confrontation with Russia.

Point of no return: after Euro-Maidan   171

The erupting violence in Ukraine forced the EU to respond. European Commission President Barroso stated that the EU had been monitoring the situation in Kiev with 'shock and dismay'.[47] He declared that

> the EU will respond to any deterioration on the ground. We therefore expect that targeted measures against those responsible for violence and use of excessive force can be agreed by our Member States as a matter of urgency, as proposed by the High Representative/Vice President.[48]

The President of the European Parliament, Martin Schulz, stated that what 'we need urgently is a *threat* of credible targeted sanctions against those involved in human rights violations'.[49] In comparison to general restrictive measures, 'targeted sanctions' can either be directed against individuals, business and groups, or can be implemented in economic sectors or against certain products, instead of being aimed at a state. The intention behind targeted sanctions is to enhance their effect 'on the actors responsible for violations, and to minimize the unintended consequences for innocent civilians'.[50] Targeted sanctions may include the expulsion of diplomats or the cancellation of both sport and cultural events. Alternatives to targeted sanctions are trade sanctions or financial sanctions, the latter entailing 'the freezing of funds or economic resources, the prohibition on financial transactions, restrictions on export credits or investments'.[51]

In the meantime, Ashton's spokesperson urged the Ukrainian authorities to ensure 'prompt de-escalation'.[52] This was reflected in the European Council conclusions on Ukraine.[53] Due to the worsening of the crisis, the Council 'introduced targeted sanctions including asset freeze and visa ban against those responsible for human rights violations, violence and use of excessive force'.[54]

Before assessing the impact of restrictive measures on the Ukraine conflict, it is important to recapitulate the circumstances under which the EU implements them. The Treaty of the European Union introduced restrictive measures as a means to attain specific goals in the EU CFSP. In 2003, the Council of the EU adopted more specific guidelines for the application of restrictive measures, such as 'monitoring and follow-up' of restrictive measures, which was the responsibility of a 'special Council body'.[55] In EU external relations, restrictive measures had been implemented to foster democracy, to strengthen human rights, to 'manage conflicts, to consolidate and assist democratic transition', as well as to provide support in the struggle against international terrorism.[56] However, the EU's imposition of sanctions against third-party states is challenged by the requirement for unanimity, meaning that individual EU member states cannot apply restrictive measures without having received the consent of both the European Council and the Council of Ministers. EU member states should ensure 'national coordination ... between all relevant government agencies, bodies and services with competence in the field of sanctions'.[57] As shown in this section, the unanimity requirement posed a severe obstacle to the EU's imposition of sanctions on Russia because of divisions within the EU regarding relations with Russia.

172 *Point of no return: after Euro-Maidan*

No sooner had the EU publicly announced its stance on the Ukraine crisis than representatives of the Russian Foreign Ministry launched an attack against the EU's involvement. After the most brutal and violent clashes in Ukraine on Kiev's Maidan cost the lives of many people in February 2014, the Russian Foreign Ministry issued a statement in which 'connivance on the part of those Western politicians and European structures' was held responsible for 'further escalation and provocation against the legitimate authority'.[58] The Russian Foreign Minister Sergei Lavrov stated that the Foreign Ministry was 'worried about the Western capitals ... influencing the situation in the country'.[59] He simultaneously denounced the EU's discussion about imposing potential sanctions against Ukraine: 'such actions can be considered blackmail'.[60]

Even though a Russian representative was sent to Ukraine to negotiate, the EU and Russia failed to come to an agreement regarding Ukraine's future political orientation. The Kremlin's spokesperson, Dmitry Peskov, stated that Yanukovich asked Putin to 'send a Russian [mediator] to [Kiev] to participate in the negotiation process with the opposition'.[61] Russian ombudsman Vladimir Lukin was chosen as a mediator because of his 'abundant experience of diplomatic service and a considerable reputation among human rights defenders'.[62] But due to the escalation of violence in Ukraine, the EU was forced to react. The German chancellor Angela Merkel informed Putin that Foreign Minister Frank-Walter Steinmeier, his French counterpart Laurent Fabius, and their Polish colleague Radoslaw Sikorski would travel to Kiev on 20 February to mediate between the opposition and President Yanukovich.[63] Before talking to President Yanukovich, the foreign ministers met with opposition leaders Arseny Yatsenyuk, Olkeg Tyagnibok and Vitaly Klitschko at the German embassy in Kiev.[64]

Merkel's plans to mediate in the crisis were condemned by Lukyanov, chairman of the Council for Foreign and Defense Policies. He criticised Germany for its 'desire to show its newly acquired taste for European leadership'.[65] He stated that the 'institutional collapse in Ukraine increases the likelihood that external players will get involved'.[66] Lukyanov criticised the US for its 'inclination ... to check an increasingly assertive Russia along with Moscow's desire to prove its pre-emptive right to dominate the post-Soviet space'.[67] This statement is one of several examples which illuminate the Kremlin's strategic foreign policy over the post-Soviet space. It is not surprising that such statements raise suspicions among politicians and commentators in the West that the Kremlin is attempting to construct an empire. Despite Lukyanov's reference to Russia's right to dominate the former Soviet space, he stated that EU–Russian cooperation 'would guarantee the preservation of Ukraine within its present borders and take on some of the responsibilities that the current state institutions seem unable to manage'.[68] Russian dominance on the one hand, and EU–Russian cooperation regarding institution-building in Ukraine on the other, are utterly contradictory objectives which demonstrate the incompatibility of EU and Russia's political approaches towards Ukraine.

The result of the German, French and Polish foreign ministers' mediation efforts was a preliminary agreement seeking to resolve the Ukraine crisis. This

Point of no return: after Euro-Maidan 173

agreement – a five point plan – was signed by the Ukrainian government and the opposition on 21 February 2014. First, the agreement urged the reestablishment of the Ukrainian constitution of 2004. Simultaneously, a coalition should be created and a national government should be formed ten days after the plan's signing. Second, constitutional reform and equalisation of the balance of power between the president, the government and the parliament should be completed by September 2014. Third, the presidential election should be held as soon as possible whilst a new Central Electoral Commission should be formed. Fourth, all acts of violence, which had shaken Ukraine, should be investigated. Fifth, the Ukrainian authorities would not impose a state of emergency and violence should be stopped.[69]

Despite this agreement, the negotiators were concerned about its limitations. Several hours after the agreement was reached, Steinmeier declared that he

> hoped that all sides make a policy out of this agreement in the next days. This framework [for the resolution of the crisis] needs to be implemented by Ukraine itself. We will keep an eye that the agreement ... will be implemented.[70]

No less critical about the agreement's success was Steinmeier's counterpart and negotiating partner Fabius. Having been asked whether the negotiations between the three EU foreign ministers and Yanukovich would result in a compromise, Fabius was hesitant to give an answer. He merely stated that in order to safeguard Ukraine's integrity, opposition between Ukraine's future political alignment with either the EU or Russia had to be avoided.[71]

The day after the agreement was signed some of the EU's internal obstacles in its foreign policy towards Ukraine surfaced. Instead of implementing sanctions against Ukraine, Romano Prodi, the former president of the European Commission, put forward two strategies, aiming at the crisis' resolution. First, he argued that the imposition of restrictive measures would not contribute to resolution of the conflict. He stated that 'European leaders should back down from their threats of sanctions against Ukraine ... which would only prolong the suffering of the Ukrainian people'.[72] Prodi urged

> European leaders [to] immediately schedule direct talks with President ... Putin ... and his top officials to find a temporary solution to stop the bloodshed and a longer-term plan that would allow Ukrainians to determine their political destiny in a peaceful and democratic fashion.[73]

At the same time he criticised 'Russian interference in Ukraine's internal affairs'.[74] He emphasised that the 'West must make clear to Moscow that Ukraine – a bridge between East and West – should not be the object of geopolitical games.'[75] In an obvious criticism of the EU's policy towards Ukraine, Prodi stated that 'to threaten sanctions, to condone violent extremists in the streets and to ignore Ukraine's financial troubles – as some European leaders seem to be doing – would be to hasten the destruction of the bridge'.[76]

174 *Point of no return: after Euro-Maidan*

Two weeks later, EU condemnation of Russia increased. On 3 March 2014, the EU Foreign Affairs Council strongly condemned the 'clear violation of Ukrainian sovereignty and territorial integrity by *acts of aggression* by the Russian armed forces', which are in 'clear breach of the UN Charter and the OSCE Helsinki Final Act and the [Ukrainian–Russian] Treaty of Friendship'.[77] Russia's failure to commit to the afore mentioned regulations severely undermined its relations with the EU. A European Council press release stated that both mutual interests and respect in EU–Russia relations 'have been put in doubt'.[78] The EU would suspend talks with Russia on visa related issues and on the PCA's renewal, should Russia fail to take 'de-escalating steps'.[79] These words carried weight. Three days later, on 6 March, the EU suspended talks on visa liberalisation with Russia.[80] A statement by the European Council published the same day revealed the actual extent of EU–Russian confrontation over Ukraine. It commenced by stating that the EU's and Russia's 'common objective of a relationship based on mutual interest and respect of international obligations *needs to be promptly restored*. It would be a matter of great regret if the Russian Federation failed to work in that direction'.[81] The fact that the word 'restored' was used demonstrated that both mutual interest and respect had been undermined in EU–Russia relations.[82] The statement emphasised the need for negotiations between the Ukrainian government and Russia to begin within five days. They should result in the resolution of the conflict 'within a limited timeframe'.[83] The failure to meet this obligation would result in the imposition of further sanctions against Russia, such as 'travel bans, asset freezes and the cancellation of the EU–Russia summit'.[84]

A day later Russia's permanent ambassador to the EU Vladimir Chizhov belittled the EU's response to the Ukraine crisis. He referred to the need to rethink the implementation of sanctions when he alluded to potential mutual economic losses caused by such restrictive measures: 'Our [EU–Russian] trade turnover … is one billion euros a day. And that is a figure that is worth considering before taking any restrictive measures'.[85] Chizhov downplayed the sanctions proposed by the West, stating that 'on certain possible measures that were announced at the [EU] Foreign Affairs Council yesterday, they do not appear to be overly impressive. I would even add that they are more restrained than the political rhetoric that surrounded them.'[86] He was disparaging about the impact of the restrictive measures when he compared the extent of the proposed sanctions with the volume of economic exchange between the EU and Russia.

The EU institutions were divided regarding the extent and severity of potential sanctions against Russia. The European Commissioner for energy Guenther Oettinger stated in an interview that it 'would be wrong to question the economic ties that have been built over decades with Russia'.[87] A possible reason for Oettinger's reluctance to impose sanctions was an attempt by the Kremlin to blackmail the EU. On 8 March, the Russian Defence Ministry announced that it would consider preventing monitoring of its nuclear power plants if economic sanctions were enforced.[88] Several members of the European Parliament were much more assertive about the imposition of sanctions against Russia than Oettinger. Johannes

Point of no return: after Euro-Maidan   175

van Baalen, a Dutch member of the European Parliament from the Liberal Party supported the imposition of sanctions despite the fact that restrictive measures would simultaneously have negative repercussions for the EU.[89]

This discrepancy among EU officials concerning the implementation of sanctions against Russia had already characterised EU foreign policy towards Russia during the second Chechen War. In 2000 a group of leaders perceived Putin's election as president as a window of opportunity for EU–Russian cooperation. The European Council, the Commission and members of the European Parliament proposed imposing sanctions on Russia, such as the suspension of trade-related clauses in the EU–Russian PCA, because of Russian human rights abuses in Chechnya. The Parliamentary Assembly of the Council of Europe also imposed a short-term ban on Russia's voting rights. Opposed to the imposition of these sanctions, a group of prominent European political figures sought a 'fresh start' to EU–Russia relations and developed plans for EU–Russian energy cooperation. As a consequence, EU condemnation of Russia's human rights violations in Chechnya were muted and 'business as usual' was resumed with Russia.[90]

The point of no return

The EU's deliberations on the implementation of restrictive measures against Russia neither resulted in resolution of the crisis nor in constraining the Kremlin's foreign policy towards Ukraine. As a consequence, EU leaders witnessed the annexation of Crimea in March 2014. This secession from Ukraine was condemned by the EU, which responded by implementing more extensive and harsher restrictive measures against Russia. At the same time, EU–Russian diplomatic relations reached the lowest point since the political crisis in 2004 after the Orange Revolution.

The EU position on Russia hardened drastically in light of Putin's planned referendum in Crimea. In a joint statement van Rompuy and Barroso mentioned that all 29 EU heads of state and government had expressed the view that the referendum contradicted both international law and the Ukrainian constitution. The EU condemned the 'unprovoked violation of Ukraine's sovereignty and territorial integrity and called on Russia to withdraw its armed forces'.[91] The EU High Representative, Catherine Ashton, stated that there should be consequences for Russia's behaviour. She announced that

> you can[not] simply sit back and say this situation can be allowed to happen. So first of all we have to think very carefully about what the response ought to be and there should be a response.... We [are] also trying to send the strongest possible signals to Russia.[92]

These statements were officially adopted in the European Council conclusions on Ukraine on 17 March, which stated that the EU abstained from recognising the 'illegal referendum in Crimea'.[93] According to the conclusion statement, the referendum 'was held in the visible presence of armed soldiers under conditions

176 *Point of no return: after Euro-Maidan*

of intimidation of civic activists and journalists, blacking out of Ukrainian television channels and obstruction of civilian traffic in and out of Crimea'.[94] Due to these developments in Crimea, the Council decided to impose additional restrictive measures, such as travel restrictions and asset freezes against individuals who were considered responsible for undermining Ukraine's territorial integrity, sovereignty and independence. The Council urged Russia to de-escalate by withdrawing its troops and by launching negotiations with the Ukrainian government to seek a solution to the conflict.[95] It warned that in the case of Russia's failure to de-escalate the situation, there would be 'additional and far-reaching consequences for relations in a broad range of economic areas between the European Union and ... the Russian Federation'.[96] It emphasised its willingness to engage in a 'constructive dialogue' and the EU's commitment to 'developing [the] EU–Russia relationship, based on mutual interest and respect for international law'.[97] In a drastic condemnation of EU–Russia relations at the time, the Council 'regret[ed] that Russia's actions contradict these objectives'.[98]

The European Council conclusions carried weight. Several days after their publication, the EU imposed sanctions against Russia. Catherine Ashton announced that 'we do regret that Russia has so far not engaged in negotiations with Ukraine. In the absence of positive steps, we have today decided to introduce additional ... restrictive measures against 21 individuals responsible for actions which undermine or threaten the territorial integrity, sovereignty and independence of Ukraine'.[99] In this context, Ashton indirectly addressed herself to the Russian political leadership by stating that 'there is still time to avoid a negative spiral and reverse current developments'.[100] Van Rompuy justified the reasons for the EU's implementation of visa bans and widening of asset freezes.[101] In a possible attempt to rebuff criticism from Russian policy makers on the imposition of these restrictive measures, he declared that

> sanctions are not a question of retaliation; they are a foreign policy tool – not a goal in themselves, but a means to an end. Our goal is to stop Russian action against Ukraine, to restore Ukraine's sovereignty – and to achieve this we need a negotiated solution.[102]

Two days after the referendum on Crimea, Putin's address to State Duma deputies, members of the Federation Council and representatives of civil society revealed Russia's open confrontation with the EU over Ukraine. He dismissed the West's condemnation of the referendum. He stated that determining Crimea's future political orientation was undertaken in 'full compliance with democratic procedures and international norms'.[103] According to Putin, 'Crimea has always been an inseparable part of Russia. This firm conviction is based on truth and justice'.[104] In an attempt to highlight the importance of Ukraine's annexation to Russia, Putin referred to the illegality of the region's accession to Ukraine. He stated that the 'decision was made in clear violation of the constitutional norms that were in place.... Naturally, in a totalitarian state nobody bothered to ask the citizens of Crimea and Sevastopol'.[105]

Point of no return: after Euro-Maidan   177

Meanwhile a group of Russian policy makers retaliated to the proposed sanctions, expressing concerns about the impact of these restrictive measures on the Russian economy. The Russian Foreign Minister Sergei Lavrov condemned the West's proposed sanctions as 'hasty and ill-considered'.[106] The Deputy Economic Development Minister Aleksey Likhachev stated that the Russian Economic Ministry hoped that 'there will only be targeted political sanctions and not a broad package affecting economic trade'.[107] Emphasising that Russia would impose sanctions against the EU and the US as a retaliatory action against the punitive economic measures, Likhachev stated that 'our sanctions will be of course similar'.[108] This was not merely empty rhetoric, as the State Duma issued legislation which would result in freezing assets of both businesses and individuals from the US and the EU in case sanctions were implemented against Russia after the referendum on Crimea.[109] In a reference condemning the West's external interference in Russian affairs, Andrey Klishas, who drafted the legislation, stated that it would give the presidents and government opportunities to 'defend our sovereignty from threats'.[110]

The immediate aftermath of the referendum in Crimea revealed both the EU's division in its response to the annexation and the helplessness of the EU in responding to the crisis. During an annual meeting of European and American politicians, the Estonian President Toomas Ilves and the Italian Foreign Minister Federica Mogherini clashed in a debate on the EU's response to the Ukraine crisis. Ilves criticised the EU for 'sitting and watching' the annexation of Crimea and for giving Russia only 'a minor slap on the wrist' by imposing visa bans. According to Ilves, Russia 'laughed at' this reaction.[111] His reaction sparked a heated debate with Mogherini, who cynically repudiated Ilves' remark by asking rhetorically 'So, let's bomb Russia? What is the solution?' Ilves retaliated that the EU should 'begin defending ourselves, because once you start ... the annexation of territories what possible intellectual reasoning could say "this won't continue"'.[112] The Prime Minister of Luxembourg Xavier Bettel summed up the EU debate on the annexation of Crimea by stating that 'among the 28 [EU member states] there are very wide gaps'.[113] The EU's internal division regarding its stance towards Russia undermined its ability to create an affirmative and unitary policy towards Moscow during the second Chechen War, as demonstrated in Chapters 2 and 3 of this book. No less constraining was the EU's lack of a common stance in its response to the Ukraine crisis.

The annexation resulted in an institutional break in EU–Russia relations. The most drastic sign of confrontation between the strategic partners over Ukraine was the cancellation of the summit, which was supposed to take place in July.[114] In addition, the European Council decided that bilateral meetings between Russia and individual EU member states would not be held either. The European Commission announced that the EU would not participate in the G8 summit, which was hosted by Putin in Sochi. Instead, the summit took place in Brussels in the context of a meeting of the G7 states. Furthermore, the Foreign Ministers of the EU member states refused to participate in a meeting on foreign policy to be held in Moscow.[115] A further sign of the culmination of the crisis in Mos-

178 *Point of no return: after Euro-Maidan*

cow's relations with the West was Russia's exclusion from the G 8.[116] Commenting on this decision, German Chancellor Angela Merkel emphasised that 'the G 8 are not only an economic community but they are also a community which shares values and that demands respect for international law'.[117] Whilst the EU–Russian confrontation was at its peak, the genuine intentions of the EU towards integration with Ukraine were confirmed when the political provisions of the EU–Ukrainian AA were signed on 21 March.[118]

Russian policy makers ridiculed the EU's limited capacities in its foreign policy towards Ukraine. The chairman of the Council for Foreign and Defense Policies, Fyodor Lukyanov, referred to the limited impact of the sanctions when he stated that 'the West can put economic pressure on Russia, but no one – especially in Europe – is ready to consider truly serious sanctions, because they would cut both ways in this globalized world'.[119] At the same time, he slated the EU's response to the conflict: 'Europe ... has already demonstrated to the world its total political failure as an international player'.[120] In a similar vein to Lukyanov, the former Russian Foreign Minister Igor Ivanov referred to the EU's inability to react to the Ukraine crisis when he ridiculed sanctions as 'a sign of weakness. [They] demonstrate a clear inability to resolve complicated problems through political and diplomatic means.'[121]

The failure of EU–Russian relations was further reflected in the Kremlin's retaliation to the implementation of sanctions. At the Economic Forum in St Petersburg, Putin warned that due to the level of interdependence in global politics, 'economic sanctions used as an instrument of political pressure have a boomerang effect that ultimately has consequences for business and economy in the countries that impose them'.[122] Putin's words carried weight. Three months later, Russia implemented import bans on agricultural products from countries which had imposed restrictive measures against Moscow.[123]

Putin condemned both the West's position on the annexation of Crimea and the EU's role in Ukraine. He condemned the West for 'trying to corner us in retaliation for ... having an independent position, for defending it, for calling things by their names and not being hypocritical'.[124] Putin criticised the West for having 'crossed the red line. They acted brutally, irresponsibly and unprofessionally'.[125] He accused the EU for breaching laws when interfering in Ukrainian domestic politics in 2004. According to Putin, 'the necessary candidate' was 'push[ed] ... through' during the presidential elections, and 'they thought up some sort of third round that was not stipulated by the law. It was absurd and a mockery of the constitution'.[126] Accusing the EU of having betrayed Russia, he stated that 'they have thrown in an organized and well-equipped army of militants'.[127] Putin declared that

> actions were aimed against Ukraine and Russia and against European integration. And all this while Russia strived to engage in dialogue with our colleagues in the West. We are constantly proposing cooperation on all key issues ... we want to strengthen our level of trust and for our relations to be equal, open and fair. But we saw no reciprocal steps. On the contrary they

Point of no return: after Euro-Maidan 179

have lied to us many times, made decisions behind our backs [and] placed us before an accomplished fact.[128]

Putin's view of the EU's role in Ukraine demonstrates the severity of the EU–Russian confrontation over Ukraine.

No less confrontational than Putin towards the West's attitude in the Ukraine crisis was Lukyanov. He stated that the West 'did not understand right away, if they understood at all, that Russia sees the Ukrainian issue not simply as a red line, but as a double solid white line'.[129] In what can be considered an obvious reference to the regime change marking the Orange Revolution, Lukyanov continued that

> [t]he space for agreement disappeared when Russia saw a neighbouring country, Ukraine being enticed by Europe and the United States into adopting other principles. Moscow has acted accordingly, with no regard for the possible costs or even the danger of curtailed relations with the West.[130]

The downing of a passenger flight by pro-Russian separatists over Eastern Ukraine marked the point of no return in EU–Russia relations. The downing forced the EU to implement further sanctions against Russia.[131] The German Foreign Minister Frank-Walter Steinmeier commented on the developments of EU–Russian relations after this catastrophe. He asserted that

> the downing of flight MH 17 has tremendously changed the situation. We need a serious and independent resolution of this crime.... All foreign ministers ... know that a common action is required. Sanctions are neither a means just for the sake of it, nor a cure against everything, but without any doubt, the Russian leadership did not do enough in the past weeks to contain separatists. Therefore ... we are ready to increase the pressure against Moscow in order to force Russia to change its behavior and to take part in de-escalation.[132]

Steinmeier's words carried weight. A week after his statement, the EU implemented the most severe sanctions yet against Russia: 'an arms embargo, a ban on the export of some sensitive technologies and a ban on the sales of bonds and equities by state-owned Russian banks in European capital markets'.[133] However, these sanctions can only be considered as short-term solutions and do not offer any long-lasting sustainable solution to ease some major sources of confrontation in EU–Russia relations.

Yet it remains difficult to see the impact of the sanctions in putting the Kremlin under pressure to terminate the Ukraine crisis by coercing separatists in Eastern Ukraine. This was already implied by Steinmeier's statement that restrictive measures were neither a 'means just for the sake of it nor a cure against everything'.[134] At the same time, sanctions do seem to be the only means the EU has at its disposal in the overly ambitious attempt to coerce Russia to change its

180 *Point of no return: after Euro-Maidan*

foreign policy. Despite the lack of impact of sanctions, they have had negative repercussions on the Russian economy. In early 2014, devaluation of the rouble, high inflation and a decrease in growth, the slowest growth rate since 1999, without taking the recession in 2009 into consideration, were partial consequences of the sanctions.[135] Professor Richard Sakwa rightly argued

> the impact of the sanctions in the end turned out to be quite severe, [but] there is no evidence that they achieved the desired effect. In fact, sanctions only impeded the path of dialogue and the emergence of mutually satisfactory outcomes.'[136]

Whilst these deliberations on the implementation of sanctions were ongoing, Mikhail Margelov, head of the Foreign Affairs Committee of the Russian Federation Council, commented on the EU's failure to draw lessons from the Russian–Georgian War. According to Margelov,

> the events of August 2008, when Russia intervened in the war unleashed by the regime of Mikhail Saakashvili ... to enforce peace in the region ... should have made clear to everyone that Russia is not only ready to make its voice heard, but is also prepared to use force when its national interests are at stake.[137]

He claimed that the Ukraine crisis would 'drag on for the foreseeable future'.[138] He rhetorically asked whether the crisis would 'result in a new Cold War and a severe reduction of all ties between Russia and the [EU]'.[139] In an attempt not to jeopardise the strategic partnership, he referred to the mutual benefits of EU–Russian economic interdependence. He acknowledged that

> each nation seeks to diversify its trade relations and reduce its risks in the global market. But who would want to lose time-tested economic partners with large markets? Russia is just as interested in exporting its energy resources to the [EU] as the EU is in importing them.[140]

In what can be considered a potential attempt to avoid overemphasising EU–Russian economic interdependency, Margelov emphasised that Russia was diversifying its political relations. He stated that 'Russia has demonstrated to the West that there are alternative economic partners to the [EU], with the demand for Russian hydrocarbons in China and other developing markets in the region just as high as in Europe'.[141] According to Margelov, Russia should develop relations with different countries to 'avoid being suspected of allying itself with any of the competing parties'.[142] Regarding the development of EU–Russia relations, Margelov stated that there remained the challenge of 'rapprochement' with the EU, 'especially considering that Russia is a European country'.[143]

Russian views on the development of relations with Europe were diverging. An article published in the Russian newspaper *Vedomosti* referred to Russia's

Point of no return: after Euro-Maidan   181

cultural, political and economic distinction from Europe. From an economic point of view, Russia diversifies its relations by cooperating with China. On a political level, in light of condemnation of the annexation of Crimea, the head of the Russian delegation to PACE and speaker of the State Duma, Sergei Naryshkin, stated that Russia would suspend its membership of PACE after Moscow was deprived of its right to vote.[144] He referred to the fact that the voting ban would have limited effects in that Russia would not 'urgently revise its foreign policy and principles'.[145] His allusion to the limited ability of the voting ban to coerce Russia to change its foreign policy was a reminder of the reaction of Duma deputies to the imposition of the sanction by PACE in April 2000.[146] On a cultural level, a draft on Russian cultural policy prepared by the Russian Ministry of Culture was quoted by Interfax: 'Russia should be treated as a unique and distinctive civilization, [which] cannot be reduced either to the "West" or to the "East"'.[147] In essence this statement alluded on the one hand to the diverging world views of Russia and the West, which became a source of confrontation in their relationship. On the other hand, this statement also made clear that due to its 'distinctive civilization', Russia would not listen to lectures given by Brussels on democracy and human rights. This tendency in Russian politics to abstain from adopting the West's self-proclaimed values was already reflected in the RMTS published in 2000 which stated that

> Russia should retain its freedom to determine and implement its domestic and foreign policies, its status and advantages of an Euro-Asian state and the largest country of the Commonwealth of Independent States, independence of its position and activities at international organizations.[148]

The fact that the Russian Ministry for Culture regarded Russia as a political entity which was neither comparable to the West nor to the East was in addition to the RMTS' rejection of closer association with the EU, a symbol of the reversal in Russia's relations with the EU.

The statement that Russia was a unique civilisation which cannot be reduced either to the West or the East demonstrates a U-turn in relations in comparison with the great expectations which had characterised EU–Russia relations in 1999. At that time President Yeltsin lamented that Russia was not an EU member.[149] Prime Minister Chernomyrdin was equally disappointed at the lack of prospect of Russia becoming part of the EU.[150] Since 2002, the gradually intensifying confrontation in EU–Russia relations was caused by the EU's increasing influence in the former Soviet space, its development of the integrative political and economic EaP, as well as growing ideational discrepancies.

Conclusion

This chapter sought to explain the reasons for the shift in Russian perceptions of the EU from an aggressive organisation seeking to increase its influence in the post-Soviet space after the Orange Revolution, to a weak actor a decade later. It

182 *Point of no return: after Euro-Maidan*

argued that this shift was influenced by three factors. First, division within the EU over implementation of restrictive measures against Russia undermined the EU's response to the Ukraine crisis. Representatives of new EU member states, such as the Estonian president, for instance, were in favour of imposing sanctions against Russia. However, other European officials, such as the Commissioner for energy, feared that the implementation of restrictive measures could harm Europe's economy and undermine long-term security of the EU's energy supply.

Second, the sanctions the EU implemented against Russia were not an appropriate means of de-escalating the crisis. The limited effect of the restrictive measures became increasingly evident as Russian politicians such as the former Foreign Minister Ivanov belittled the impact of sanctions after the EU announced further restrictive measures following Russia's annexation of Crimea.

The third factor which contributed to the shift in Russian perceptions of the EU was the fact that the EU was incapacitated by the Kremlin's foreign policy. According to Lukyanov, Russian foreign policy was

> marked by renunciation of the integration idea and by a concept according to which Russia should retain the freedom of action and seek the consolidation of its independent position on all issues. This is a time of 'strategic breakthrough' to a basically new status of Moscow in the international arena.[151]

Lukyanov's statement reflects Putin's foreign policy towards Ukraine, especially since the annexation of Crimea. According to Lukyanov, Russia has gained 'greater self-reliance in international affairs and ... greater confidence in the country's ability to solve its problems on its own terms'.[152] Russia's independence and confidence in its foreign policy resulted in the Kremlin's reluctance to heed EU condemnation of Russia's ruthless foreign policy towards Ukraine.

The EU does not possess the political means to influence Russia's ruthless foreign policy. In the future, when dealing with such an idiosyncratic partner, the EU's external relations towards Moscow would need to comprise elements of both soft and hard power. However, this policy recommendation is merely based on two academic concepts with limited practical applicability. This policy recommendation is challenged by the dynamic nature of EU politics. The various and continuing changes, such as the rotating European Council Presidencies and divergent stances among EU member states regarding relations with Russia, hamper the EU's ability to develop and maintain a unitary stance in its relations with Moscow. Since 2006, this internal friction has been aggravated by a division between 'old' and 'new' member states. The relations between new member states and Russia have been shaped by history. As a consequence, EU foreign policy towards Russia was often marked by internal divisions, resulting in deadlocks in EU–Russia relations. This was the case in 2006, when Poland and Lithuania both vetoed the renewal of the EU–Russian PCA because of bilateral disputes with Russia.

Point of no return: after Euro-Maidan   183

In addition to the challenges to the EU's foreign policy towards Moscow, fundamental questions regarding Ukraine's political development remain. Ukraine's future political orientation is challenged by three factors. First, the EU's declaration at the EaP summit in Riga in May 2015 that it did not anticipate further accessions until 2020 has increased doubts about Ukraine's future political direction. Second, the conflict in Eastern Ukraine constrains the development of a bright political future for Ukraine as a country which is not torn between affiliation to the EU or Russia. Third, any predictions about Kiev's future political development remain hypothetical at this stage because it depends on the ability of the EU and Russia to overcome the deadlock over Ukraine. However, reducing the strained relations between the EU and Russia merely to the Ukraine conflict is to provide a narrow examination of the reasons for the deterioration of the former strategic partnership. The book's conclusions refer to the diverse dynamics which gradually culminated in confrontation between the EU and Russia after their blooming aspirations for a strategic partnership in 1999.

Notes

1 Kondrashov (2005).
2 BBC News (2013).
3 Lithuanian Presidency of the Council of the European Union (2013a).
4 European Commission (2013).
5 Lithuanian Presidency of the Council of the European Union (2013b).
6 EurActiv (2013a).
7 Glazyev (2013).
8 BBC Monitoring (2013).
9 Ibid.
10 Interfax (2013).
11 ITAR-TASS (2013a
12 European Commission (2013).
13 Ibid.
14 Ibid.
15 Ibid.
16 ITAR-TASS (2013b).
17 Medetsky (2013).
18 President of Ukraine (2013).
19 Ibid.
20 Ibid.
21 Sakwa (2015), p. 79.
22 Lithuanian Presidency of the Council of the European Union (2013a).
23 Ibid.
24 Ibid.
25 Ibid.
26 Ibid.
27 Ibid.
28 Ibid.
29 EurActiv (2013b).
30 Zamyatina (2013).
31 Gardiner (2004).

184 *Point of no return: after Euro-Maidan*

32 Zamyatina (2013).
33 Sakwa (2015), p. 41.
34 ITAR-TASS (2014a).
35 Ibid.
36 Interfax (2014).
37 Ibid.
38 European Commission (2014a).
39 Croft and Pawlak (2014).
40 Kravtsova (2014).
41 European Council (2014a).
42 European Commission (2014a).
43 Lukyanov (2014a).
44 *Rossiyskaya Gazeta* (2014).
45 Ibid.
46 Ibid.
47 European External Action Service (2014a).
48 Ibid.
49 European External Action Service (2014b). Emphasis added.
50 Quoted in Giumelli (2013), p. 22.
51 Giumelli, F. (2013), p. 23.
52 European External Action Service (2014c).
53 Council of the European Union (2014a).
54 Ibid.
55 Council of the European Union (2007). Until 2004, the notion of a sanction was not used within the EU. See Portela (2015).
56 Giumelli (2013), p. 24.
57 Council of the European Union (2007), p. 24.
58 *Wall Street Journal* (2014).
59 ITAR-TASS (2014b).
60 Ibid.
61 The Voice of Russia (2014).
62 Ibid.
63 Auswaertiges Amt (2014a).
64 *Guardian* (2014a).
65 Lukyanov (2014b).
66 Ibid.
67 Ibid.
68 Ibid.
69 *Guardian* (2014b).
70 Auswaertiges Amt (2014a).
71 France Diplomatie (2014).
72 Prodi (2014).
73 Ibid.
74 Ibid.
75 Ibid.
76 Ibid.
77 Council of the European Union (2014b), emphasis added; United States Department of State (2014); McMahon (2014).
78 Council of the European Union (2014b).
79 Ibid.
80 The Federal Government of Germany (2014).
81 European Council (2014b). Emphasis added.
82 Ibid.
83 Ibid.

Point of no return: after Euro-Maidan 185

84 Ibid.
85 EurActiv (2014b).
86 Ibid.
87 Gardner (2014a).
88 Gardner (2014b).
89 Keating (2014).
90 See Chapter 2 of this book.
91 European Council (2014c).
92 European External Action Service (2014d).
93 Council of the European Union (2014c).
94 Ibid.
95 Ibid.
96 Ibid.
97 Ibid.
98 Ibid.
99 European External Action Service (2014e).
100 Ibid.
101 European Council (2014d).
102 European Council (2014e).
103 The Kremlin (2014).
104 Ibid.
105 Ibid.
106 *Russia Today* (2014a).
107 Ibid.
108 Ibid.
109 Ibid.
110 Ibid.
111 Pop (2014).
112 Ibid.
113 Neuger, Wishart and Sterans (2014).
114 European Council (2014d).
115 European Commission (2014b).
116 *Guardian* (2014c).
117 Chancellor of Germany (2014).
118 European Council (2014f).
119 Lukyanov (2014c).
120 Ibid.
121 Ivanov (2014).
122 Sakwa (2015), p. 195.
123 Ibid.
124 *Russia Today* (2014b).
125 Ibid.
126 The Kremlin (2014).
127 Ibid.
128 Ibid.
129 Lukyanov (2014c).
130 Ibid.
131 Auswaertiges Amt (2014b); BBC News (2014).
132 Auswaertiges Amt (2014b).
133 Deutsche Welle (2014).
134 Auswaertiges Amt (2014b).
135 Sakwa (2015), p. 189.
136 Ibid., p. 199.
137 Margelov (2014).

186 *Point of no return: after Euro-Maidan*

138 Ibid.
139 Ibid.
140 Ibid.
141 Ibid.
142 Ibid.
143 Ibid.
144 Nechepurenko (2015); *Vedomosti* (2014).
145 EurActiv (2014a).
146 For a discussion on voting ban against Russia imposed by PACE see Chapter 2.
147 *Vedomosti* (2014).
148 The Delegation of the European Union to Russia (1999).
149 Isachenkov (1999).
150 McEvoy (1997).
151 Lukyanov (2008), p. 1116.
152 Sakwa (2008), p. 882.

Bibliography

Auswaertiges Amt. (2014a). Vereinbarung zur Loesung der Krise in der Ukraine unterzeichnet. 21 February 2014. Retrieved 24 July 2014 from: www.auswaertiges-amt.de/DE?Aussenpolitik/Laender/Aktuelle_Artikel/Ukraine/140221_Ukraine-Vereinbarung.html

Auswaertiges Amt. (2014b). 'Wir sind zu einer Erhoehung des Drucks auf Moskau bereit'. 22 July 2014. Retrieved 24 July 2014 from: www.auswaertiges-amt.de/DE/ Infoservice?Presse?interviews?2014/140722-BM_Rzesczpospolita.html?nn+385808

BBC Monitoring. (2013). Moscow Centre TV. Russian presidential aide slams pro-EU 'fifth column' in Ukraine. 25 November 2013.

BBC News. (2013). EU–Russia rivalry looms over Vilnius summit. 28 November 2013. Retrieved 29 July 2014 from: www.bbc.com/news/world-europe-25133721

BBC News. (2014). EU set to widen sanctions on Russia over Ukraine. 22 July 2014. Retrieved 29 July 2014 from: www.bbc.com/news/world-europe-28539254

Chancellor of Germany. (2014). Bundeskanzlerin. Die Woche der Kanzlerin. (2.6–7.6.2014). Retrieved 24 July 2014 from: www.bundeskanzlerin.de/Content/DE/AudioVideo/2014/ Video/_woche_der_kanzlerin/2014-06-07-woche-der-kanzlerin/2014-06-07-textversion-wdk.html

Council of the European Union. (2007). Restrictive Measures/ EU Best Practices for the effective implementation of restrictive measures. Brussels, 9 July 2007.

Council of the European Union. (2014a). Foreign Affairs Council Meeting. Brussels, 20 February 2014.

Council of the European Union. (2014b). Press release. 3305th Council meeting. Foreign Affairs. 7196/14. Brussels, 3 March 2014.

Council of the European Union. (2014c). Council conclusions on Ukraine. Foreign Affairs Council Meeting. Brussels, 17 March 2014.

Croft, A. and Pawlak, J. (2014). EU meets Russia for 'clear the air' talks with Putin. Reuters. 28 January 2014.

Deutsche Welle. (2014). EU adopts broad economic sanctions against Russia. 29 July 2014. Retrieved 30 July 2014 from: www.dw.de/eu-adopts-broad-economic-sanctions-against-russia/a-17820786

EurActiv. (2013a). EU 'refines its thinking' on its Ukraine–Russia relations. 27 November 2013.

Point of no return: after Euro-Maidan 187

EurActiv. (2013b). Ashton to visit Kiev amid Ukraine's anti-government protests. 9 December 2013. Retrieved 10 December 2013 from: www.youtube.com/watch?v=BbGfPjDIDow.

EurActiv. (2014a). Russia was suspended from the parliamentary assembly of European human rights watchdog the Council of Europe on Thursday in protest at Moscow's behavior towards Ukraine and the annexation of Crimea. 10 April 2014. Retrieved 17 July 2015 from: www.euractiv.com/sections/europes-east/council-europe-assembly-suspends-russias-voting-rights-301506

EurActiv. (2014b). Chizhov: For Russia Ukraine is more important than G 8. 5 March 2014. Retrieved 30 July 2014 from: www.euractiv.com/europes-east/chizhov-russia-ukraine-important-interview-533921.

European Commission. (2013). Joint statement by the President of the European Commission Jose Manuel Barroso and the President of the European Council Herman Van Rompuy on Ukraine. 25 November 2013. Memo. Retrieved 10 December 2013 from: http://europa.eu/rapid/press-release_MEMO-13-1052_en.htm.

European Commission. (2014a). 32nd EU–Russia summit. Brussels. 28 January 2014. Press release. IP/14/72. 24 January 2014. Retrieved 3 July 2014 from: http://europa.eu/rapid/press-release_IP-14-72_en.htm

European Commission. (2014b). The Hague declaration following the G 7 meeting on 24 March. Press Release. The Hague. 24 March 2014.

European Council. (2014a). Remarks by President of the European Council Herman van Rompuy following the 32nd EU–Russia summit. EUCO 27/14. PRESSE PR PCE 21. Brussels, 28 January 2014. Retrieved 3 July 2015 from: www.consilium.europa.eu/en/press/press-releases/2014/01/pdf/remarks-by-president-herman-van-rompuy-following-the-32nd-eu-russia-summit/

European Council. (2014b). Statement of the Heads of State or Government on Ukraine. Brussels, 6 March 2014.

European Council. (2014c). Joint statement on Crimea by president of the European Council Herman van Rompuy and President of the European Commission Jose Manuel Barroso. Brussels 16 March 2014. EUCO 58/14 PRESSE 140 PR PCE 53

European Council. (2014d). Joint statement by European Council. Conclusions on Ukraine approved by the European Council. Brussels, 20 March 2014. Retrieved 17 July 2015 from: www.consilium.europa.eu/uedocs/cms_data/docs/pressdata/en/ec/141707.pdf

European Council. (2014e). EU strengthens sanctions against actions undermining Ukraine's territorial integrity. Brussels, 21 March 2014. PRESSE 174. 8049/14.

European Council. (2014f). Statement by President of the European Council. Herman van Rompuy at the occasion of the signing ceremony of the political provisions of the Association Agreement between the European Union and Ukraine. EUCO 68/14 PRESSE 176 PR PCE 61. Brussels, 21 March 2014. Retrieved 3 July 2015 from: www.consilium.europa.eu/en/press/press-releases/2014/03/pdf/statement-by-president-herman-van-rompuy-at-the-signing-ceremony-of-the-political-provisions-of-the-association-agreement-between-the-eu-and-ukraine/.

European External Action Service. (2014a). Statement by EU leaders on Ukraine. Statement by President Barroso on Ukraine. 19 February 2014. Retrieved 17 June 2014 from http://eeas.europa.eu/delegations/russia/press_corner/all_news/news/2014/20140219_2_en.htm.

European External Action Service. (2014b). Statement by EU leaders on Ukraine. European Parliament President Schulz on Ukraine: further bloodshed must be avoided at all costs. 19 February 2014. Retrieved 17 June 2014 from: http://eeas.europa.eu/delegations/russia/press_corner/all_news/news/2014/20140219_2_en.htm.

188　*Point of no return: after Euro-Maidan*

European External Action Service. (2014c). Statement by EU leaders on Ukraine. Statement by the spokesperson of EU High Representative Catherine Ashton on the deterioration of the situation in Ukraine. 19 February 2014. Retrieved 17 June 2014 from http://eeas.europa.eu/delegations/russia/press_corner/all_news/news/2014/20140219_2_en.htm.

European External Action Service. (2014d). Remarks by EU High Representative Catherine Ashton upon arrival at the Foreign Affairs Council, 17 March 2014. 140317/01. Retrieved 29 November 2014 from: http://eeas.europa.eu/statements/docs/2014/140317_04_en.pdf

European External Action Service. (2014e). Remarks by High Representative of Catherine Ashton following the Foreign Affairs Council. Brussels, 17 March 2014. 140317/01. Retrieved 17 July 2015 from : http://eeas.europa.eu/statements/docs/2014/140317_04_en.pdf

France Diplomatie. (2014). Ukraine – Entretien de Laurent Fabius avec <<Europe 1>>. 21 February 2014. Retrieved 24 July 2014 from: www.diplomatie.gouv.fr/fr/dossiers-pays/ukraine/la-france-et-l'ukraine/evenements-3762/article/ukraine-entretien-de-laurent

Gardner, A. (2014a). A gas blowback for Russia? *European Voice.* 13 March 2014.

Gardner, A. (2014b). Facing sanctions, Russia threatens to put nuclear sites off-limit to EU. *European Voice.* 13 March 2014.

Gardiner, B. (2004). World leaders welcome new Ukraine vote. *Associated Press Online.* 3 December 2004.

Giumelli, F. (2013). *The Success of Sanctions. Lessons learned from the EU experience.* Ashgate.

Glazyev, S. (2013). Who stands to win? Political and Economic Factors in Regional Integration. *Russia in Global Affairs.* Retrieved 13 July from: http://eng.globalaffairs.ru/number/Who-stands-to-win-16288.

Guardian. (2014a). EU foreign ministers agree sanctions against Ukrainian officials. 21 February 2014. Retrieved 25 July 2014: www.theguardian.co/world/2014/feb/20/ukraine-eu-foreign-ministers-agree-sanctions-officials.

Guardian. (2014b). Agreement on the Settlement of the Crisis in Ukraine – full text. 21 Friday 2014. Retrieved 24 July 2014 from: www.theguardian.com/world/2014/feb/21/agreement-on-the-settlement-of-crisis-in-ukraine-full-text.

Guardian. (2014c). G 7 Countries snub Putin and refuse to attend planned G 8 summit in Russia. 24 March 2014. Retrieved 10 June 2014 from: www.theguardian.com/world/2014/mar/24/g7-countries-snub-putin-refuse-attend-g8-summit-russia

Interfax. (2013). Russian MP: Eastern Partnership policy of 'amputation' of post-Soviet states. 27 November 2013.

Interfax. (2014). EU, Russia need frank discussion of European, Eurasian integration – Ushakov. 24 January 2014.

Isachenkov, V. (1999). Yeltsin meets with German, EU leaders. Associated Press. 18 February 1999.

ITAR-TASS. (2013a). Ukrainian economy will not withstand European integration. 28 November 2013.

ITAR-TASS. (2013b). Putin offers to depoliticize Moscow-Kiev-EU relations issue. 26 November 2013.

ITAR-TASS. (2014a). Putin to participate in Russia–EU summit in Brussels. 28 January 2014.

ITAR-TASS. (2014b). Russia's position on political crisis in Ukraine. The West's threat to impose sanctions on Ukraine is a blackmail and double standards, Russian Foreign Minister Sergei Lavrov said. 20 February 2014.

Ivanov, I. (2014). Western sanctions are a sign of weakness. *Moscow Times.* 27 March 2014.

Point of no return: after Euro-Maidan 189

Keating, D. (2014). Call for sanctions on Russia. *European Voice*. 13 March 2014.

Kondrashov, D. (2005). Front protiv Rossii: napravlenia agressii. Regnum. 28 March 2005. Retrieved 23 October 2011 from: www.regnum.ru/news7428347.html

Kravtsova, Y. (2014). Putin rebukes EU actions in Ukraine. *Moscow Times*. 29 January 2014.

Lapczynski, M. (2009). The European Union's Eastern Partnership: Chances and perspectives. *Caucasian Review of International Affairs* 3(2).

Lithuanian Presidency of the Council of the European Union. (2013a). Eastern Partnership Summit. Press Conference. 29 November 2013. Retrieved 4 December 2013 from: www.eu2013.lt/en/video/highlights-of-eastern-partnership-summit

Lithuanian Presidency of the Council of the European Union. (2013b). The third Eastern Partnership Summit in Vilnius. Retrieved 20 June 2014 from: www.eu2013.lt/en/vilnius-summit

Lukyanov, F. (2008). Russia–EU: The partnership that went astray. *Europe–Asia Studies*. 60(6): 1107–1119.

Lukyanov, F. (2014a). Third Decade Diplomacy. Valdai Discussion Club/Gazeta.ru. 16 January 2014.

Lukyanov, F. (2014b). In Ukraine. No choice and no future. The current violence in Kiev is more reminiscent of Moscow in October 1998 than the Orange Revolution. Gazeta.ru. 20 February 2014. Retrieved 26 February 2014 from: http://rbth.com/opinion/2014/02/20/in_ukraine_no_choice_and_no_future_34367.html

Lukyanov, F. (2014c). Perestroika 2014. The reasons behind Moscow's firm stance on Ukraine. Valdai Discussion Club. 19 March 2014. Retrieved April 17 2015 from: http://valdaiclub.com/opinion/highlights/perestroika_2014_the_reasons_behind_moscow_s_firm_stance_on_ukraine/

Margelov, M. (2014). Russia–West–East. 17 July 2014. Valdai Discussion Club. Fostering a Global Dialogue about Russia. Retrieved 17 July 2015 from: http://valdaiclub.com/russia_and_the_world/70320.html

McEvoy, J. (1997). Russia restates EU membership ambitions. Reuters. 18 July 1997.

McMahon, R. (2014). Ukraine in Crisis. 6 March 2014. Council on Foreign Relations. Backgrounder. Retrieved 17 July 2015 from: www.cfr.org/ukraine/ukraine-crisis/p32540

Medetsky, A. (2013). Ukraine offers new deadline for EU deal. *Moscow Times*. 27 November 2013.

Nechepurenko, I. (2015). Council of Europe exit to cut Russia away from Europe. *Moscow Times*. 4 February 2015. Retrieved 17 July 2015 from: www.themoscowtimes.com/news/article/council-of-europe-exit-to-cut-russia-away-from-europe/515449.

Neuger, J. G., Wishart, I. and Sterans, J. (2014). Merkel warns on rush to Russia Sanctions, reflecting EU split. *Bloomberg*. 20 March 2014.

Pop, V. (2014). Russia to Europe: we can do whatever we want. *EUobserver*. 22 March 2014.

Portela, C. (2015). The EU, ENP and the Politics of Sanctions. Lecture on the framework of College of Europe's PhD Summer School. 'The ENP under pressure: The EU and the Eastern and Southern Neighbourhoods'. Natolin. 26 June 2015.

President of Ukraine. (2013) President Viktor Yanukovich's speech at plenary session of the Eastern partnership summit. Vilnius, 29 November 2013. Retrieved 29 November 2013 from: http://president.gov.ua/en/news/29616.html.

Prodi, R. (2014). How Ukraine can be solved. 21 February 2014. *The International New York Times*.

Remarks by EU High Representative Catherine Ashton upon arrival at the Foreign Affairs Council, 17 March 2014. 140317/03.

190 *Point of no return: after Euro-Maidan*

Rossiyskaya Gazeta. (2014). Fyodor Lukyanov, Fight for interspace. 29 January 2014.

Russia Today. (2014a). Russia won't exclude sanctions to counter US and EU-Ministry. 13 March 2014. Retrieved 17 July 2015 from: www.rt.com/business/russia-us-eu-sanctions-546/

Russia Today. (2014b). Putin: Crimea similar to Kosovo, West is rewriting its own rule book. 18 March 2014. Retrieved 17 July 2015 from: www.rt.com/news/putin-address-parliament-crimea-562/

Sakwa, R. (2008). Putin's Leadership. Character and consequences. *Europe–Asia Studies* 60(6): 879–897.

Sakwa, R.P. (2015). *Frontline Ukraine. Crisis in the borderlands*. London: I.B. Tauris.

The Delegation of the European Union to Russia. (1999). The Russian Federation's Middle Term Strategy towards the EU (2000–2010). Retrieved 18 November 2009 from: www.delrus.ec.europa.eu/en/p_245.htm

The Federal Government of Germany. (2014). Extraordinary Meeting of EU Heads of State and Government. Support for Ukraine reaffirmed. 6 March 2014. Retrieved 30 May 2014 from: www.bundesregierung.de/Content/EN/Reiseberichte/2014/2014-03-06-eu-sonderrat-ukraine.html

The Kremlin. (2014). Address by the President of the Russian Federation. Kremlin.ru. 18 March 2014. Retrieved 6 April 2014 from: http://en.kremlin.ru/events/president/news/20603

The Voice of Russia. (2014). Russia's Putin sending envoy to Kiev as mediator at request of Yanukovych. 20 February 2014.

United States Department of State. (2014). Diplomacy in Action. US/UK/Ukraine press statement on the Budapest memorandum meeting. 5 March 2014. Retrieved 30 May 2014 from: www.state.gov/r/pa/prs/ps/2014/03/222949.htm.

Vedomosti. (2014). Ot redaktsii: Bolshe ne evropeits. 7 April 2014.

Wall Street Journal. (2014). Ukraine gets ugly. Amid rioting and a regime crackdown in Kiev, the EU and U.S. stay on the sidelines. 19 February 2014.

Zamyatina, T. (2013). Attempts at foreign interference in Ukrainian home affairs – act of vengeance by indignant EU. ITAR-TASS. 11 December 2013.

Conclusions

The deterioration of EU–Russia relations from courtship in 1999 to confrontation in 2015 unfolded on three levels. First, on the geopolitical level, a Russian discourse on EU membership aspirations in 1999 emerged alongside the Kremlin's advancement of its own project for integration with countries in the post-Soviet space. As soon as the EU was able to exert influence in this region, its relations with Russia deteriorated. The most prominent demonstration of the Kremlin's hostility towards EU involvement in Russia's 'near abroad' was after the Orange Revolution. At that moment, Russian policy makers perceived the EU as an 'aggressive organisation' which sought to entice Ukraine to integration with the EU at the expense of the Kremlin's wish to keep Kiev within its orbit. In contrast, during the Kosovo War, when the EU's underdeveloped institutional structure impeded its ability to develop an affirmative foreign policy, Russian policy makers treated the EU as a diplomatic partner in seeking to resolve the crisis in the Serbian province.

An examination of the ideological underpinnings of the evolution of EU–Russia relations between 1999 and 2015 demonstrated the partners' diverging stances regarding the importance of values in their relations. The shaping of a mutual EU–Russian understanding concerning the role of values was challenged by two factors. The EU's emphasis on values in its relationship with Russia oscillated between pragmatic foreign policy goals and normative considerations. This was affected by division within the EU over a clear policy towards Russia. Friction within the EU increased during the second Chechen War because of the limited and decreasing EU influence on Moscow over Russian human rights violations in Chechnya. This was in contrast to the pragmatism of the French European Council Presidency in launching a joint energy policy with Russia. There was a brief moment of unity in the EU's stance towards Russia during the second Chechen War during the European Council summit in Helsinki in December 1999. Although the EU warned Russia about the potential suspension of trade clauses in the PCA and reduced the aid Russia received through the TACIS programme, criticism of Russian human rights violations was muted and the EU took a pragmatic approach to cooperation with Russia. The EU's prioritisation of long-term economic considerations over humanitarian concerns at the time of the continuing war with Chechnya was condemned by European human rights defenders.

192 *Conclusions*

However, the EU's use of sanctions and public diplomacy to exert influence on human rights in Russia faced limitations. The Kremlin refused to listen to lectures from Brussels on the need to safeguard human rights as the price of Russia's closer integration with or membership of the EU. The RMTS rejected the idea of EU membership whilst emphasising Russia's ambition to be a Eurasian great power.[1] This prevented the EU from using potential accession to the EU as leverage to convince Russia to implement reforms, to abide by the values set out in the pre-amble to the PCA, and to divert Russia's gradual drift into authoritarianism and curbing of democracy during Putin's second term in office. Mikhail Khodorko-vsky's arrest in 2003,[2] the reforms Putin announced after the hostage crisis in Beslan in 2004, the Kremlin's reluctance to undertake any measures to liberalise its energy market in 2006, Russia's annexation of Crimea in 2014, as well as the launch of the Eurasian Union a year later, were further signs of the gradually increasing authoritarianism in Putin's Russia. These have been widely interpreted in the West as evidence of Russia's attempt to regain its strength as a great power. Russia's rejection of membership of the ENP further strengthened this view. Russia's refusal to join the ENP demonstrated the Kremlin's reluctance to implement political and economic reforms as the price of future integration with the EU. As a consequence, the EU was no longer able to use EU membership as an incentive to encourage Russia to conform to the values the EU aspired to uphold.

On an economic level, Russia transformed from a reliable partner in the supply of energy to an enlarging EU, to a major threat to the long-term security of EU energy supplies. The year 2000 was marked by the launch of the EU–Russian Energy Dialogue, the first crucial step towards cooperation in energy policy, despite Russia's continuing military invasion of Chechnya. Prior to the Energy Dialogue, EU–Russian energy diplomacy was rather vaguely alluded to in the PCA. The interruption of supply to Ukraine by Gazprom in 2006 and 2009 contributed to the perception of Russia as an unreliable guarantor for the long-term security of EU energy supplies.[3] The first disruption of supply, which undermined deliveries to nine EU member states, was a wakeup call for the EU in seeking to diversify its energy supply by attempting to find alternative suppliers. At the same time, the EU urged Russia to liberalise its energy market by ratifying the European ECT. The Russian government refused to ratify this Charter and responded to the EU's request by increasing state control over its energy sector. In a further attempt to decrease the Kremlin's control of the energy market, the EU sought to use the update of the PCA as an opportunity to include a clause on the 'Early Warning Mechanism', which would put Russia under a contractual obligation to inform the EU as soon as possible about any potential interruptions of supply. Russia refused to fulfil this request. As a result, the EU developed plans for alternative supply routes, including the Nabucco pipeline from Turkey to Austria. However, a number of challenges have impeded the final construction of this pipeline. The pursuit of alternative energy supplies reflects strains in the relationship between the EU and Russia in an area where there was previously potential for cooperation.

Conclusions 193

This book endeavoured to explain the reasons for the deterioration of EU–Russia relations from 1999 to 2015. In 1999, the outlook was promising for mutually fruitful diplomacy between Brussels and Moscow. During the Kosovo War, Russia's relations with the US and NATO culminated in the most severe crisis since the end of the Cold War. In contrast, Russian policy makers recognised the EU as a trustworthy partner in seeking to resolve this conflict. The adoption of a peace plan for Kosovo was a joint and successful EU–Russian effort, which marked the beginning of diplomatic relations following the PCA's entrance into force. Four months after this successful diplomacy, Javier Solana, in his role as NATO's Secretary-General, emphasised the significance of an EU–Russian 'strategic partnership', stating that the partnership 'offers the greatest opportunity to affect the cause of world affairs in a manner, which will truly affect the course of history, *for the better*'.[4]

By 2015, it had become evident that Solana's aspirations for the evolution of EU–Russia relations had not materialised. The Kremlin's pressure on the Ukrainian government to become a member of the Eurasian Union at the expense of closer political and economic integration with the EU, as well as Russia's illegal annexation of Crimea, are the latest in a series of examples which lead Western analysts to argue that EU–Russia relations have reached the point of no return.

The main contention of this book is that the reversal in the relationship, from courtship in 1999 to the height of confrontation in 2015, was the result of major changes within the EU and Russia which led to increasing divergence. In 1999 the EU lacked coherent external representation, which resulted in Russian perceptions of the EU as the 'acceptable face of the West'. The EU's evolution as a political actor, with increasing influence in foreign policy, soon had an impact on the Kremlin. The European Commission's imposition of visas on Russians travelling to and from Kaliningrad directly impinged upon the lives of Russian citizens and confirmed that the EU could impact on the post-Soviet space. Despite vehement attempts by Russian diplomats and policy makers to reverse the introduction of visas, which they condemned as an infringement of the right of free movement of persons, the EU held firm to this policy course.

However, EU policy towards Russia was not always as consistent as in the case of Kaliningrad. When the Russian government perpetrated human rights violations during the second Chechen War, the European Parliament condemned Russia's actions, urging an immediate ceasefire. In contrast, the European Council took a firmer line as exemplified by the reduction of aid to Russia from the TACIS programme and the Council's proposal to freeze some PCA provisions. However, the EU was internally divided regarding the development of relations with Russia. Some prominent heads of state and government did not want to jeopardise relations with Russia, the EU's most important trading partner and the main supplier of energy to an enlarging EU. Even the initially more outspoken critics of Russia's conduct in the North Caucasus gradually toned down their protests because of the plan to launch the EU–Russia Energy Dialogue, the strategic partners' first major deal for energy cooperation.

194 *Conclusions*

In contrast to the Chechen War, at the time of the Orange Revolution, the EU managed to pursue strategic and carefully planned diplomacy towards Ukraine, which led to the first political crisis between the EU and Russia since 1999. The EU was able to exert influence in Ukraine by refusing to accept the results of the fraudulent elections and by requesting a rerun of the presidential election, resulting in victory for the pro-Western candidate. Russian policy makers perceived the EU's involvement in resolution of the Ukraine crisis as a deliberate attempt to draw Kiev into its sphere of influence to the detriment of the Kremlin's interests. This view was further strengthened by the launch of the EaP in 2009, which set out a political and economic integrative framework for six countries from the former Soviet space, including Ukraine.

The institutionalisation of the EaP resulted in a major EU–Russian confrontation, which has characterised the former strategic partnership since November 2013. In the continuing crisis over Ukraine, the EU did not pursue a clear agenda regarding its future relations with Kiev. The EaP summit in Riga in May 2015 demonstrated the absence of a streamlined integrative policy with Kiev. At the Riga summit, the EU revealed that further enlargement would not be a foreign policy priority for the EU over the next few years. The unwillingness of the EU to fulfil the ambitions of pro-EU politicians for integration with the EU, and Eastern Ukraine's dominance by Russian separatists make it impossible to predict Ukraine's future political orientation.

The examination of the deterioration of EU–Russia relations between 1999 and 2015 raises the question whether these sources of confrontation will impact on relations in the years to come. An assessment of the future development of EU–Russia relations in the short-term faces several fundamental challenges. First, an attempt to address the future development of EU–Russian diplomacy necessitates a reference to the Ukraine crisis. Chapter 7 sought to demonstrate that the origins of this crisis, which emerged in November 2013, can be traced back to open confrontation between the EU and Russia after the Orange Revolution in 2004. Due to the inability of both Russia and the EU to draw lessons from their initial clash over Ukraine, the West was simply paralysed by the deteriorating Ukraine crisis, which culminated in Crimea's annexation to Russia. The sudden brutality of the dynamics in Ukraine in 2013 and 2014 made a prediction of future developments in Ukraine impossible. Such an assessment would require the examination of domestic factors in Ukrainian politics, such as attempts by the Ukrainian government to negotiate with separatists in Eastern Ukraine, which goes beyond the objectives of this book but could form the basis for future research.

Second, seeking to assess the future development of EU–Russia relations depends on the possibility of the partners dealing with their divergent understandings of the role of values in their relationship. Their inability to establish a set of mutually agreed values as a basis for the development of relations becomes evident when looking at the preamble to the PCA. According to this, the European Community and the Russian Federation are

Conclusions   195

convinced about the paramount importance of the rule of law and respect for human rights, particularly those of minorities, the establishment of a multi-party system with free and democratic elections and economic liberalization aimed at setting up a market economy.[5]

Such statements are only meaningful when they go beyond political rhetoric and are implemented in the EU's relations with Russia. This examination of EU–Russia relations between 1999 and 2015 has demonstrated that dialogue over both respect for human rights and economic liberalisation broke down. In 2000, during the second Chechen War, EU officials and institutions condemned Russian human rights abuses in the North Caucasus before, but this posturing on human rights did not bring about the intended effect – to coerce Russia to end the war. The EU's lack of an affirmative position on continuation of its relations with Russia – despite the continuation of war in Chechnya – further undermined the EU's ability to seek to uphold the values set out in the PCA preamble.

The ever growing intensity of the confrontation over Ukraine and the annexation of Crimea raises the question of why the PCA was not put on hold as a demonstration that the EU and Russia could not continue their relationship on the basis of 'business as usual'. In order to address this question, the EU's previous intentions to use the PCA as a coercive measure need to be concisely examined. In the diplomatic history of EU–Russia relations since the adoption of the PCA in 1997, the agreement was used twice as leverage by the EU. The initial implementation of the PCA was put on hold because of the outbreak of the first Chechen War in 1994. After it was signed in 1997, the European Council proposed freezing some of the trade provisions and strictly applying the political clauses in the agreement. The EU response to this proposal was incoherent and therefore prevented the implementation of this proposition. Nine years later, during the Russian–Georgian War, the European Council postponed negotiations regarding an update of the PCA for about two months as an expression of the EU's condemnation of Russia's war with Georgia. However, whilst this restrictive measure was announced, the European Council emphasised that there

is no desirable alternative to a strong relationship, based on cooperation, trust and dialogue, respect for the rule of law and [the EU] call[s] on Russia to join with us in making this fundamental choice in favour of mutual interest, understanding and cooperation.[6]

In light of this statement, the failure to suspend the PCA during the ongoing crisis in Ukraine, in which Russia allegedly supports Ukrainian separatists in the East, is not surprising.

In endeavouring to explain the reasons for the reversal of relations between 1999 and 2015, this book does not claim to offer an exhaustive analysis of the evolution of the relationship. The book was not intended to illuminate underlying motives of Putin and the Russian power elite. As a consequence, it remains uncertain to what extent conflicts with the EU were driven by ideological

196 *Conclusions*

conceptions or by advantages for individual policy makers. It will only be possible to fill in the gaps in our understanding of decision-making processes in Russia when the Kremlin's archives are opened decades from now. An examination of documents from these archives would help to clarify the thinking of the Russian leadership and how it impacted on Russia's relations with the EU from 1999 until 2015. Obtaining access to documents in these archives, as well as interviews with key Russian officials, on the question of whether the EU intended to promote its values in relations with Russia would result in a more nuanced assessment of the role of values in the former strategic partnership.

EU decision making, which moulded EU–Russia relations at various stages during the time period covered by this book, like the Kremlin's, is far from transparent. At this stage, it remains unclear what motives have driven EU member states in their interaction with Russia during their chairmanship of the European Council Presidency. The thinking behind the Portuguese European Council Presidency's accommodating stance towards Russia during the second Chechen War and behind Berlusconi's advocacy of Putin's policy in Chechnya still remains obscure.

No less significant than the need to assess *internal* aspects of both the EU's and Russia's political decision making in the attempt to understand changes in their diplomatic relations, is the need to assess current *external* political developments. As a consequence, future research on EU–Russia relations requires an examination of the repercussions of Russia's current involvement in Syria for both EU–Russia relations and for the future of the ENP. Russia's increasing engagement in Syria raises the question of why, after Russia's pressure on Ukraine – a member of the EU's Eastern Neighbourhood, the Kremlin is currently seeking to interfere in the EU's Southern Neighbourhood as well. Russia's engagement is demonstrated by its allegedly military support in Syria's fight against Islamic State and rebel groups. Some political commentators speculate that Russia will seek the EU's support in an attempt to find a political resolution to the conflict in Syria.[7] It is difficult to predict the potential shortcomings of the ENP and its future development, Russia's motivations, developments and the outcomes of its involvement in Syria. The publication of a Russian proposal on 11 November 2015 for reforms of the Syrian constitution followed by elections raised hopes that conflict resolution was gaining momentum.[8] Two days later, France and the world was traumatised by the terrorist attacks in Paris, which were claimed by Islamic State.[9] Time will tell if President Putin and President Obama's agreement on a 'Syrian led and Syrian-owned political transition' at the G20 summit in Antalya on 15 November can be considered effective in both resolving the Syrian crisis and eliminating the root causes of extremism, which has become a threat to international security.[10] At the same time, it remains to be seen if this seemingly common goal, the combat of extremism, can be considered a first step in the rapprochement between Russia and the West.

Russia's current engagement in Syria and pressure on Ukraine raise questions about potential shortcomings of the ENP and its future evolution. Time will tell

Conclusions 197

whether the development of a practical approach to revising the ENP by the European Commission, involving Russia in deliberations on enhanced integration between the EU and the CIS, will help to ease tensions between the EU and Russia. The publication of the ENP review will demonstrate if the Commission envisages a fresh approach to the core principles of the ENP focusing on differentiation, focus, flexibility, ownership and visibility.[11] The feasibility of reducing EU–Russian confrontation over the shared neighbourhood through the application of these principles can only be assessed by examining empirical evidence on the development of the EU's relations with ENP member states such as Syria and Ukraine in the context of those countries' trilateral relations with the EU and Russia in the years to come.

Predicting developments in EU–Russia relations requires examination of another crucial factor which has influenced relations – energy policy. Recent developments regarding the EU's diversification of energy policy are very likely to have a direct impact on long-term cooperation between the EU and Russia. The interruption of gas supply to Ukraine in 2006 and 2009 increased Brussels' calls for diversification in energy supply. As soon as the EU presented concrete plans for diversification, including construction of the Nabucco pipeline, Russian officials played down the significance of the EU–Russian energy trade by referring to China as an alternative market for Russian resources. The validity of Russia's claim of a proposed reorientation towards a different market was borne out by negotiations to finalise an agreement on Russian–Chinese energy cooperation in June 2014. This deal includes the first concrete evidence of measures which might eventually shift the balance in the EU–Russian energy supply in the long term. The first deliveries of gas are expected to commence in 2018.[12] It remains to be seen if this deal will materialise through construction of the necessary pipelines.[13] It would be premature to predict whether this Russian–Chinese energy deal will jeopardise the security of the EU's energy supply in the long term before the first supplies of gas are delivered.

Notes

1 The Delegation of the European Union to Russia (1999).
2 Sakwa (2014), p. xix.
3 De Jong, Wouters and Sterkx (2013) pp. 140–164.
4 Solana (1999). Emphasis added.
5 European Commission (1997).
6 Council of the European Union (2008).
7 Marcus (2015); BBC News (2015a).
8 BBC News (2015b).
9 BBC News. (2015c).
10 Murphy (2015).
11 European Commission (2015).
12 Wright (2014).
13 Rapoza (2015).

198 *Conclusions*

Bibliography

BBC News. (2015a). Syria conflict: Assad in surprise visit to Moscow. 21 October 2015. Retrieved 2 November 2015 from: www.bbc.com/news/world-europe-34590561

BBC News. (2015b). Syria conflict: Russia 'peace plan' revealed ahead of key summit. 11 November 2015. Retrieved 11 November 2015 from: www.bbc.com/news/world-middle-east-34784276

BBC News. (2015c). Paris attacks 'planned from Syria' – French PM Valls. 16 November 2015. Retrieved 16 November 2015 from: www.bbc.com/news/world-europe-34830233

Council of the European Union. (2008). Revised presidency conclusions. Extraordinary European Council, Brussels. 1 September 2008 (OR.fr) 12549/2/08 REV 2. CONCL 3. Brussels, 6 October 2008.

De Jong, S., Wouters, J. and Sterkx, S. (2013). *The EU and Multilateral Security Governance*. London: Routledge.

European Commission. (1997). Agreement on partnership and cooperation establishing a partnership between the European Communities and their Member States, of one part, and the Russian Federation, of the other part. Official Journal L 327 , 28/11/1997 P. 0003 – 0069. Retrieved 27 October 2015 from: http://trade.ec.europa.eu/doclib/docs/2003/november/tradoc_114138.pdf

European Commission. (2015). Press Release Database. European Commission – Press release. Towards a new European Neighbourhood Policy: the EU launches a consultation on the future of its relations with neighbouring countries. 4 March 2015. IP/15/4548. Retrieved 2 November 2015 from: http://europa.eu/rapid/press-release_IP-15-4548_en.htm

Marcus, J. (2015). Syria crisis: Russia's strategy and endgame? BBC News. Europe. 8 October 2015. Retrieved 18 October 2015 from: www.bbc.com/news/world-europe-34474362

Murphy, K. (2015). G 20 – Barack Obama and Vladimir Putin agree to Syrian-led transition. *Guardian*. 15 November 2015. Retrieved 16 November 2015 from: www.theguardian.com/world/2015/nov/16/g20-barack-obama-and-vladimir-putin-agree-to-syrian-led-transition

Rapoza, K. (2015). Russia, China get energy deals under way. 3 June 2015. Forbes. Retrieved 19 October 2015 from: www.forbes.com/sites/kenrapoza/2015/06/03/russia-china-get-energy-deals-under-way/

Sakwa, R. (2014). *Putin and the Oligarch. The Khodorkovsky-Yukos affair*. London and New York: I.B.Tauris.

Solana, J. (1999). The EU–Russia Strategic Partnership. Speech by the High Representative designate of the European Union for Common Foreign and Security Policy. Stockholm, Wednesday 13 October 1999. Retrieved 25 April 2015 from: www.consilium.europa.eu/uedocs/cms_data/docs/pressdata/EN/discours/59417.pdf

The Delegation of the European Union to Russia. (1999). The Russian Federation's Middle Term Strategy towards the EU (2000–2010). Retrieved 18 November 2009 from: www.delrus.ec.europa.eu/en/p_245.htm

Wright, C. (2014). $400 billion gas deal shows Russia looking to China to replace Western money. 22 May 2014. Forbes. Retrieved 19 October 2015: www.forbes.com/sites/chriswright/2014/05/22/400-billion-gas-deal-shows-russia-looking-to-china-to-replace-western-money

Appendix

List of interviews

Anonymous. Former spokesman for EU external relations, Directorate General EU External Relations (DG RELEX), European Commission. Interview at European Commission, Brussels. 23 June 2010.

Anonymous. Expert in the Directorate General Energy, European Commission. Email interview. 4 May 2011.

Anonymous. Former seconded national expert at the Unit for Relations with Russia and the Northern Dimension Policy, DG RELEX, European Commission. Email interview. 30 June 2015.

Anonymous. Chief of Cabinet/Political adviser to the EU Special Representative for the South Caucasus and the Crisis in Georgia. Email interview. 30 July 2015.

Anonymous. Former official in the Unit for Relations with Russia, DG RELEX, European Commission. Interview at European Commission, Brussels. 28 August 2015.

Grønbjerg, Lars. Former seconded national expert, Unit for Relations with Russia and the Northern Dimension Policy, DG RELEX. Interview at DG RELEX, European Commission, Brussels. 16 June 2010, 23 June 2010.

Email interviews. 16 October 2010, 20 February 2011, 3 March 2011, 4 March 2011. 4 January 2012, 17 July 2012, 6 October 2012.

Petritsch, Dr Wolfgang. Former European chief negotiator of the Balkan Contact Group and EU envoy for Kosovo, October 1998 to July 1999. Email interview. 20 August 2011.

Tkeshelashvili, E. Former Georgian Foreign Minister and current President of the Georgian Institute for Strategic Studies, Tbilisi. Telephone interview. 13 July 2015.

Index

Abkhazia 137–8, 141–4, 146–8, 150–1, 156
Adamkus, V. 92–3, 98–9
Ahtisaari, M. 8, 13–16, 20
Akayev, A. 96
Albright, M. 18
annexation 138, 140–1, 175–8, 181–2, 192–5
anti-terrorist operation 29, 34, 41
Ashton, C. 168–71, 175–6
asset freezes 174, 176
Azerbaijan 1, 128, 143, 150

Berlusconi, S. 46, 57, 66–9, 71, 75, 147, 196
Beslan hostage crisis 58, 72–5, 122, 140, 192
bronze soldier, Tallinn 125–7

ceasefire 32, 38, 140, 142–5, 149, 156, 193
Central Election Commission 89
Charter for European Security 33–4
Chechnya 1, 12, 28–56, 60, 62, 64, 68–73, 75–6, 100–1, 103, 117, 119, 129, 139, 147, 149, 155, 175, 191–2, 195–6
Chernomyrdin, V. 8, 13–17, 20, 88, 181
China 37, 82, 116, 135, 180–1, 197
Chizhov, V. 60, 66, 118–20, 127, 154, 174
civil society 4, 155, 176
Clinton, B. 9, 18
coloured revolutions 97, 115
common EU external energy policy 114, 116
common EU line in EU–Russia relations 101, 123–4
Common Foreign and Security Policy 2
'common neighbourhood' of Russia and the EU 101, 126, 145, 148
constructive EU–Russia relationship 139
Crimea 138, 140–1, 175–8, 181–2, 192–5; *see also* annexation; referendum

dash to Pristina 17–18
Deep and Comprehensive Free Trade Agreement (DCFTA) 165–6
democracy 1–2, 17–18, 32, 36–8, 60, 65–6, 71–2, 74–5, 88, 91–2, 95–7, 100, 118, 149, 154, 171, 181, 192
Directorate for Interregional and Cultural Ties with Foreign Countries and the CIS 99
diversity in energy policy 114
Dubrovka theatre siege 62–3
Duma's Committee for International Affairs 59

Eastern Partnership 1, 13
Eastern Partnership Summit, Riga 183, 194
Eastern Partnership Summit, Vilnius 61, 154, 165, 167
economic benefits to SES 87
election campaigns in former Soviet space 2, 4, 84–93, 96–8
electoral fraud 84, 90
Energy Charter Treaty *see* Russia's reluctance of ratification
energy policy 2–3, 43–4, 47, 102, 113–16, 118–20, 123, 126, 128–9, 139, 149, 155, 191–2, 197
energy security 2–3, 28, 44
Estonian–Russian dispute 113, 118, 125–7
'EU as an aggressive organisation' 98, 101, 103, 126, 145, 148, 150, 164, 181, 191
EU enlargement 47, 57, 59, 67–8, 84, 87
EU Foreign Affairs Council 174
EU High Representative for Common Foreign and Security Policy 10, 116, 168, 170, 175
EU–Russia summit 1, 9–10, 32, 39, 41, 43, 46–7, 59, 61–4, 67, 70–1, 74, 88–91,

100–2, 116–17, 121–2, 126–7, 139, 148, 151, 155, 174
EU–Russian Energy Dialogue *see* launch of Eurasian Union
EU's Common Strategy on Russia 18, 30, 35
EU's diplomacy in Kiev 169
EU's internal division concerning Russia 28–9, 46, 67, 69, 74, 103, 118, 120, 122–4, 148, 156, 177, 182
EU's limitations as an actor in Ukraine 164, 169–70, 174, 177–8
EU's and Russia's understanding of values 124
European Energy Strategy 149
European Monitoring Mission, Georgia 144–5
European Neighbourhood Policy 1, 4, 57, 64, 95, 192, 196–7; *see also* Russia's objections to ENP Membership
European Parliament's Committee of Foreign Affair's report on EU–Russia relations 69
European values 41, 71, 86, 88, 99, 155
extremism 41, 45, 196

Facilitated Transit Document 63
Federalnaya Sluzba Bezopasnosti (FSB) 115, 140
financial sanctions 171
Fogh Rasmussen, A. 63–4
Foreign Policy Concept of the Russian Federation 58
Four Common Spaces 100, 102, 153
freedom of the press 123, 139
Fyodorov, B. 9

G8 states 15–16, 177
G20 summit 196
Gama, J. 39–40
Gazprom 104, 113–16, 119, 129, 192
Gazprom's interruption of supply to Ukraine 129
general restrictive measures 171
Georgia 1–2, 120, 129, 137–56, 169, 180, 195
Georgian Foreign Minister 141, 199
Glazyev, S. 188
Glucksmann, A. 43, 73
Gorbachev, M. 11

human rights 1–2, 6, 10, 17–19, 28–9, 34–5, 38, 40, 42–7, 50–2, 54, 56–7, 60, 62, 65–6, 68–72, 81–3, 92, 97, 100–4, 109, 113–14, 117–23, 126–9, 139, 148–9, 154–5, 171–2, 175, 181, 187, 191–3, 195

impeachment process against Yeltsin 9
Islamic state 196
Ivanov, L. 3–35, 39–41, 45, 67–8, 98, 139, 178, 182

Kaczynski, J.L. 121–2
Kaliningrad 1, 57–64, 66, 68, 74–7, 79–83, 170, 193, 208
KFOR 16–17
Khodorkovsky, M. 67–8, 73, 115, 192
Klitschko, V. 172
Kosovo Contact Group 9, 18
Kosovo war 8–20, 39, 98, 103, 125, 191, 193
Kosovo's Declaration of Independence 138
Kouchner, B. 142–4
Kovalev, S. 42–5
Kremlin's hostility towards the EU 2, 90, 96, 98, 137, 150, 156, 191
Kuchma, L. 87–8, 90–1, 93–4, 150, 169
Kwasniewski, A. 91–3, 98–9, 102
Kyrgyzstan 2, 85, 96–7

launch of Eurasian Union 165–6, 192–3
liberalisation of Russian energy market 114, 117, 120, 128
Likhachev, A. 177
Lithuanian–Russian dispute 113, 118, 121, 126, 128
Litvinenko, A. 122
Lukin, V. 33, 61, 172
Lukyanov, F. 135, 152, 166, 169–70, 172, 182

Maidan 89, 92, 164, 170, 172
Margelov, M. 180
Mashkadov, A. 29
Medvedev, D. 1, 99, 115, 139–40, 142–3, 145–7, 151, 155
meeting of all EU heads of state and Putin 117–20, 124, 128
Merkel, A. 123, 126–7, 172, 178
MH 17 179
Miller, A. 116
Milosevic, S. 11, 13, 15–16, 43
Mogherini, F. 177

Nabucco pipeline 127–9, 192, 197
Naryshkin, S. 181

202 Index

NATO *see* dash to Pristina; KFOR; NATO enlargement; NATO Membership Action Plan; NATO Summit, Bucharest; NATO–Russia Permanent Joint Council
NATO enlargement 138
NATO Membership Action Plan 138
NATO–Russia Permanent Joint Council 11
NATO Summit, Bucharest 138
Nazarbayev, N. 87
normative considerations 28, 31, 65, 72, 75, 126, 128, 154–5, 191

Obama, B. 196
Oettinger, G. 174
opposition in Russia 126
Orange Revolution 2–5, 66, 75, 84–112, 137–8, 140, 150, 152, 164–5, 169–70, 175, 179, 181, 189, 191, 194
Orange Revolution's geopolitical repercussions for Russia 93–4, 102–3
OSCE 10, 15, 32–6, 48, 53, 55, 89–90, 96–7, 142–4, 150, 157, 162, 168, 174, 209; *see also* rift over Russia's financial contribution to OSCE

Parliamentary Assembly of the Council of Europe 28, 38, 175
Partnership and Cooperation Agreement between the EU and Russia 9–10, 35–6, 44, 46, 71, 102, 104, 113, 120–7, 137, 139, 147–8, 153–4, 156, 159, 174–5, 182, 191–5
Partnership for Modernisation 153, 160–1
Patten, C. 29–30, 32, 35–6, 44, 58, 61, 64, 68, 73, 94–5
Pavlovsky, G. 4, 87, 98–9
PCA 9–10, 36, 44, 46, 71, 102, 104, 113, 120–7, 130, 137, 139, 147–8, 153–4, 156, 169, 174–5, 182, 191–5, 209
peace plan for Russian–Georgian war 142–4, 156
Peskov, D. 167, 172
Petritsch, W. 10, 13–14
Polish–Russian dispute 121–2, 126
political benefits to SES 87–8
political conditionality 65
Politkovskaya, A. 117–18, 122–3
postponement of EU–Russia summit 88
pragmatic foreign policy goals 191
Primakov, Y. 8, 11, 13
Pristina *see* dash to Pristina
Prodi, R. 10, 30, 33–5, 41–7, 50, 55, 59, 61, 68–9, 173

Rambouillet, Interim Agreement for Peace and Self-Governance 10, 13–14
referendum 175–7
refugees 15–16, 34, 53, 141
reorientation of the EU's policy towards Russia 69
restrictive measures 37, 146, 148, 156, 164, 170–1, 173–9, 182
review of EU–Russia relations 70, 138, 147–9, 153, 161
rift over Russia's financial contribution to OSCE p. 97–8
'Russia as a unique and distinctive civilisation' 181
Russia as ally in struggle against terrorism 29, 45–7
Russian Medium Term Strategy for Relations with the EU 2, 30–1, 38, 46, 58, 66, 75, 88, 100, 124, 152, 155, 181, 192
Russian youth movement *Nashi* 125
Russian–Chinese energy deal 197
Russian–Ukrainian gas deal 167
Russia's increasing authoritarianism 2, 72, 74, 101, 117–18, 125, 128, 192
Russia's objections to ENP Membership 57–8, 65–6, 75, 155
Russia's reliability of supply of energy resources 113–14, 117, 127
Russia's reluctance of ratification 117, 119
Russia's 'self-reliance in international affairs' 182

Saakashvili, M. 142–3
Sakwa, R. 138, 169, 180
sanctions *see* asset freezes; financial sanctions; general restrictive measures; trade sanctions visa bans
Sarkozy, N. 142–4, 149–50, 156, 162
Schengen zone 57, 59–61
Schroeder, G. 9, 11, 13–14, 16, 19–20, 34, 36–8, 45–6, 67, 74, 91–2
Semneby, P. 142
separatists 138, 179, 194–5
September 11, 2001 29, 45, 47
Sikorski, R. 144, 172
Single Economic Space (SES) 85, 87–8, 150; *see also* economic benefits to SES; political benefits to SES
Slutsky, L. 166
Solana, J. 1–2, 18–19, 30, 33, 36–7, 39, 46, 67, 89, 92–3, 96–7, 101, 116, 125, 149, 193

South Ossetia 137–8, 140, 145, 147–8, 151, 156
sovereign democracy 2, 6, 32, 38
spread of revolutions in post-Soviet space 97, 100, 115
State Duma 9, 42, 93, 99–100, 115, 166, 176–7, 181
Steinmeier, F.-W. 125, 141–2, 145, 155, 172–3, 179
'strategic partnership' 1, 20, 64, 67, 94, 104, 128–9, 139, 147, 151, 168, 170, 183, 193–6
Stubb, A. 142–5
Syria 65, 196–8

TACIS 37, 42, 70, 191, 193
terrorist attacks, Paris 2015 196
'threat of bipolar Europe' 85
Tkeshelashvili, E. 141–4
trade sanctions 171
Tyagnibok, O. 172

Ukraine 1–5, 37, 66, 75–6, 80, 84–99, 102–5, 107–15, 120, 129, 132–3, 135, 137–8, 140, 145, 148, 150–2, 156, 162, 164–80, 182–3, 186–92, 194–7, 211
Ukrainian presidential election 4, 12, 36, 84–5, 87–8
UN 10, 14–17, 21, 24, 36, 53–5, 81, 107, 143, 174

unanimity requirement 171
UNMIK 17
USA 2, 22, 98
Ushakov, Y. 169

values 2–5, 29, 31, 36, 41–2, 46, 57, 60, 65–6, 70–2, 74–5, 82, 86, 88, 91–2, 95–7, 99, 101, 113–14, 118, 121, 124–5, 128–9, 139, 148–9, 152, 154–5, 178, 181, 191–2, 194–6
van Rompuy, H. 153, 166–9, 175–6
visa abolition 147
visa bans 37, 171, 176–7
visa-free travel 60, 91, 169
vulnerability of EU energy supply 116

Wider Europe Initiative 64–5
World Chechen Congress 62–4
World Trade Organisation (WTO) 102

Yanukovich, V., integration with Russia at core of his election campaign 85–8
Yatseny, A. 87
Yatsenyuk, A. 172
Yeltsin, B. 1–2, 4–5, 8–9, 11–16, 18, 20, 30, 32–4, 36, 46, 88, 181
Yukos 67–9, 115
Yushchenko, V., integration with the EU at core of his election campaign 85–6

# Taylor & Francis eBooks

Helping you to choose the right eBooks for your Library

Add Routledge titles to your library's digital collection today. Taylor and Francis ebooks contains over 50,000 titles in the Humanities, Social Sciences, Behavioural Sciences, Built Environment and Law.

Choose from a range of subject packages or create your own!

Benefits for you
- Free MARC records
- COUNTER-compliant usage statistics
- Flexible purchase and pricing options
- All titles DRM-free.

REQUEST YOUR FREE INSTITUTIONAL TRIAL TODAY

Free Trials Available
We offer free trials to qualifying academic, corporate and government customers.

Benefits for your user
- Off-site, anytime access via Athens or referring URL
- Print or copy pages or chapters
- Full content search
- Bookmark, highlight and annotate text
- Access to thousands of pages of quality research at the click of a button.

eCollections – Choose from over 30 subject eCollections, including:

Archaeology	Language Learning
Architecture	Law
Asian Studies	Literature
Business & Management	Media & Communication
Classical Studies	Middle East Studies
Construction	Music
Creative & Media Arts	Philosophy
Criminology & Criminal Justice	Planning
Economics	Politics
Education	Psychology & Mental Health
Energy	Religion
Engineering	Security
English Language & Linguistics	Social Work
Environment & Sustainability	Sociology
Geography	Sport
Health Studies	Theatre & Performance
History	Tourism, Hospitality & Events

For more information, pricing enquiries or to order a free trial, please contact your local sales team:
www.tandfebooks.com/page/sales

 | The home of Routledge books

www.tandfebooks.com